GOSPEL ASSURANCE AND WARNINGS

Recovering the Gospel

The Gospel's Power and Message

The Gospel Call and True Conversion

Gospel Assurance and Warnings

GOSPEL ASSURANCE AND WARNINGS

PAUL WASHER

Reformation Heritage Books
Grand Rapids, Michigan

Reformation Heritage Books
2965 Leonard St. NE
Grand Rapids, MI 49525
616-977-0889 / Fax 616-285-3246
e-mail: orders@heritagebooks.org
website: www.heritagebooks.org

Printed in the United States of America
14 15 16 17 18 19/10 9 8 7 6 5 4 3 2 1

Library of Congress Cataloging-in-Publication Data

Washer, Paul, 1961-
  Gospel assurance and warnings / Paul Washer.
    pages cm. — (Recovering the Gospel)
  ISBN 978-1-60178-294-6 (pbk. : alk. paper) 1. Assurance (Theology) 2. Salvation—Christianity. I. Title.
  BT785.W37 2014
  234—dc23
                              2013050598

For additional Reformed literature, request a free book list from Reformation Heritage Books at the above address.

Contents

Series Preface: Recovering the Gospel

The gospel of Jesus Christ is the greatest of all treasures given to the church and the individual Christian. It is not *a* message among many but *the* message above them all. It is the power of God for salvation and the greatest revelation of the manifold wisdom of God to men and angels.[1] It is for this reason that the apostle Paul gave the gospel the first place in his preaching, endeavored with all his might to proclaim it clearly, and even pronounced a curse upon all those who would pervert its truth.[2]

Each generation of Christians is a steward of the gospel message, and through the power of the Holy Spirit, God calls upon us to guard this treasure that has been entrusted to us.[3] If we are to be faithful stewards, we must be absorbed in the study of the gospel, take great pains to understand its truths, and pledge ourselves to guard its contents.[4] In doing so, we will ensure salvation both for ourselves and for those who hear us.[5]

This stewardship drives me to write these books. I have little desire for the hard work of writing, and there is certainly no lack of Christian books, but I have put the following collection of sermons in written form for the same reason that I preached them: to be free from their burden. Like Jeremiah, if I do not speak forth this message, "then…in my heart [it becomes] like a burning fire shut up in my bones; and I was weary of holding it back, and I could not."[6] As the apostle Paul exclaimed, "Woe is me if I do not preach the gospel!"[7]

---

1. Romans 1:16; Ephesians 3:10.
2. 1 Corinthians 15:3; Colossians 4:4; Galatians 1:8–9.
3. 2 Timothy 1:14.
4. 1 Timothy 4:15.
5. 1 Timothy 4:16.
6. Jeremiah 20:9.
7. 1 Corinthians 9:16.

As is commonly known, the word *gospel* comes from the Greek word *euangélion*, which is properly translated "good news." In one sense, every page of Scripture contains the gospel, but in another sense, the gospel refers to a very specific message—the salvation accomplished for a fallen people through the life, death, resurrection, and ascension of Jesus Christ, the Son of God.

In accordance with the Father's good pleasure, the eternal Son, who is equal with the Father and is the exact representation of His nature, willingly left the glory of heaven, was conceived by the Holy Spirit in the womb of a virgin, and was born the God-man: Jesus of Nazareth.[8] As a man, He walked on this earth in perfect obedience to the law of God.[9] In the fullness of time, men rejected and crucified Him. On the cross, He bore man's sin, suffered God's wrath, and died in man's place.[10] On the third day, God raised Him from the dead. This resurrection is the divine declaration that the Father has accepted His Son's death as a sacrifice for sin. Jesus paid the penalty for man's disobedience, satisfied the demands of justice, and appeased the wrath of God.[11] Forty days after the resurrection, the Son of God ascended into the heavens, sat down at the right hand of the Father, and was given glory, honor, and dominion over all.[12] There, in the presence of God, He represents His people and makes requests to God on their behalf.[13] All who acknowledge their sinful, helpless state and throw themselves upon Christ, God will fully pardon, declare righteous, and reconcile unto Himself.[14] This is the gospel of God and of Jesus Christ, His Son.

One of the greatest crimes committed by this present Christian generation is its neglect of the gospel, and it is from this neglect that all our other maladies spring forth. The lost world is not so much gospel hardened as it is gospel ignorant because many of those who proclaim the gospel are also ignorant of its most basic truths. The essential themes that make up the very core of the gospel—the justice of God, the radical depravity of man, the blood atonement, the nature of true conversion,

---

8. Acts 2:23; Hebrews 1:3; Philippians 2:6–7; Luke 1:35.
9. Hebrews 4:15.
10. 1 Peter 2:24; 3:18; Isaiah 53:10.
11. Luke 24:6; Romans 1:4; Romans 4:25.
12. Hebrews 1:3; Matthew 28:18; Daniel 7:13–14.
13. Luke 24:51; Philippians 2:9–11; Hebrews 1:3; Hebrews 7:25.
14. Mark 1:15; Romans 10:9; Philippians 3:3.

and the biblical basis of assurance—are absent from too many pulpits. Churches reduce the gospel message to a few creedal statements, teach that conversion is a mere human decision, and pronounce assurance of salvation over anyone who prays the sinner's prayer.

The result of this gospel reductionism has been far-reaching. First, it further hardens the hearts of the unconverted. Few modern-day "converts" ever make their way into the fellowship of the church, and those who do often fall away or have lives marked by habitual carnality. Untold millions walk our streets and sit in our pews unchanged by the true gospel of Jesus Christ, and yet they are convinced of their salvation because one time in their life they raised a hand at an evangelistic campaign or repeated a prayer. This false sense of security creates a great barrier that often insulates such individuals from ever hearing the true gospel.

Secondly, such a gospel deforms the church from a spiritual body of regenerated believers into a gathering of carnal men who profess to know God, but by their deeds they deny Him.[15] With the preaching of the true gospel, men come to the church without gospel entertainment, special activities, or the promise of benefits beyond those offered by the gospel. Those who come do so because they desire Christ and are hungry for biblical truth, heartfelt worship, and opportunities for service. When the church proclaims a lesser gospel, it fills up with carnal men who share little interest in the things of God, and the maintenance of such men is a heavy burden upon the church.[16] The church then tones down the radical demands of the gospel to a convenient morality, and true devotion to Christ gives way to activities designed to meet the felt needs of its members. The church becomes activity-driven rather than Christ-centered, and it carefully filters or repackages the truth so as not to offend the carnal majority. The church lays aside the great truths of Scripture and orthodox Christianity, and pragmatism (i.e., whatever keeps the church going and growing) becomes the rule of the day.

Thirdly, such a gospel reduces evangelism and missions to little more than a humanistic endeavor driven by clever marketing strategies based upon a careful study of the latest trends in culture. After years of witnessing the impotence of an unbiblical gospel, many evangelicals seem convinced that the gospel will not work and that man has somehow

---

15. Titus 1:16.
16. 1 Corinthians 2:14.

become too complex a being to be saved and transformed by such a simple and scandalous message. There is now more emphasis on understanding our fallen culture and its fads than on understanding and proclaiming the only message that has the power to save it. As a result, the gospel is constantly being repackaged to fit what contemporary culture deems most relevant. We have forgotten that the true gospel is always relevant to every culture because it is God's eternal word to every man.

Fourthly, such a gospel brings reproach to the name of God. Through the proclamation of a lesser gospel, the carnal and unconverted come into the fellowship of the church, and through the almost total neglect of biblical church discipline, they are allowed to stay without correction or reproof. This soils the purity and reputation of the church and blasphemes the name of God among the unbelieving.[17] In the end, God is not glorified, the church is not edified, the unconverted church member is not saved, and the church has little or no witness to the unbelieving world.

It does not become us as ministers or laymen to stand so near and do nothing when we see "the glorious gospel of our blessed God" replaced by a gospel of lesser glory.[18] As stewards of this trust, we have a duty to recover the one true gospel and proclaim it boldly and clearly to all. We would do well to pay heed to the words of Charles Haddon Spurgeon:

> In these days, I feel bound to go over the elementary truths of the gospel repeatedly. In peaceful times, we may feel free to make excursions into interesting districts of truth which lie far afield; but now we must stay at home, and guard the hearts and homes of the church by defending the first principles of the faith. In this age, there have risen up in the church itself men who speak perverse things. There be many that trouble us with their philosophies and novel interpretations, whereby they deny the doctrines they profess to teach, and undermine the faith they are pledged to maintain. It is well that some of us, who know what we believe, and have no secret meanings for our words, should just put our foot down and maintain our standing, holding forth the word of life, and plainly declaring the foundation truths of the gospel of Jesus Christ.[19]

---

17. Romans 2:24.

18. 1 Timothy 1:11.

19. Charles H. Spurgeon, *The Metropolitan Tabernacle Pulpit* (repr., Pasadena, Tex.: Pilgrim Publications), 32:385.

Although the Recovering the Gospel series does not represent an entirely systematic presentation of the gospel, it does address most of the essential elements, especially those that are most neglected in contemporary Christianity. It is my hope that these words might be a guide to help you rediscover the gospel in all its beauty, scandal, and saving power. It is my prayer that such a rediscovery might transform your life, strengthen your proclamation, and bring the greatest glory to God.

Your brother,
Paul David Washer

PART ONE
Biblical Assurance

Examine yourselves as to whether you are in the faith. Test yourselves. Do you not know yourselves, that Jesus Christ is in you?—unless indeed you are disqualified.

—2 Corinthians 13:5

These things I have written to you who believe in the name of the Son of God, that you may know that you have eternal life.

—1 John 5:13

CHAPTER ONE

False Assurance

They profess to know God, but in works they deny Him, being abominable, disobedient, and disqualified for every good work.

—Titus 1:16

Many will say to Me in that day, "Lord, Lord, have we not prophesied in Your name, cast out demons in Your name, and done many wonders in Your name?" And then I will declare to them, "I never knew you; depart from Me, you who practice lawlessness!"

—Matthew 7:22–23

With this third book in the Recovering the Gospel series, we have come to a crucial place in our study of the gospel and salvation. We must ask ourselves this question: How can I know I have been born again, that I am truly a child of God? How can I know that I have believed unto eternal life? The relevancy of these questions becomes apparent as we consider that we live in an age when many claim to have some sort of eternal hope in Christ yet reflect so little of His teachings in their lives.

The seriousness of the matter becomes even more acute because twentieth-century preaching and evangelism have radically altered the content of the gospel, the gospel call, and the means by which people obtain assurance of salvation. Many preachers today now present the gospel as a series of concise, convenient statements that, while inherently true, are often left unexplained and hollowed of their true evangelical meaning and power. The gospel call to repent and believe has been replaced with a call to accept Christ and repeat the sinner's prayer, which is often at the end of tracts and the conclusion of emotional and often manipulative public invitations. Many people no longer obtain assurance of salvation by a careful consideration of their conversion and lifestyle in light of the Scriptures. Rather, it is granted by a well-meaning minister who is quick to pronounce the full benefits of salvation upon any who have prayed to receive Christ with any degree of apparent sincerity.

The result of these drastic alterations in the gospel is that multitudes of individuals demonstrate little evidence of saving grace, yet walk with the greatest assurance of salvation and respond with the greatest offense to anyone who would question their confession. They believe themselves saved, carry their assurance in their heart, and have the affirmation of a religious authority. They have seldom heard a gospel warning to empty confessors of faith or been admonished to examine themselves in light of the Scriptures or test themselves for objective evidences of conversion.[1] They sense no urgency and find little need to make their calling and election sure.[2]

A WARNING TO MINISTERS

Many who serve as gospel ministers must accept the greater blame for people's prevalent nonchalant attitude toward salvation and superficial view of assurance. These erroneous opinions and careless attitudes toward the gospel and conversion did not spring forth from a careful reading of the Scriptures or a serious study of the great confessions and preaching of former centuries. Rather, these faulty, dangerous opinions are the result of ministers who preach carelessly, handle the gospel with little trepidation, and deal with people's souls in a superficial manner.

This depreciation and poor handling of the gospel results from the twentieth century's gradual but decisive departure from a serious and devout study of biblical truth, which alone has the power to give men a high view of God, a right esteem for the gospel, and a healthy fear to discharge the solemn responsibility that has been laid upon ministers. Thus, men have traded their mantles for methodologies, prophecy for pragmatism, and the power of the Holy Spirit for cleverly devised marketing strategies. The school of the prophets now looks more like a leadership-training seminar for future CEOs and junior executives. The pastor's presentation of life principles is given priority over gospel preaching, the rapid growth and mobilization of the congregation has become more important than the purity of the church, and the conversion of the

---

1. Matthew 7:13–27; 2 Corinthians 13:5; Titus 1:16.
2. 2 Peter 1:10.

congregant is assumed if he has prayed the sinner's prayer and partici-pates in the advancement of the church's mission statement.

As ministers to whom much has been given and from whom much will be required, we must guard through the Holy Spirit the treasure that has been entrusted to us.[3] We must return to the ancient paths marked out by the Word of God.[4] We must be absorbed in the Scriptures, that our progress in piety and our usefulness in the gospel ministry might be evident to all.[5] We must be diligent to present ourselves approved to God as workers who have no cause for shame, accurately handling the word of truth.[6] We must pay close attention to ourselves and our teach-ing—especially as we teach the gospel—for as we do, we will ensure both our own salvation and that of our hearers.[7] As ministers of the gospel, we cannot be uninformed or careless with regard to our preaching of the gospel, our calling people to repentance and faith, and our counseling of seekers. People's eternal destiny and the church's reputation depend upon our diligence and fidelity in these high matters.

We must remember that Jesus Christ has a church made up of those who have been regenerated by the Holy Spirit, who have repented and believed unto salvation, and who continue walking and growing in grace. This church is God's creation and one of His most spectacular works.[8] It is the instrument God has ordained through which to display His glory and make known His manifold wisdom to the rulers and authorities in heavenly places.[9] The church is an important enterprise, and all of us, ministers and laymen alike, who have been called to contribute to her edi-fication, must take extreme care. We must do all within our means to see that our service adds to her edification and beauty rather than weakens her or does insufferable damage to her testimony. This present threat is what gave rise to the apostle Paul's admonition to the church in Corinth:

> For no other foundation can anyone lay than that which is laid, which is Jesus Christ. Now if anyone builds on this foundation with gold, silver, precious stones, wood, hay, straw, each one's work will

---

3. Luke 12:47–48; 2 Timothy 1:14.
4. Jeremiah 6:16.
5. 1 Timothy 4:15.
6. 2 Timothy 2:15.
7. 1 Timothy 4:16.
8. Ephesians 2:10.
9. Ephesians 3:10.

become clear; for the Day will declare it, because it will be revealed by fire; and the fire will test each one's work, of what sort it is. If anyone's work which he has built on it endures, he will receive a reward. If anyone's work is burned, he will suffer loss; but he himself will be saved, yet so as through fire. (1 Cor. 3:11–15)

Jesus Christ is the Great Cornerstone[10] of the church; therefore, her foundation is unshakable. As Paul wrote to young Timothy, "The solid foundation of God stands, having this seal: 'The Lord knows those who are His'" (2 Tim. 2:19). On the other hand, we have been called to build upon that foundation with a fear and trembling that flow from two fountains. First, we know that our contributions to the church have the power to strengthen or weaken and beautify or spoil her. Second, we know that we will be judged for the quality of our ministry toward the church. On that great day, the value of our labor will be revealed by fire. Though we will be saved by God's grace and the blood of the Lamb, we may well witness the burning of all our labors. These thoughts should move the gospel minister to be careful in every aspect of his ministry, but especially in his preaching of the gospel and care for souls. If this first stone is out of place, then the entire wall will be weakened, and the church's reputation, which is more precious than gold, will be soiled.

THE DANGERS OF FALSE ASSURANCE

Although what I have been discussing so far is a hard saying and difficult to understand,[11] good evidence suggests that it is an accurate description of much of modern evangelicalism. Many have handled the gospel carelessly, generalizing its essential truths and reducing its content to the lowest common denominator in order to include the largest number of professions into a fellowship. The glorious gospel of our blessed God[12] has become a shallow creed made up of a few spiritual laws or principles. If an individual is willing to give even the most superficial assent to this creed, we authoritatively declare him born again, welcome him into the family of God, and place his name on the church roll. Although a few converts are actually converted, far too many either never return to the

---

10. Psalm 118:22; Isaiah 28:16; Matthew 21:42; Mark 12:10; Luke 20:17; Acts 4:11; Ephesians 2:20; 1 Peter 2:6–7.
11. John 6:60.
12. 1 Timothy 1:11.

fellowship or disappear from the congregation after only a few months. Others who keep their association with the church often demonstrate a great dullness toward Christ, a frightening apathy toward holiness, and a disregard for ministry. They are not bound to the church by a vital union with Christ but by all that the congregation with its vibrant leadership and programs can offer them: a wholesome community, exciting relationships, a place for their children to grow, and a constant catering to their felt needs.

Because of an evangelical pulpit weakened by ignorance, pragmatism, and fear, the professing church is filled with individuals who have never really been confronted with the gospel of Jesus Christ, have never heard any of the gospel's warnings, and have little understanding of genuine biblical assurance. Furthermore, evangelicals explain away these individuals' lack of sanctification and worldliness with one of the most dangerous terms that has ever come forth: the carnal Christian. It is the doctrine that a genuine believer in Jesus Christ, a person regenerated and indwelt by the Holy Spirit, can actually live out his entire life in worldliness, indulging in fleshly desires and evidencing little concern for the things of God. This doctrine is a direct contradiction of the teachings of Christ and the apostles. Furthermore, it opens the door for carnal and unregenerate people to find assurance of salvation by looking to the apparent sincerity of their past decision to accept Christ, even though their manner of living contradicts such a profession.[13]

In contrast to this doctrine, the Scriptures admonish those professing faith in Christ to find assurance of their salvation not only by a close examination of their conversion experience but also by a close examination of their manner of living after that experience. Do they demonstrate ongoing evidence of God's sanctifying work, without which no one will see the Lord?[14] Is the God who began a good work perfecting it?[15] Does the person have fruit in keeping with genuine repentance and faith?[16] Is his profession proven or evidenced by genuine works of piety?[17]

---

13. Titus 1:16.
14. Hebrews 12:14.
15. Philippians 1:6.
16. Matthew 3:8.
17. James 2:18.

LORDSHIP SALVATION

Among evangelicals is a great deal of debate over what has been termed "lordship salvation." The proponents of this teaching believe that salvation requires that a person not only receive Jesus Christ as Savior but also as Lord. Those on the other side of the debate teach that in order to be saved a person need only receive Christ as Savior; the issue of lordship is an entirely independent matter. Consequently, they argue that to demand submission to the lordship of Christ is to contradict the doctrine of salvation by grace alone through faith alone.[18] If a person must submit to the lordship of Christ to gain salvation, then it is no longer on the basis of grace but of works.[19]

While I applaud every sincere effort to protect the essential doctrine of salvation by grace alone through faith alone, I must disagree with this opinion. I argue that the call to submission to the lordship of Jesus is an inherent and essential aspect of the gospel call to sinners. Furthermore, I argue that a professing Christian's growth or gradual progress in submission to the Lord Jesus Christ is an evidence of genuine conversion. My convictions are founded upon the following truths.

First, Christ Himself taught the absolute necessity of a sincere and practical submission to His lordship as an essential aspect of salvation. Not only does salvation require a confession of lordship but also a proof of that confession. In the conclusion of the Sermon on the Mount, Christ strongly warned His hearers that submission to His lordship was the great litmus test of true confession. In His words, the gate is small and the way is narrow that leads to life, and there are few who find it, even among those who emphatically declare Him to be Lord: "Not everyone who says to Me, 'Lord, Lord,' shall enter the kingdom of heaven, but he who does the will of My Father in heaven" (Matt. 7:13–14, 21).

Christ is not teaching a works-based salvation but rather a truth that runs through the entire course of Scripture. Submission to the lordship of God and His Christ (i.e., obedience to the will of God) is the evidence of saving faith. While it is heretical even to entertain the thought that faith plus works equals salvation, it is biblical, orthodox, and historically Christian to believe and proclaim that works are the result of salvation and a test of its authenticity.

---

18. Ephesians 2:8.
19. Romans 11:6.

Second, submission to the lordship of Jesus Christ was an essential aspect of the apostolic proclamation of the gospel. No one can deny that the apostles solemnly testified to both Jews and Greeks that God had made this Jesus, whom the world crucified, both Lord and Christ.[20] Furthermore, according to the apostolic proclamation of the gospel, a person's confession of Christ's universal lordship is essential for salvation. Here the apostle Paul is emphatic: "that if you confess with your mouth the Lord Jesus and believe in your heart that God has raised Him from the dead, you will be saved" (Rom. 10:9).

This is one of the most important confessional statements in the Scriptures. Furthermore, it is one of the most widely employed among evangelicals for the purpose of evangelism. Are we, or the apostle for that matter, merely calling sinners to an empty confession of the lordship of Christ? Are they only to confess Jesus as Lord without any intentions to submit to His will? Can a person believe a truth as great as this in his heart and confess it with his mouth without experiencing any practical influence upon the purpose, direction, and manner of his life? It is wrong to suggest the possibility. Furthermore, we have just considered that any confession of the lordship of Christ that does not manifest itself in the doing of His will is empty and will result in eternal ruin.[21]

Third, the objections often raised against lordship salvation seem to result from a misunderstanding of the nature of salvation, especially of the doctrines of regeneration and perseverance. When the Scriptures teach that practical and discernible submission to the lordship of Jesus[22] is an essential evidence of salvation and a means of assurance, they in no way infer that salvation or the believer's perseverance is the result of works. The believer's submission to the lordship of Christ neither causes nor preserves salvation, but rather is the result of God's great work of salvation in the believer. This work is twofold. First, the person who repents and believes unto salvation has been regenerated by the Holy Spirit, which is a supernatural and recreating work of God that results in a real change (as opposed to a poetic or metaphorical change) in the believer's nature. The Christian has become a new creature[23] with new affections

---

20. Acts 2:36; 20:21; 1 Corinthians 2:8.

21. Matthew 7:23.

22. Submission to the lordship of Jesus is synonymous with fruit (Matt. 7:16, 20), obedience to Jesus' will (Matt. 7:21), and works (James 2:14–26).

23. 2 Corinthians 5:17.

for righteousness and a new inclination toward godliness and true piety. Second, the person who repents and believes unto salvation has become the workmanship of God.[24] God's continuing work of grace after salvation assures that every genuine believer will make degrees of progress in sanctification. This is not the result of self-will or works springing forth from the believer's own determination but the result of God's work in the believer. He who began the good work at conversion continues working until that final day. Progress in sanctification throughout a believer's life will be evident because it is God who works "both to will and to do" for His good pleasure (Phil. 2:13).

Because of the Spirit's regenerating and sanctifying work, every genuine believer will grow in submission to the lordship of Jesus Christ and in conformity to Him. This neither means that all believers grow at the same pace or to the same degree nor does it require that a believer show evidence of progress at any given moment. Even the most sincere believer will fall into periods of carnality in thought, word, and deed. What it does mean is that through the full course of the believer's life there will be discernible growth in submission to the lordship of Christ, works of righteousness, and fruit-bearing. The 1689 London Confession and the Westminster Confession agree in chapter 13, articles 1–3:

> They who are united to Christ, effectually called, and regenerated, having a new heart and a new spirit created in them through the virtue of Christ's death and resurrection, are also further sanctified, really and personally, through the same virtue, by His Word and Spirit dwelling in them; the dominion of the whole body of sin is destroyed, and the several lusts thereof are more and more weakened and mortified, and they more and more quickened and strengthened in all saving graces, to the practice of all true holiness, without which no man shall see the Lord.
>
> This sanctification is throughout the whole man, yet imperfect in this life; there abideth still some remnants of corruption in every part, whence ariseth a continual and irreconcilable war; the flesh lusting against the Spirit, and the Spirit against the flesh.
>
> In which war, although the remaining corruption for a time may much prevail, yet through the continual supply of strength from the sanctifying Spirit of Christ, the regenerate part doth overcome; and so the saints grow in grace, perfecting holiness in the fear of

---

24. Ephesians 2:10.

God, pressing after an heavenly life, in evangelical obedience to all the commands which Christ as Head and King, in His Word hath prescribed them.

As if the Westminster and London Confessions were not enough to demonstrate that genuine, saving faith is evidenced by sanctfication and the bearing of fruit, we can also turn to the esteemed Belgic Confession of Faith (1561) and its remarkable comments in articles 22 and 24. Here again we see the agreement between the doctrine of salvation by faith alone and the clear teaching of Scripture that such saving faith is evidenced by works:

> Therefore, to say that Christ is not enough but that something else is needed as well is a most enormous blasphemy against God—for it then would follow that Jesus Christ is only half a Savior.... And therefore we justly say with Paul that we are justified "by faith alone" or by faith "apart from the deeds of the law" (Romans 3:28).

> We believe that this true faith, produced in man by the hearing of God's Word and by the work of the Holy Spirit, regenerates him and makes him a "new creation" (2 Corinthians 5:17) causing him to live the "newness of life" (Romans 6:4) and freeing him from the slavery of sin.... So then, it is impossible for this holy faith to be unfruitful in a human being, seeing that we do not speak of an empty faith but of what Scripture calls "faith working through love" (Galatians 5:6) which leads a man to do by himself the works that God has commanded in His Word.

Salvation is by grace alone through faith alone, yet the nature of salvation guarantees that saving faith will have real and practical evidences. Thus, those who have truly believed in Christ unto salvation may gain greater assurance of their salvation not only through examining their conversion experience in light of the Scriptures but also by thoroughly examining their life since the moment of their conversion. Although all believers are subject to many failings and can fall before the smallest temptation, their determination to continue in the faith and their gradual and progressive sanctification are great evidences of salvation and provide a solid ground for assurance.

CHAPTER TWO

Examining Yourself

---

*Examine yourselves as to whether you are in the faith. Test yourselves.
Do you not know yourselves, that Jesus Christ is in you?—unless indeed
you are disqualified.*

—2 Corinthians 13:5

*These things I have written to you who believe in the name of the Son of
God, that you may know that you have eternal life.*

—1 John 5:13

We will now consider one of the essential doctrines regarding the believer's relationship with God: assurance. What is the basis for the believer's assurance that his sins have been forgiven and that he has been reconciled with God?

All who are truly Christian recognize that salvation is the result of faith in the person and work of Christ: His deity, incarnation, impeccable life, atoning sacrifice, resurrection from the dead, and ascension to the right hand of God. Yet how do we know that we have believed unto sal-vation[1] and that we are not merely deceived by a false faith? After all, the Scriptures are filled with many grave and solemn warnings against those who profess faith in Christ but by their deeds deny Him; who emphatically declare His lordship yet are turned away on the day of judgment; who believe themselves to be sheep yet are counted with the goats and sent away into eternal punishment.[2] The frightening parable of the marriage feast, by which Jesus reminds His listeners that "many are called, but few are chosen," tells of an invited guest who arrived unprepared, was speechless when beckoned before the king, and was finally bound

---

1. Romans 1:16; 10:10; 2 Timothy 3:15; 1 Peter 1:5.
2. Matthew 7:21–23; 25:41–26; Titus 1:16.

hand and foot and thrown into a place of outer darkness, where there is weeping and gnashing of teeth.[3] Salvation is by grace alone through faith alone, but how do we know that the saving faith required is the faith we possess? Salvation is given to those who believe, but how do we know that we truly believe?

THE NEED FOR SELF-EXAMINATION

The church in Corinth was unusually blessed. By the apostle Paul's own admission, they were enriched in Christ in all speech and knowledge so that they were not lacking in any gift.[4] However, there were also great problems in the church. There was division among the members, jealousy and strife, superiority and pride, immorality, lawsuits, worldliness, abuses of liberty, disorder in the meetings, and a near denial of the doctrine of the resurrection.[5] In light of these things, the apostle had every reason to rebuke the congregation sternly: "And I, brethren, could not speak to you as to spiritual people but as to carnal, as to babes in Christ. I fed you with milk and not with solid food; for until now you were not able to receive it, and even now you are still not able; for you are still carnal. For where there are envy, strife, and divisions among you, are you not carnal and behaving like mere men?"[6]

We should carefully note Paul's choice of words. He does not coddle the Corinthians but reproves them with the strongest possible language. At best, he denounces them as baby Christians who are yet unable to receive and appropriate solid food, or mature teaching. At worst, he speaks to them as to fleshly or unregenerate men who do not have the Spirit of God and who walk as the Gentiles.[7] In light of the Corinthians' ungodly behavior, Paul was merely putting forth two possibilities. The first was that the Corinthians were immature Christians who had fallen into error for a time and needed both reproof and instruction to be set back on the road of true piety and godliness. The second possibility was that at least some of the members were still unconverted. They were walking like "mere men" because they were following the lusts of the

---

3. Matthew 22:8–13.
4. 1 Corinthians 1:4–7.
5. 1 Corinthians 1:10; 3:3; 4:7–8; 5:1; 6:1–6, 9–20; 8:1–9:27; 11:1–14:40; 15:1–58.
6. 1 Corinthians 3:1–3.
7. Ephesians 4:17–19.

flesh, indulging in the desires of the flesh, and unable to accept the things of the Spirit of God.[8] Only time and their appropriate response to Paul's reproof would demonstrate the validity of their faith.

Here we find the modus operandi of the faithful, well-instructed minister when those who are professing a faith contradicted by their manner of living confront him. Since he does not have omniscience at his disposal, he must seek to discern one of two possibilities. The first possibility is that those professing faith are immature or wayward believers who can and will be restored through the providence of God, the Spirit's aid, and the proper administration of God's Word: teaching, reproof, correction, and training.[9] The second possibility is that those professing faith are still unconverted. They are holding to a form of godliness and yet denying its power; professing faith in Christ and yet denying Him with their lives.[10] At the minister's rebuke these people will repent and believe unto salvation, ignore the warning and continue in their sin, or mend their ways for a time and then return to their folly as "'a dog returns to his own vomit,' and 'a sow, having washed, to her wallowing in the mire'" (Prov. 26:11; 2 Peter 2:22). In this way, the true and false convert are discerned.

Before we continue, we must once again clearly state that the genuine Christian is not wholly sanctified in this life. The flesh will not be fully eradicated until his final glorification in heaven.[11] There will always be, even in the most devout life, a constant battle against sin and moral failure and a need for repentance, confession, and restoration.[12] However, there will be a great difference between the weakest sincere believer who struggles against sin and makes only minimal progress in sanctification and the false convert who professes faith in Christ yet lives in a near-constant state of worldliness with little offense to his conscience, brokenness over sin, or heartfelt confession. It is because of these distinguishable differences between the true and false convert that the apostle Paul gives the following authoritative directive to the wayward Corinthians at the end of his second letter to them: "Examine yourselves as to whether you

---

8. 1 Corinthians 2:14; Ephesians 2:3.
9. 2 Timothy 3:16.
10. 2 Timothy 3:5; Titus 1:16.
11. Galatians 5:17.
12. 1 John 1:8–10.

are in the faith. Test yourselves. Do you not know yourselves, that Jesus Christ is in you?—unless indeed you are disqualified" (2 Cor. 13:5).

From Paul's letters to the church in Corinth, we understand that false apostles and prophets among them were constantly subjecting Paul's life and ministry to critical examination, casting doubt upon his appointment as an apostle, and even questioning the sincerity of his faith.[13] Paul turns the tables on his opponents and those who were listening to them and tells them to test *themselves* and examine *themselves*[14] with regard to the authenticity of their profession because they were living a life that did not conform to their declaration of faith and purported identification with Christ.

Paul's admonishment to the professing Christians in Corinth to examine themselves and look for evidences of conversion proves that God's work of salvation in the believer will not only result in justification but also in real, practical, and observable sanctification. God not only frees the believer from the condemnation of sin but also continues to work in the believer to free him from the power of sin. Every genuine believer in Jesus Christ has been regenerated by the Holy Spirit and has become a new creature with new affections for God and His righteousness. Furthermore, the Spirit who regenerates a believer now works to sanctify him. The believer has become the workmanship of God, and God who began a good work will finish it.[15]

The rediscovery of this truth in modern-day evangelicalism is essential. A great multitude of professing Christians in the West and around the world live in an almost continuous state of worldliness, carnality, and fruitlessness. Yet they sit at ease in Zion with the greatest assurance of their salvation and without the slightest fear that they have believed in vain. Many are not even actively believing in or looking to Christ, but they are trusting in a decision they made years ago that has had little discernible impact upon their lives. To make a bad situation worse, well-meaning ministers who seem to understand too little about the nature and power of salvation affirm them in their dangerous state. These ministers have become like the prophets of Jeremiah's day: "They have also

---

13. 1 Corinthians 9:1–3; 2 Corinthians 10:1–12:21; 13:3.

14. The Greek is emphatic. Paul uses the reflexive pronoun *eautou* three times: test *yourselves*, examine *yourselves*, recognize this about *yourselves*.

15. Ephesians 2:10; Philippians 1:6.

healed the hurt of My people slightly, saying, 'Peace, peace!' when there is no peace" (Jer. 6:14).

Do we not realize that so many of our converts are clouds without water, autumn trees without fruit, doubly dead, and uprooted?[16] They long for the day of the Lord, thinking it will be light, but for them it will be a day of darkness and inescapable judgment, as when a man flees from a lion and runs into a bear or leans his hand against the wall of his home and is bitten by a venomous snake.[17] They are confident, even adamant, that they will receive a rich welcome into the eternal kingdom of our Lord and Savior Jesus Christ,[18] but they will be turned away with the words, "'I never knew you; depart from Me, you who practice lawlessness!'" (Matt. 7:23).

The Lion has roared! Will we not fear and prophesy?[19] Will the watchmen not sound the trumpet and warn the wicked?[20] Will we let them sit at ease in Zion while certain judgment is visible from the watchtower? Should we not cry out to them:

> Awake, you who sleep,
> Arise from the dead,
> And Christ will give you light. (Eph. 5:14)

> Examine yourselves as to whether you are in the faith. Test yourselves. (2 Cor. 13:5)

> Make your call and election sure. (2 Peter 1:10)

Understand that this is not a call for ministers or laypeople to become the judges of others, but to put away the belief in and proclamation of a superficial and powerless gospel that is granting assurance to millions, making them resistant against a biblical gospel and sealing their eternal condemnation. We must learn to console and assure the weakest saint who is broken over his many sins, but we must also learn to warn the false convert whose life is a barren and fruitless tree and whose settled manner of living is a contradiction to the gospel.

The remedy for most of the maladies afflicting the evangelical church in the West is to return to a scriptural view of salvation that is as powerful

---

16. Jude v. 12.
17. Amos 5:18–20.
18. 2 Peter 1:11.
19. Amos 3:8.
20. Ezekiel 3:17–22; 33:1–9.

as it is marvelous. We must turn away from those who would seek to save the church by introducing novel strategies and avant-garde methodologies that will take us even further from the Scriptures. "To the law and to the testimony! If they do not speak according to this word, it is because there is no light in them" (Isa. 8:20). Let us look to the rock from which we were hewn and to the quarry from which we were dug.[21] Let us stand in the way and see, and ask for the ancient paths, where the good way is, and walk in it. Then we will find rest for our souls and for those who have been entrusted to us.[22] Then we will rebuild the ancient ruins and raise up the former devastations of many generations.[23]

Let us consider the men who walked before us with great eternal success and benefit to the church—men such as George Whitefield, Jonathan Edwards, Joseph Alleine, Charles Spurgeon, Martyn Lloyd Jones, and A. W. Tozer. True instruction was in their mouths, and unrighteousness was not found on their lips. They walked with God in peace and uprightness, and they turned many back from iniquity.[24] Let us adopt the simplicity of their evangelistic methodology. They preached the gospel, called listeners to repentance and faith, encouraged the weakest saint in the love of God, and, like their Master, warned empty confessors that not everyone who calls Jesus Lord will enter into the kingdom of heaven, but he who does the will of the Father in heaven will enter.[25] They were wholly loyal to the doctrine of salvation by grace alone through faith alone, but they also understood and preached that the grace that saves also sanctifies and that true assurance of salvation cannot be gained apart from examining oneself in the light of Scripture.

THE STANDARD OF SELF-EXAMINATION

The Scriptures command us to examine ourselves to see if we are in the faith, to test ourselves that we might discern whether we are truly Christian.[26] However, this admonition leads us to an extremely important question: What is the authoritative standard by which we are to evaluate

---

21. Isaiah 51:1.
22. Jeremiah 6:16.
23. Isaiah 61:4.
24. Malachi 2:6.
25. Matthew 7:21.
26. 2 Corinthians 13:5.

the validity of our faith? Against what sure rule can we examine our lives? Who is able to judge us and help us understand our case?

The apostle John warns us that we should not simply trust the dictates of our heart in such matters in that it might wrongly approve or condemn us.[27] The apostle Paul instructs us that it is unwise to measure ourselves by our own standard or to compare ourselves with others in our own circle of fellowship.[28] If we use the carnal man who professes Christ as our standard, we may be lulled into a false assurance. However, if we compare ourselves to the most mature Christian in our fellowship, we may find ourselves falsely condemned. Furthermore, although it is wise to seek the counsel of others in this matter, we cannot base our assurance of salvation merely on their opinions. Some may wrongly assure us because of their low view of salvation,[29] and others may wrongly condemn us by demanding proofs that exceed the dictates of Scripture, laying heavy burdens upon us that they themselves are not willing or able to bear.[30] What, then, should be our standard? Against what pattern should we evaluate the sincerity of our faith and the reality of our conversion?

We can be thankful that the standard we seek is not hopelessly hidden within the weave of Scripture nor is it an unfathomable mystery open only to the greatest minds. On the contrary, it is specifically and clearly laid out for us in the Scriptures. In fact, the standard, or tests of genuine conversion, are laid out for us most clearly, concisely, and completely in the apostle John's first epistle.

One of the most amazing and helpful characteristics about John's gospel and first epistle is that he clearly sets forth the reason for which they were written:

> And truly Jesus did many other signs in the presence of His disciples, which are not written in this book; *but these are written that you may believe that Jesus is the Christ, the Son of God, and that believing you may have life in His name.* (John 20:30–31, emphasis added)

> These things I have written to you who believe in the name of the Son of God, *that you may know that you have eternal life"* (1 John 5:13, emphasis added)

---

27. 1 John 3:19–20.
28. 2 Corinthians 10:12.
29. Jeremiah 6:14–15.
30. Matthew 23:4.

Demonstrating both the inspiration and unity of the Scriptures, John wrote his gospel so that his readers might believe in Jesus Christ and receive eternal life. Correspondingly, he wrote his first epistle so that those who had truly believed might possess full assurance that eternal life had been granted to them.

Throughout his first epistle, John sets forth a series of tests by which the true believer might examine his life in order to prove the authenticity of his profession of faith and gain an assurance of salvation based upon the infallible Word of God. Nevertheless, the epistle also serves a secondary purpose, in that it exposes the false assurance of the unbeliever who professes faith in Christ but bears none of the marks of true conversion. Several authorities support this understanding of John's purpose in writing his epistle. John R. W. Stott writes, "Throughout the epistle, John has been giving [his readers] criteria (doctrinal, moral, social) by which to test themselves and others. His purpose is to establish their assurance.... Putting together the purposes of Gospel and Epistle, John's purpose is in four stages, that his readers should hear, hearing should believe, believing should live, and living should know." D. Edmond Hiebert observes, "The author's practical purpose is evident. It is his basic desire to ground them in the assurance of their salvation.... He provides them with a series of tests whereby they may test their own faith and conduct and so reassure their own hearts.... The assurance John has in view is not the result of wishful thinking but is firmly grounded in the varied evidences set forth in the epistle." Finally, Colin G. Kruse asserts:

> The author's primary reason for writing the letter was to bolster their assurance by counteracting the false teaching of the secessionists. The author sought to do this by pointing out that it was his readers who had truly received eternal life, who truly knew God, not the secessionists. It was his readers who manifested the authentic marks of those who have eternal life; they were the ones who continued in the teaching first proclaimed by the eyewitnesses; they were the ones who continued to obey the commands of the Lord; and they were the ones who loved the children of God, which is the essential mark of those who have eternal life.[31]

---

31. John R. W. Stott, *The Epistles of John: An Introduction and Commentary* (London: Tyndale, 1964), 184–85; D. Edmond Hiebert, *The Epistles of John: An Expositional Commentary* (Greenville, S.C.: Bob Jones University Press, 1991), 19, 52; and Colin G. Kruse, *The Letters of John* (Grand Rapids: Eerdmans, 2000), 188–89.

John has given his readers various doctrinal and moral criteria by which they may test themselves regarding the authenticity of their claim to salvation. He seeks to establish their assurance of salvation not upon wishful thinking, religious feelings, or a mere confession of faith but upon the demonstration or manifestation of the authentic marks of Christianity in their lives. According to John's doctrine, those who profess faith in Christ can have a biblical assurance of salvation only to the degree that their lives conform to the tests he presents in this first letter.

In summary, it is important for us to remember that John is not setting forth the means of conversion but rather the results of it. We can have a biblical assurance of salvation to the degree that the evidences set forth in John's epistle are realities in our lives. If after testing ourselves we find little reality of these evidences, we should be greatly concerned. If our manner of living stands in great contrast to John's description of the true believer, then we must seriously consider one of two possibilities. First is the possibility that we are a genuine child of God who has strayed from His will and is in great need of repentance. If we do truly repent and return to the will of God as a practice of life then there is great hope that we have truly believed and possess eternal life. The second is that we have never truly come to know the Lord and that both our faith and our confession have been false from the beginning. In this case, we must seek the Lord and call upon Him. If we are truly repentant, we may seek Him with great confidence, knowing that a broken and contrite spirit He will not despise, that whoever comes to Him He will certainly not cast out, that whoever calls on the name of the Lord will be saved, and that whoever believes in Him will not be disappointed.[32]

In the chapters that follow, we will explain and expound upon each test in the order that they occur in John's letter. The reader is encouraged to study through each chapter carefully and prayerfully. The Scriptures call upon us to test ourselves to determine whether we are truly Christian.[33] In the chapters that follow, we will be obeying this command.

---

32. Psalm 51:17; John 6:37; Romans 10:11, 13.
33. 2 Corinthians 13:5.

CHAPTER THREE

Walking in God's Revelation

This is the message which we have heard from Him and declare to you, that God is light and in Him is no darkness at all. If we say that we have fellowship with Him, and walk in darkness, we lie and do not practice the truth. But if we walk in the light as He is in the light, we have fellowship with one another, and the blood of Jesus Christ His Son cleanses us from all sin.

—1 John 1:5–7

John wrote his first epistle with a specific purpose—that those who believe in Jesus Christ might possess a great assurance that they have eternal life.[1] To accomplish this purpose, the apostle set forth several evidences, or essential characteristics, of genuine conversion by which we may examine our lives and test the authenticity of our confession. The first of these characteristics may be summarized by this statement:

> The Christian will walk in the light. His manner of living will conform to what God has revealed to us about His nature and will.

GOD IS LIGHT

First John 1:5 begins with an extremely important declaration: "God is light and in Him is no darkness at all." John commonly uses the words "light" and "darkness" in his writings,[2] and it is of particular importance that we discover their meaning in this text. At first glance, John's contrast of light and darkness may lead us to think of them primarily as moral terms: the distinction between good and evil or the great divide between

---

1. 1 John 5:13.
2. See John 1:4–5; 3:19; and 1 John 2:8–10 for several examples of this common theme in John's gospel and epistles.

the holy and the profane. This interpretation would certainly agree with what the Scriptures tell us about God's holiness. However, when John writes that God is light he is not only denoting His moral purity but also indicating that He is a God who has made Himself known. The God of Scriptures is not hidden or dark; He is light. He has revealed Himself to mankind through creation, history, Scripture, and especially through the incarnation and redemptive work of His Son, Jesus Christ.

This understanding of God being light becomes even more evident when we consider the historical context of John's first epistle. The church or churches to whom John was writing had come under the influence of a false teaching that later evolved into one of the greatest heresies ever to confront the church—Gnosticism, a mixture of Greek philosophy, Jewish mysticism, and Christianity. It was an esoteric religion filled with mysteries, secret knowledge, and a hidden god who could be known only by the truly initiated or the upper echelons of the super-spiritual.

To combat this dangerous and destructive heresy, the apostle John explains to the church that God is light, and He has made Himself and His will known to them through the testimony of the apostles, who were eyewitnesses of the incarnation, and through the teaching of the Holy Spirit, whom they had all received.[3] God was not hidden, as the false teachers supposed, nor was His truth the exclusive possession of only a handful of self-proclaimed super-apostles. God had revealed Himself and His will to everyone who had believed in Christ and been born of God. John powerfully sets forth this truth in his closing argument at the very conclusion of the epistle: "And we know that the Son of God has come and *has given us an understanding,* that we may know Him who is true; and we are in Him who is true, in His Son Jesus Christ. This is the true God and eternal life" (1 John 5:20, emphasis added).

Based upon what we know about the internal evidence of the epistle and the historical context in which it was written, we may confidently conclude the following: the declaration that "God is light" not only refers to His impeccable moral character but also to His relationship to every believer in Jesus Christ and His revelation to them. God has not hidden Himself from His people but has graciously and abundantly revealed both His nature and will to them. He has made Himself known to us as the Lord who delights in and exercises lovingkindness, justice, and

---

3. 1 John 1:1–4; 2:20; 2:27.

righteousness on the earth.[4] He has told us what is good and what He requires of us.[5] In this, Jeremiah's prophecy concerning the new covenant has been fulfilled: "No more shall every man teach his neighbor, and every man his brother, saying, 'Know the LORD,' for they all shall know Me, from the least of them to the greatest of them, says the LORD. For I will forgive their iniquity, and their sin I will remember no more" (Jer. 31:34).

THE MEANING OF FELLOWSHIP

We will now consider the word "fellowship" and seek to discern its proper meaning. The word is derived from the Greek noun *koinonía*, which was commonly used to denote association, fellowship, communion, or joint participation. In the context of this epistle, a person who claims fellowship with God professes faith in Him and declares himself to be His child. Those who are outside of fellowship with God are yet unconverted, dead in their trespasses and sins, and under the wrath of God.[6]

In recent times, the meaning of "fellowship" in this context has been greatly misconstrued. Some now believe and teach that John is not making a distinction between those who truly believe unto salvation and those who are yet unconverted, but that he is drawing a distinction between spiritual Christians who commune with God and carnal Christians who are out of fellowship with Him. This interpretation not only departs from the true meaning of the text but also betrays the purpose for which John has written the entire epistle. He does not say, "These things I have written to you who believe in the name of the Son of God so that you may know whether you are spiritual or carnal Christians." Furthermore, verse 7 teaches us that only those who walk in the light can count on the cleansing blood of God's Son. If those who walk in the darkness are carnal Christians, then they are outside of the cleansing efficacy of Christ's blood. This is an impossibility for any Christian.

In light of these truths, we rightly conclude that to have fellowship with God is to be a Christian possessing all the benefits and blessings of Christ's atoning work. On the other hand, to be outside of God's fellowship is to be yet unconverted, separated from God, and in danger of eternal destruction.

---

4. Jeremiah 9:24.
5. Micah 6:8.
6. Ephesians 2:1–3; 5:6.

THE CHRISTIAN WALKS IN THE LIGHT

We will now consider the first characteristic of the genuine Christian: he walks in the light. The word "walk" is translated from the Greek verb *peripatéo*, which literally means to walk about or around. Metaphorically, it is used to denote a person's manner of life or conduct. It is important to note that "walk" is in the present tense, which also denotes a continuous action and further establishes that John is using it in reference to a person's style of life, manner of living, or settled practice. Thus, the first characteristic of a true child of God is that he walks in the light. His style of life conforms to what God has revealed about both His nature and will. On the other hand, the false convert walks in darkness. His style of life reflects a self-imposed ignorance of God, and His conduct demonstrates little conformity to God's nature or will as they are revealed through the Scriptures.

As we consider this first test of genuine faith, we must take care to understand that John is not teaching that a Christian can or will attain to some level of sinless perfection, an erroneous view that Christians can attain a level of sanctification in this life in which they no longer sin. Neither is he suggesting that the Christian's life will always be a perfect reflection of God's character and will. He is simply stating that the genuine believer's style of life or overall conduct will reflect conformity to what God has revealed about Himself and His will. Furthermore, although the believer's life may be battered by great struggles and tainted by intermittent failure, there will be a marked difference between his life and conduct and that of an unbeliever. The evidence of salvation is not perfectionism or the ability always to walk in the light of God's revelation. Rather, the evidence of salvation is that upon careful examination of our lives, we see a real and growing conformity to God's nature and will. However, if we discover a life unchanged and a consistent manner of conduct that contradicts what God has revealed in His Word about His nature and will, then we should be greatly concerned.

It is important to note that when we speak of self-examination, we are not referring to a moment in time or a single event but to the full course of our lives since the moment of our professed conversion. We cannot determine the validity of God's saving work in us by examining our conduct through the course of only one day. Even the most mature Christian will have momentary moral lapses and times of pruning when there seems to be little fruit. It would be presumptuous for us to confirm our salvation based on the careful examination of one good deed, and it would be equally foolish for us to condemn ourselves for one fall into sin. To correctly examine our profession of faith requires that we consider the entirety of our lives since the moment of our professed conversion until the present. We must ask ourselves if over the full course of our Christian life there is evidence of greater and greater conformity to the person and will of God. The following illustration may be helpful.

If we were to observe a professing Christian for only a short period of time and then take a snapshot at the very moment he committed a moral failure, we could not use the photograph as proof of his unconverted state. It tells us little about his style of life since his conversion. However, if we were to follow the same professing Christian for several years with a digital camera that recorded constantly, we would be able to gather ample evidence to argue either for or against his confession of faith. If he was truly Christian, we would still not see a perfect life unstained by sin, but we would see a life that was both changed and changing, gradually growing in conformity to God's nature and will. The weakness would be evident, the battles would be hard won, and the progress would often be three steps forward and two steps back. Nevertheless, over the full course of this Christian's life, there would be discernible evidence of greater and greater conformity to the nature and will of God.

DO WE WALK IN THE LIGHT?

Now that we understand the meaning of the text, we must apply its truths to ourselves: Do we walk in the light? Does our style of life reflect a growing conformity to what God has revealed to us in the Scriptures about His nature and will? Is there a detectable distinction between our manner of living and that of an unbeliever? If an impartial observer were to study each of our lives over a period of several months, would he be able to gather enough proof to argue for the validity of our faith in a court of law, or would his case be thrown out of court for a lack of evidence?

"God is light and in Him is no darkness at all" (1 John 1:5). Do we bear any resemblance to that light? Do we walk as children of light, bearing the fruit of the light that consists in all goodness, righteousness, and truth?[7] Or do we walk as the unbelievers walk, in the futility of our

---

7. Ephesians 5:8–9.

minds, darkened in our understanding, and excluded from the life of God?[8] Is our confession of Jesus as Savior and Lord proven sincere by a life that is marked by submission to the Father's will, or is it proven false by a lifestyle of spiritual neglect, lack of conformity to the nature of God, and rebellion against the revelation of His will?[9]

If we say that we are truly Christian and yet walk in the darkness, we are lying. It makes little difference whether such lying is intentional or we have been deceived by the superficial gospel of our time. We must acknowledge that we have entered through the wide gate and are walking in the broad way that leads to destruction.[10] We must admit that we have a name that we are alive, even though we are dead in our trespasses and sins.[11] We must flee from the wrath to come and draw near to God with repentance and faith.[12] We must seek Him until He is found.

If we say that we have fellowship with God and we walk in the light, then we have passed John's first test on the way to a full assurance of salvation. We have laid the first stone in a wall of hope that will be founded upon the Scriptures and impregnable to the enemy's fiery darts of doubt. We should be encouraged but not presumptuous. We must continue on to John's other tests and examine our lives in light of them.

---

8. Ephesians 4:17–20.
9. Matthew 7:21, 23.
10. Matthew 7:13.
11. Ephesians 2:1; Revelation 3:1.
12. Matthew 3:7; Luke 3:7; James 4:8.

CHAPTER FOUR

Confessing Sin

If we say that we have no sin, we deceive ourselves, and the truth is not in us. If we confess our sins, He is faithful and just to forgive us our sins and to cleanse us from all unrighteousness. If we say that we have not sinned, we make Him a liar, and His word is not in us.

—1 John 1:8–10

The second test of true conversion may be one of the most remarkable in that it proves that the believer's assurance of salvation is not based on the absence of sin in his life but upon his proper response when his sin is brought to his attention. The mark of the true believer is not sinless perfection but that sin becomes more and more repugnant to him, more and more antagonistic to his desires. The reality of sin leads him to repentance and confession. This truth is supported by some of the greatest declarations in the Scriptures regarding the believer and his attitude toward sin.

> The sacrifices of God are a broken spirit,
> A broken and a contrite heart—
> These, O God, You will not despise. (Ps. 51:17)

> "But on this one will I look:
> On him who is poor and of a contrite spirit,
> And who trembles at My word." (Isa. 66:2)

> "Blessed are those who mourn, for they shall be comforted." (Matt. 5:4)

> "Blessed are those who hunger and thirst for righteousness, for they shall be filled." (Matt. 5:6)

The evidence that we have become children of God is that when we become aware of our sin we respond with humility, brokenness, contrition, mourning, and trembling at the law we have spurned. That God presents this truth to us at the beginning of our self-examination demonstrates the greatness of His wisdom. If the truth of this text had come later, we may have been too severe with our self-examination and fallen under a false condemnation leading to hopelessness. We could easily have misinterpreted and misapplied the first test that we considered, leading us to believe that our all-too-frequent wanderings from the light prove our unconverted state. Yet here at the very beginning of our self-examination, God proves to us that our frequent struggling against sin does not disprove our profession of faith but rather confirms it. We know that we have come to know Him not because we are without sin but because our attitude toward sin has been radically altered: we have a growing hatred for it, are broken over it, and confess it.

THE BELIEVER'S NEW RELATIONSHIP WITH SIN

A recent convert will often break the news of his conversion by declaring that he has a new relationship with God. However, little does he understand that the adverse is also true: he has a new relationship with sin. In fact, the validity of his claim to a new relationship with God can be affirmed only to the degree that his relationship with sin has changed.

Prior to regeneration and conversion, the sinner is a lover of self and pleasure and a hater of God and good.[1] Job observed that unconverted men thirst for iniquity and drink it down like water.[2] The wisdom of Solomon exposes the natural man as one who not only leaves the paths of uprightness to walk in the ways of darkness but also delights in doing evil and rejoices in the perversity of it.[3] The reason for this inclination and fellowship with evil is made clear to us throughout all of Scripture but particularly in the counsel of the prophet Jeremiah, who described fallen man's heart as "deceitful above all things, and desperately wicked." In fact, Jeremiah was so taken back by the radical depravity of the human heart that he declared in astonishment, "Who can know it?" (Jer. 17:9). This fallen human heart produces in natural man his great affections for sin and his equally great disdain of God and righteousness.

---

1. Romans 1:30; 2 Timothy 3:2–4.
2. Job 15:16.
3. Proverbs 2:13–14.

However, in the titanic work of conversion, God recreates the heart after His likeness in true righteousness and holiness.[4] This radically altered heart has new and radically altered affections. Its love for self has been replaced by a love for God, and its thirsting for iniquity has been replaced by a hungering and thirsting for righteousness.[5] To put it simply, the Christian now loves the God he once hated and hates the self he once loved; he now desires the righteousness he once spurned and despises the unrighteousness of which he once boasted.

Some may argue that this description of the believer's radically altered heart is unrealistic, the result of an overrealized eschatology that ascribes to the believer blessings of salvation in the present that will only be realized in his ultimate glorification. They may argue that this description is even unbiblical. They may respond with the question, "If this is so, then why do I still struggle with sin?" The answer is clearly set forth in the Scriptures. Although we must never diminish the believer's great and ongoing struggle with sin, we must not explain away or diminish the power of regeneration. The believer's struggle against sin is not because regeneration is any less powerful than I have described but because the believer's new heart is still opposed by a great and seemingly undaunted enemy—the flesh. Although the concept of "the flesh" is difficult to define, we must accept that there is some remnant of the old man that remains with the believer until it is ultimately eradicated in the believer's glorification.[6] There is some unredeemed aspect of the believer's person that makes him susceptible to temptation and wars against the new man he has been recreated to be. Paul sets forth the reality of such a battle in the following words to the churches in Galatia: "For the flesh lusts against the Spirit, and the Spirit against the flesh; and these are contrary to one another, so that you do not do the things that you wish" (Gal. 5:17).

Even though the believer will battle with sin and at times suffer loss, both his heart and affections have been transformed. His sin is no longer a cause for delight and boasting but of mourning and confession. In fact, this mourning that leads to confession is one of the greatest evidences of his conversion. He is no longer a child of the devil or a son

---

4. Ephesians 4:24.
5. Matthew 5:6.
6. John MacArthur, *The MacArthur Study Bible* (Nashville: Thomas Nelson, 1997), 1704.

of disobedience but a child of God and a new creature in Christ Jesus.[7] Therefore, he can no longer stomach the sin upon which he once fed with delight, but is repulsed by it and nauseated by his participation in it. Thus, he must confess it and be rid of it.

TRUE CONFESSION

In 1 John 1:9, John tells us that one of the great marks of genuine conversion is a person's confession of sin. Therefore, it is important that we discover exactly what confession is. The word "confess" is translated from the Greek word *homologéo,* which is a compound of the word *homos,* meaning "same," and *lógos,* meaning "word." It literally means "to speak the same thing." Therefore, to confess is to agree verbally with God that we have sinned and that our sin is heinous. When such confession is genuine, it is also accompanied by sorrow or brokenness.

Although the believer's life will be marked by a growth in holiness and greater power over sin, he will never be completely free from its influence until he stands glorified in heaven. Even the most mature believer will sin. However, his response to that sin will prove that he is no longer an unregenerate son of disobedience living estranged from God and outside of His fatherly providence but has become a child of God, a member of His household, subject to both divine instruction and discipline.[8] When the believer sins, God is faithful to expose his sin and convict him of his guilt[9] through the ministry of the Holy Spirit.[10] Although God may use many natural means to expose the believer's sin, such as the study of Scripture, the rebuke of a faithful brother, or even the censure of the church, it is nonetheless a supernatural work of God's providence. In response, the believer acknowledges his sin and the gravity of it. He then turns to God with a broken and contrite heart, confesses his sin, and asks for pardon.

---

7. John 8:44; 2 Corinthians 5:17; Ephesians 2:2; 1 John 3:12.

8. Ephesians 2:2, 19; Hebrews 12:5–11.

9. The words *convict* and *conviction* have been greatly misunderstood. *Convict* is translated from the Greek word *elégcho,* which is best illustrated by the work of a prosecuting attorney who diligently presents evidence to prove the guilt of a defendant. The end result is not merely that the believer feels convicted, but he is convicted and thus admits or confesses his trespass before God.

10. John 16:8, 13; Romans 8:14; 1 John 2:27.

A very instructive example of biblical confession is displayed in Psalm 51:1–4, which David penned after his fall into sin with Bathsheba and, subsequently, Nathan the prophet's rebuke:

> Have mercy upon me, O God,
> According to Your lovingkindness;
> According to the multitude of Your tender mercies,
> Blot out my transgressions.
> Wash me thoroughly from my iniquity,
> And cleanse me from my sin.
> For I acknowledge my transgressions,
> And my sin is always before me.
> Against You, You only, have I sinned,
> And done this evil in Your sight—
> That You may be found just when You speak,
> And blameless when You judge.

Notice first that although David is broken over his sin, he is not paralyzed with fear or given to hopeless despair. God's lovingkindness and great compassion give him the necessary confidence to confess his sin with the greatest expectation of pardon. How much more then should we who are in Christ be encouraged to draw near and confess our sins to God? Has not God promised us that He is "faithful and just to forgive us our sins and to cleanse us from all unrighteousness" (1 John 1:9)? Have we not been told by the most reliable of sources that we have a High Priest who can sympathize with our weaknesses because He was tempted in all things as we are, yet remained without sin? Does not God Himself encourage us to draw near with confidence to the throne of grace, so that we may receive "mercy and find grace to help in time of need" (Heb. 4:15–16)? Dear Christian, if in the midst of our sin and defeat we ever hear instruction to flee *from* God rather than *to* Him, we must recognize that its origin is not from the heights of heaven but from the pit of hell.

Second, we should notice David's great loathing of his sin and his desire to be cleansed of it. The unregenerate person does not desire to be cleansed of his sin; he only wants to avoid its publication and to be liberated from its adverse consequences. Furthermore, if he were to be cleansed, he would find it unacceptable. His lusts would be ravenous and his heart without rest until he was once again feeding from the same filthy trough and sleeping in the same stinking mire. In stark contrast, the Christian hates the sin he has committed. He loathes even the garments he wore at the moment of his moral failure and considers them to be polluted, unclean, and contagious.[11] His heart is broken, contrite, and filled with remorse and mourning. In the end, his reaction demonstrates that he is indeed a new creature, the old has gone and the new has come![12] The sin that was once a delightful meal to him has become a barrel of filth; the life of sin that was once his fragrant bed has become a miry wallow of dung.

Third, we should note David's justification, or vindication, of God. When Nathan the prophet denounced him and accused him of his secret sin, he made no excuse but openly confessed before all, "I have sinned against the Lord."[13] In Psalm 51:3–4, he is even more explicit:

> For I acknowledge my transgressions,
> And my sin is always before me.
> Against You, You only, have I sinned,
> And done this evil in Your sight—
> That You may be found just when You speak,
> And blameless when You judge.

David begins by declaring that he knew his sin.[14] He had come to view it through God's eyes and to understand something of its heinous nature and dreadful consequences. He also realized that though he had sinned against Uriah by murder, Bathsheba by adultery, and the people of Israel by violating his oath as king and shepherd, he had ultimately sinned against God. And it was this aspect of his sin that made it so loathsome.

Finally, David acknowledged that God was justified in His assessment and judgment of his sin. When God confronted him with his first trespass in the garden, Adam passed the blame to the woman and ultimately to God: "Then the man said, 'The woman *whom You gave to be with me*, she gave me of the tree, and I ate'" (Gen. 3:12, emphasis added). In contrast, David attempted no such diversion of guilt but openly acknowledged that what God said about him was true. He agreed with God about his sin and spoke the same thing. This is the mark of true confession.

---

11. Leviticus 13:52–57; 15:4, 7; Jude v. 23.
12. 2 Corinthians 5:17.
13. 2 Samuel 12:13.
14. The word *know* is translated from the Hebrew word *yada'*, which means to know, perceive, or acknowledge; to know a person intimately or a thing by experience.

THE CHRISTIAN IS MARKED BY CONFESSION

Some have concluded that the believer's growth in holiness will result in a diminishing need for confessing sin; however, the opposite is true. As the believer grows in sanctification, he will experience greater liberty from the power of sin and walk in a greater victory over it. Yet, at the same time, he will develop a more acute understanding of the holiness of God and a keener sensitivity to sin in his life. As a result, his life will be marked by greater depths of brokenness and profound confession. The mature saint will walk in greater holiness than the recent convert, yet his sorrow for sin and the depth and frequency of his confession will exceed that of the babe in Christ. This is simply because God's holiness and his own sin are greater realities to him.

Jesus taught us that the genuine Christian life is marked by mourning.[15] However, it is not a mourning that overpowers all other godly emotions or ends in despair. The grieving of which Jesus speaks always leads to comfort and joy. As the Christian grows in his knowledge of God, his knowledge of self and sin is also amplified. Such a revelation properly comprehended will result in a more profound mourning, but not despair. For as the Christian grows in the knowledge of God, he also comes to a greater understanding of the grace of God in the person and work of Jesus Christ. Such grace leads the Christian to openly confess his sin and receive pardon with joy unspeakable and "full of glory" (1 Peter 1:8). However, the most wonderful thing about this transformation is that the believer finds joy less and less in his own performance and more and more in the perfect and immutable work of Christ. Thus, gradually, the believer is being weaned away from the idolatry of finding joy and assurance in himself as Christ becomes his only source of both.

The devil would convince us that our concern for sin will eventually lead to deadly introspection and that the open confession of our sin will bring us under the cruel censure of God. However, nothing could be further from the truth. A greater awareness of our sin and inability will lead us to turn our eyes to the perfect work of Christ, and our open confession of sin will result in forgiveness and cleansing from a heavenly Father. Taking serious inventory of the sin in our lives is not a downward spiral leading to debilitating remorse. If we correctly understand the gospel, it is the path to freedom, assurance, and joy.

---

15. Matthew 5:4.

BLIND PERFECTION

The Scriptures confirm that one of the greatest evidences of genuine conversion is a life marked by a recognition of sin, a broken and contrite spirit, and open and honest confession of sin before God. However, to the same degree, one of the greatest evidences of false conversion is a blindness to sin, a hardness of heart, and a life with no genuine confession.

In 1 John 1:8–10, the apostle John reaches three terrible conclusions about the person who professes faith in Christ yet sees little reason for either repentance or confession. First, that person is deceiving himself. How deluded must a person become to believe that he has lived a number of days or even hours in absolute and perpetual conformity to God's law?[16] To what heights of vanity must he ascend to see himself perfect as our heavenly Father is perfect?[17] How long must the hot iron lay against his conscience to make him bold enough to stand beside Jesus Christ and put forth the challenge, "Which of you convicts Me of sin?"[18] Such perfect blindness seems impossible, yet the delusion is not uncommon. A multitude of professing Christians sit in evangelical churches every Lord's Day, yet their sin is rarely exposed to them or pressed upon their conscience with enough force to break their hearts or pry open their mouths in even the most meager confession toward God. Although some of this can be attributed to the modern pulpit's weakness and its refusal to preach against sin, these cannot be the only causes. While it is true that the Holy Spirit works through preaching, He is not confined to it. If this multitude truly belonged to God, He would show them their sin and lead them to confession, with or without the aid of the contemporary preacher. How is it, then, that so many in the evangelical church are unaware of their sin and unmarked by confession? It is because they are largely unconverted. They sit at ease in Zion and rehearse her songs by rote, but there is no understanding in them.[19] They have a name that they are alive, but they are dead.[20] They believe themselves rich and without need, and they do not know that they are wretched, miserable, poor, blind, and naked.[21]

---

16. Galatians 3:10; James 2:10.
17. Matthew 5:48.
18. John 8:46; 1 Timothy 4:2.
19. Deuteronomy 32:28; Isaiah 29:13; Amos 6:1.
20. Revelation 3:1.
21. Revelation 3:17.

It is well known among pastors that whenever God moves to expose sin and break hearts in a congregation, it is almost always the most devout and dedicated who are moved to tears and an open confession of sin, while the most carnal and apathetic church members sit in their pews as cold as a stone. They are unmoved by the Spirit of God, and even the open contrition and confession of the better people around them has no effect upon them. What is the reason for such a contrast in the same congregation? The answer is as simple as it is brutal: We are merely witnessing a preview of the great day of judgment when the goats are distinguished from the sheep and separated from them. The sheep are those who are sensitive to the Spirit's work of conviction and are brought to confession, while the goats are those who see no spot or blemish upon themselves and are perfectly content in their comfortable religion. Again, making matters worse, their failure to react is rarely exposed from the pulpit, so the silence of the preacher seals their doom.

The second conclusion John reaches is that those who make a claim to have no sin are devoid of the truth. This also includes those who profess faith in Christ but are either blind or unconcerned about the ongoing sin in their lives. Such things as the conviction of sin, contrition, and confession are all but absent from their daily routine. Furthermore, they would view such brokenness over sin as a strange emotion found only in those whose introspection is extreme and whose religious zeal has surpassed the bounds of civility and respectability. They would never claim sinless perfection for themselves, but in the absence of any degree of brokenness or confession, they live as though they possess it.

To counter such a vain and dangerous delusion, John gives his readers a double warning within the space of only three verses:

If we say that we have no sin,…the truth is not in us. (v. 8)

If we say that we have not sinned,…His word is not in us. (v. 10)

It is important that we understand the exact meaning of John's warning. He is not merely scolding a few immature believers for holding to a superficial view of sin. Instead, he is telling them that those who see no sin in their lives and find no reason for confession are devoid of the gospel and its accompanying salvation. They are blind guides to the blind with one foot already in the ditch.[22]

---

22. Matthew 15:14.

To receive the word of the gospel is to receive the key that unlocks the door to a correct view of reality, especially the reality of one's own person. Only in the gospel can the philosopher's admonition, "Know thyself," be truly obeyed. Those who have a saving knowledge of the gospel have been shown the depravity of their own hearts and the heinous nature of their sin. They have been made aware of what they were apart from Christ, and it was this knowledge that drove them to Him. Once converted, their sensitivity to sin continues to increase along with their disdain for sin and their confession of it.

In contrast, those who have only a form of religion but have never experienced the power of a justifying and regenerating gospel remain blissfully unaware of both the presence and repugnance of the sin in their lives. They go on seeing but do not perceive, they hear but do not understand.[23] They continue to "walk, in the futility of their mind, having their understanding darkened, being alienated from the life of God, because of the ignorance that is in them, because of the blindness of their heart" (Eph. 4:17–18). Though they dress themselves in religious garb and are confident that they are a guide to the blind, a light to those who are in darkness, a corrector of the foolish, and a teacher of the immature,[24] they are ignorant to one of the greatest realities in the universe—their own sin.

Third, the apostle John concludes that the person who claims no sin is making God a liar. The universality of sin is one of the most prominent and consistent themes running throughout the full course of Scripture: "All have sinned and fall short of the glory of God" (Rom. 3:23). "There is no one who does not sin" (1 Kings 8:46). "We all stumble in many things" (James 3:2). Not even among the most pious Old Testament saints or the apostles do we have one example of perfectionism or any recorded claim that anyone among the sons of Adam, except Christ, has ever reached the rung of sinless perfection. Even the great apostle Paul, who was able to say in 1 Corinthians 11:1, "Imitate me, just as I also imitate Christ," never made a claim to perfection but rather gave the following testimony in Philippians 3:12–14:

> Not that I have already attained, or am already perfected; but I press
> on, that I may lay hold of that for which Christ Jesus has also laid

---

23. Isaiah 6:9; Jeremiah 5:21; Ezekiel 12:2; Matthew 13:14; Mark 4:12; Luke 8:10; John 12:40; Romans 11:8.

24. Romans 2:19–20.

hold of me. Brethren, I do not count myself to have apprehended; but one thing I do, forgetting those things which are behind and reaching forward to those things which are ahead, I press toward the goal for the prize of the upward call of God in Christ Jesus.

There is no text in the Scriptures that even hints at the possibility of sinless perfection in the reprobate or the saint. If we believe that God is the author and preserver of the Scriptures and that every word proceeds out of His mouth,[25] then we must concede that a person who argues in defense of his own moral rectitude argues against God. He has set himself against God's opinion and is declaring Him to be mistaken at best or a liar at worst. This is not the opinion, attitude, or action of a child of God.

IS CONFESSION A REALITY IN OUR LIVES?

In conclusion, we must embrace the truths that we have learned. First, the very nature of salvation[26] ensures that if we are Christian, we will walk in the light of God and gradually grow in conformity to His nature and will. Second, we may rightly conclude that those who confidently profess faith in Christ but continue to walk in a manner that is contrary to the person and will of God are guilty of presumption, possibly unconverted, and in danger of eternal destruction. Third, the evidence of genuine conversion is not sinless perfection but a life marked by genuine repentance and confession. Finally, the one who professes faith in Christ yet lives in sin with little or no brokenness or divine discipline should be greatly concerned.

Having learned these important truths, we must now examine our lives and our Christian profession in light of them. Are we growing in our knowledge of God's holiness and, in turn, becoming more and more sensitive to the sin in our lives? Do we react to our sin with a greater sense of repugnance and disdain? Do we battle against it? Does the weight of our sin, coupled with the kindness of God, lead us to repentance and confession?[27] If we have answered yes, there is some evidence that God has done a saving work in us.

---

25. Matthew 4:4; 2 Timothy 3:16.

26. For too long in evangelicalism, God's work of salvation has been viewed only in terms of justification. The other aspects of salvation such as regeneration and sanctification have been neglected.

27. Romans 2:4.

CHAPTER FIVE

Keeping God's Commandments

Now by this we know that we know Him, if we keep His commandments. He who says, "I know Him," and does not keep His commandments, is a liar, and the truth is not in him. But whoever keeps His word, truly the love of God is perfected in him.

—1 John 2:3–5

So far we have considered two great evidences of genuine conversion. First, the genuine Christian will learn to walk in the light of God's revelation and grow in conformity to His nature and will. Second, the Christian will reflect a new relationship with sin. He will grow in his aversion toward it, and when he does sin, he will both repent of it and confess it openly before God.

As John continues in chapter 2 of his epistle, we find a third evidence of genuine conversion: the believer will keep God's commandments. In this chapter we will endeavor to understand what this means and how we are to apply it to our lives.

TESTS OF FAITH

We must remind ourselves of the overall purpose of John's first epistle: he wrote these truths so that believers in Jesus Christ might have a biblical confirmation of their faith, that they might know that they have eternal life.[1] Consequently, John begins this third test with a restatement of that purpose: "Now by this we know that we know Him, if we keep His commandments" (2:3).

We must remind ourselves that throughout this epistle John is not making a distinction between two types of Christians or drawing a line

---

1. 1 John 5:13.

between the spiritual and carnal among the people of God. John is separating the sheep and the goats. Although his primary purpose is to give true believers a biblical assurance of salvation, he subsequently exposes those who profess faith in Christ, yet remain unconverted. For many today, this is a hard saying and difficult to accept. Nevertheless, John is simply following a teaching and pattern established by the Lord in Matthew 7:17–19: the proof of a good tree is the good fruit it bears, for a tree is known by its fruit.

Although this is biblical truth, recognized throughout the history of the church by its most prominent ministers and established confessions, the majority of contemporary evangelicals deem such language judgmental, harsh, and unloving. This unusual reaction can be attributed to a superficial view of salvation and all that accompanies it. In contemporary evangelicalism, salvation has been reduced to nothing more than a human decision to accept Christ, and the life that follows depends entirely upon the convert's continued right choices. It is believed that since God's love is not coercive or manipulative, the Christian may simply choose not to grow. He may rebel against the gentle promptings of God and never enter into any form of true discipleship. He may remain carnal until the day he is ushered into glory and transformed. Although there is some truth in this, as a whole it must be rejected as utter heresy. It is true that God's love is not coercive or manipulative, and it is equally true that the exercise of the human will is a necessary element in both conversion and sanctification.

However, this opinion ignores or even denies at least three major doctrines that are inseparable from salvation. The first is the doctrine of regeneration. The person who has repented of sin and believed in the Lord Jesus Christ has been regenerated. He has become a new creature with a new nature and transformed affections. Although he must still battle against the flesh, the world, and the devil, and although he will not be perfected until his ultimate glorification in heaven, he will, nonetheless, exhibit the characteristics of the new person he has become. A rule to remember is that the will and affections of a rational person are determined by the nature of that person.

The second and third doctrines are the inseparable truths of sanctification and divine providence. If we believe in the inspiration of Scripture and the faithfulness of God, then with the apostle Paul we must be persuaded that the God who began a good work will complete it in the life of every believer.[2] For it is God who is at work in the believer, both to will and to work for His good pleasure.[3] The true believer will be taught of God and led by His Spirit.[4] And when the believer sins or rebels against God's fatherly hand, he will be disciplined so that he might share in God's holiness and the sanctification without which no one will see the Lord.[5] He will be trained by discipline even to the point of sorrow and suffering so that he might yield the peaceful fruit of righteousness.[6] If someone claims sonship with God through faith in Christ yet lives in carnality with no intervention on God's part, then the Scriptures condemn him as a false convert and an illegitimate child: "If you endure chastening, God deals with you as with sons; for what son is there whom a father does not chasten? But if you are without chastening, of which all have become partakers, then you are illegitimate and not sons" (Heb. 12:7–8).

The nature of salvation, the strength of God's providence, and the enduring faithfulness of His promises ensure that the believer will grow, mature, and exhibit the characteristics of the new life that is in him. It is for this reason that Jesus can say, "You will know them by their fruits" (Matt. 7:16–20). It is because of these truths that Paul can admonish believers to test and examine themselves to see if they are in the faith.[7] It is upon this foundation that John can provide in this epistle a biblical standard by which they may do so.

OBEDIENCE TO GOD'S COMMANDMENTS

According to this text and many others like it throughout the New Testament, obedience to God's commandments is one of the great indicators of true conversion and a right relationship with Him. Obedience to the Word is the great litmus test of salvation. This truth comes out most clearly in James 2:17–20:

> Thus also faith by itself, if it does not have works, is dead. But someone will say, "You have faith, and I have works." Show me your faith without your works, and I will show you my faith by my works.

---

2. Philippians 1:6.
3. Philippians 2:13.
4. John 6:45; Romans 8:14; Philippians 3:15; 1 John 2:27.
5. Hebrews 12:10, 14.
6. John 15:8, 16; Hebrews 12:11.
7. 2 Corinthians 13:5.

You believe that there is one God. You do well. Even the demons believe—and tremble! But do you want to know, O foolish man, that faith without works is dead?

Those who hold to the inerrancy and uniformity of Scripture recognize that there is no contradiction between the writings of James and the doctrine of justification by faith alone that the apostle Paul so clearly taught[8] and tenaciously embraced and the Reformers propagated.[9] The two inspired writers are simply addressing the issue of salvation from different sides of the same coin. The apostle Paul is addressing the cause of salvation, while James is addressing the result. Thus, from both writers we gain a comprehensive view of God's work in salvation.

Salvation is by faith alone, and those who would believe or teach otherwise are under a curse.[10] However, salvation by faith results in works, or obedience to the law. Yet we are not to attribute even these works to the one who performs them but to the God who gives grace.[11] The person who has been saved by faith begins to live a life of increasing conformity to God's commandments, not by some newfound strength of will but because he has been regenerated;[12] he has been given a new nature, he has become a new creature, and he has been indwelt by the Spirit of God.[13] In the words of Paul, he has died to the old man he once was and has been raised to walk in a newness of life.[14] All these things are from God, who reconciled us to Himself through Christ, and when we properly understand them, we attribute them back to God in worship.[15]

This truth is also supported by a Pauline text that is probably quoted more than any other in defense of salvation by faith alone: "For by grace you have been saved through faith, and that not of yourselves; it is the gift of God, not of works, lest anyone should boast. For we are His workmanship, created in Christ Jesus for good works, which God prepared beforehand that we should walk in them" (Eph. 2:8–10).

---

8. Romans 3:19–22; 4:1–25; Galatians 2:16.

9. It is no exaggeration to say that the doctrine of justification by *sola fide* (Latin for "by faith alone") was the truth that sparked the Reformation.

10. Galatians 3:10.

11. 1 Corinthians 15:10; Ephesians 3:7.

12. John 3:3, 7; 1 Peter 1:3, 23.

13. Ezekiel 36:26–27; Romans 8:9–11; 2 Corinthians 5:17.

14. Romans 6:1–6.

15. 2 Corinthians 5:18.

In the first two verses, Paul argues to the point of redundancy: salvation is *by grace* and *through faith; not of oneself* but *a gift of God; not as a result of works* so that *no one may boast.* It would be difficult to be more explicit or thorough without insulting the reader's intelligence. How much clearer must Paul be to convey the timeless truth taught and defended on every page of Scripture? In Galatians 2:16 he says, equally clearly, "A man is not justified by the works of the law but by faith in Jesus Christ…. Not by the works of the law; for by the works of the law no flesh shall be justified."

Having written as clearly as he could in Ephesians 2:8–9 to declare faith as the only means of justification, Paul then turns his attention to two accompanying doctrines: the providence of God and His work of sanctification in the believer's life. Those who have been justified by faith are God's workmanship, created in Christ Jesus for good works that God prepared for them before the foundation of the world so that they would walk in them. God does not justify and then abandon. He has not demonstrated His power to save from the condemnation of sin only to then demonstrate His impotence to save from the power of sin. Why are so many modern-day pulpits so blind to this truth? The God who is able to justify the foremost of sinners is also able sanctify the foremost of sinners.[16] Countless individuals sit in pews every Sunday, carnal and unsanctified, not because the promises of God have failed but because they are yet unconverted. They have a form of godliness but have denied its power.[17] They identify themselves with Christ, but they "practice lawlessness," as though He never gave them a law to obey. They call Him "Lord, Lord," but they do not do what He says (Luke 6:46). On the final day, they will hear the most terrifying sentence passed upon them: "I never knew you; depart from Me" (Matt. 7:23).

This is why the tests in John's first epistle are so vitally important, especially the one before us now. The evidence of salvation is not sinless perfection or a perfect scorecard of obedience, but a new relationship with God's commandments, a real inclination toward them, a genuine desire to do them, a growing practical application of them, and a real contrition when our neglecting them becomes obvious. Prior to a person's conversion, he has no such relationship with God's commandments but lives as though God had never given a law to be obeyed or a precept

---

16. 1 Timothy 1:15.
17. 2 Timothy 3:5.

of wisdom to be admired and applied. He does not set himself to know God's law and is not diligent to apply it. His nearly constant disobedience has no effect upon his conscience to move him to repentance. However, when this person is made alive by the Spirit of God through the preaching of the gospel, he not only enters into a new relationship with God but also with God's Word. He finds in himself a growing appreciation for the wisdom and beauty of God's commandments. He discovers a real desire to know what God has said and to walk accordingly. Although he previously lived in total neglect of God's commandments, he is now extolling their merits. To his bewilderment and the surprise of those who knew him before he was converted, he finds himself arm in arm with the greatest saints of Zion, declaring:

> The law of the LORD is perfect, converting the soul;
> The testimony of the LORD is sure, making wise the simple;
> The statutes of the LORD are right, rejoicing the heart;
> The commandment of the LORD is pure, enlightening the eyes;
> The fear of the LORD is clean, enduring forever;
> The judgments of the LORD are true and righteous altogether.
> More to be desired are they than gold,
> Yea, than much fine gold;
> Sweeter also than honey and the honeycomb.
> Moreover by them Your servant is warned,
> And in keeping them there is great reward. (Ps. 19:7–11)

To what can we attribute this newfound appreciation for the Word of God? Lest it be an idolatrous love, it must be traced back to a newfound love for God. For this reason John writes, "But whoever keeps His word, truly the love of God is perfected in him" (2:5). This cannot refer to God's love for the believer, for it is perfect from the beginning. The love of which John writes is that which comes from the regenerated heart of the Christian. He loves God, and this love is proved, demonstrated, and comes to its perfect end through his growing adherence to God's commands. The beloved Puritan sage Matthew Henry offers insight that is both eloquent and edifying:

> Now light is to kindle love; and love must and will keep the word of God; it enquires wherein the Beloved may be pleased and served, and, finding He will be so by observance of His declared will, there it employs and exerts itself; there love is demonstrated; there it has its perfect (or complete) exercise, operation, and delight; and hereby (by

this dutiful attendance to the will of God, or Christ) we know that we are in Him, we know that we belong to Him, and that we are united to Him by that Spirit which elevates and assists us to this obedience.[18]

This does not mean that the one who has been genuinely converted will never again neglect the law or turn from it in disobedience. There is no person who does not sin, and none of us is exempt from the apathy that sometimes overcomes our souls and blinds our reason. There is no believer this side of heaven who loves God as he ought, who desires God's law as is appropriate, or who is as zealous in its application as he would desire to be. However, it does mean that those who have been regenerated by the Spirit of God will have a marked difference in their opinion and application of the Word compared to those who are yet unconverted and still in the world. This is the truth that John seeks to set before us.

AN EMPTY CONFESSION

Next, John turns his attention toward exposing those who would identify themselves with Christianity yet have no reason for such a confidence. Here again, John's boldness is a bit overwhelming to the modern ear that has grown accustomed to smoother speech. Nevertheless, his words are inspired, and his love is unquestionable. He writes: "He who says, 'I know Him,' and does not keep His commandments, is a liar, and the truth is not in him" (1 John 2:4).

If we believe that John's words are too harsh or severe, we should at least recognize that his language is common in the Old and New Testaments. Jesus exposes false converts with even harder language when He calls them "you who practice lawlessness" (Matt. 7:23). The apostle Paul denounces them as those who profess to know God, but whose deeds deny Him. He even goes on to berate them as "abominable, disobedient, and disqualified for every good work" (Titus 1:16). James, the half brother of our Lord, refers to their character and deeds as worse than that of demons, for at least demons have the sense to tremble.[19] But these who confess Christ yet neglect Him and His commands do so without fear of either temporal or eternal repercussions. They will confidently declare,

---

18. Matthew Henry, *Commentary on the Whole Bible* (New York: Fleming H. Revell, n.d.), 6:1066.
19. James 2:19.

"I know Him" and then adamantly defend their relationship against all the evidence to the contrary. They are severely offended, crushed in heart, and even filled with rage at the slightest suggestion that they do not know the Lord or that He does not know them. Therefore, those who would suggest this to them would do well to take into consideration our Lord's warning: "Do not give what is holy to the dogs; nor cast your pearls before swine, lest they trample them under their feet, and turn and tear you in pieces" (Matt. 7:6).

There are two reasons for this obstinacy in the face of such overwhelming evidence. The first lies in human nature. The unregenerate heart is full of pride and every evil intention.[20] However, it loves to cloak itself in a thin veneer of religion and piety. Only the slightest thrust of the sword breaks through that thin veneer of feigned godliness, and then the true character of the false converted comes at you like a deluge or a ravenous wolf. The second reason for the seemingly impenetrable wall around false converts' delusion is the preaching to which they have been exposed. Rather than warning the congregation to prepare to meet their God, to make their calling and election sure, and to test themselves to see if they are in the faith, the modern-day pulpit seems to lull them into a dangerous sleep by declaring "'Peace, peace,' when there is no peace."[21] Many preachers are building their ministries on the dry bones of unconverted church members, and they plaster over their feeble walls with the whitewash of creative marketing, entertainment, and the hewing of broken cisterns designed to meet the felt needs of dying people who need the gospel.[22] When the torrential rains and violent winds of God's judgment break out against them, their wall will fall and the remains of it will be forgotten.[23] The preacher himself may be saved, but only as by fire. His work will be consumed.[24]

Those who profess faith in Christ but have nothing to do with His commandments should be greatly concerned. Even though they adamantly protest that they truly love God—but do not show it in their actions—they must be shown that the Scriptures acknowledge no such

20. Genesis 6:5; Mark 7:21–23.
21. Jeremiah 6:14; Amos 4:12; 2 Corinthians 13:5; 2 Peter 1:10.
22. Jeremiah 2:13; 14:3; Ezekiel 13:10–11.
23. Jeremiah 9:11–14; Ezekiel 13:10–16.
24. 1 Corinthians 3:15.

love, but rather denounce it as meaningless dribble.[25] Furthermore, those who claim to wear a prophet's mantle must awaken them so that they arise from the dead. Then Christ will truly shine upon them.[26]

OUR ASSURANCE AND GOD'S COMMANDMENTS

John's voice has been clear in this third test of faith he has set before us: "Now by this we know that we know Him, if we keep His commandments" (1 John 2:3). Does this test strengthen or weaken our assurance of salvation? If our relationship with God's commandments was compared to that of an unbeliever, would we recognize any real or observable difference? How would we describe our relationship with God's will as it is revealed in His Word? Do we study God's Word to show ourselves approved?[27] Are we doers of the Word—or merely hearers who delude ourselves?[28]

In summary, we can say the following things about the person who has been truly converted. First, we must confirm his weakness. Even the most mature saint must often struggle against the distractions of this world and the apathy in his heart toward the Word of God. Every Christian has lamented his too-frequent disregard of God's Word and violations of its commandments. However, it is this lamenting and repenting that provide strong evidence of conversion. The unregenerate have no such concerns.

Second, in spite of the true believer's real weaknesses, there will be notable differences between his relationship with the commandments of God and that of the unconverted. The Christian will grow in his delight in the commandments of God, and he will make progress in applying them in obedience. Although his progress will often be three steps forward and two steps back, it will be real progress. Although there will be times of pruning and divine discipline, there will be victory and fruitfulness. Over the full course of the believer's life and through the continuing and sanctifying work of God, his attitude and conduct will reflect greater and greater submission to the will of God revealed in His commands.

Third, the believer's mourning over disobedience will increase with his desire for obedience. As the believer grows in his understanding of

---

25. 1 John 2:5, 15.
26. Ephesians 5:14.
27. 2 Timothy 2:15.
28. James 1:22.

God's worthiness and his appreciation for God's Word, he will suffer great regret at any form of disobedience in his life. Yet his regret will not lead to despair because his earthly pilgrimage has revealed God's faithfulness, and he knows by experience that a broken and contrite heart He "will not despise" (Ps. 51:17).

If you are able to identify with the things John sets forth regarding the Christian's new and unique relationship with the commandments of God, then you have greater cause for assurance of salvation. If, however, your estranged or nonexistent relationship with God's commands has been exposed, you have cause for great concern. You must cry out to God and examine your life in the light of His Word. A broken and contrite heart God will not despise, none who come to Him will be cast out,[29] and "whoever calls upon the name of the LORD shall be saved" (Rom. 10:13).

---

29. John 6:37.

CHAPTER SIX

Imitating Christ

---

*By this we know that we are in Him. He who says he abides in Him ought
himself also to walk just as He walked.*

—1 John 2:5–6

We have just considered possibly the greatest evidence of genuine conversion: enduring obedience to God's commandments. In light of its
magnitude, we might easily overlook the significance of the test that follows. However, it is of such great importance that we ought to give it our
undivided attention. How do we know that we have come to know Him
in a saving relationship? The answer is as powerful as it is concise. We
walk as He walked!

At first glance, this test might fill us with doubt and even despair.
After all, who would dare think, let alone declare, that he has lived a life
equal to that of Christ when He walked upon this earth? Nevertheless,
once we overcome our initial misunderstanding of the text, it will prove
to be a tremendous consolation for even the weakest saint.

THE LIFE THAT JESUS LIVED
To begin our study, it will be helpful to consider briefly the magnificent
life that Jesus lived during His pilgrimage upon this earth. The Scriptures begin by affirming that the Son of God came to this world in the
likeness of sinful human flesh.[1] This does not mean that Christ merely
resembled sinful flesh but that He really and truly assumed a human
nature, undefiled and without sin, yet subject to the same limitations,
frailties, afflictions, and anguish of fallen humanity. William Hendriksen

---

1. Literally, "in likeness of flesh of sin" (Rom. 8:3).

explains it this way: "He took on that human nature not as it came originally from the hand of the Creator, but weakened by sin, though remaining itself without any sin."[2]

It would have been an incomprehensible humiliation if the Son of God had taken the nature of humanity when it was in its full glory and strength before the fall. However, He was sent in the likeness of human flesh and took upon Himself a nature that was exposed to all the terrible consequences of our fallenness. He knew our weakness, suffered our humiliation, and was tempted in all things as we are, yet without sin.[3] He remained "holy, harmless, undefiled" (Heb. 7:26).

To understand the magnitude of this truth, it is helpful to draw a comparison between the greatest and most pious saints that ever walked the planet and the unique person of Jesus Christ. There was never one moment in the life of even the apostle Paul in which he loved God as God deserves to be loved. He never performed one deed for God that he could say he had done for the glory of God exclusively, entirely, without any competing motivations. Yet we know that Christ never had one moment in His life when He did not love the Lord His God with all His heart, soul, mind, and strength.[4] Every deed He accomplished He carried out with the perfect motivation to glorify God alone. Whether He ate, drank, or did even the most menial of tasks, He did it all for the glory of God.[5]

Jesus' sinless perfection was so outstanding and irrefutable that, without the slightest hesitancy, He bore witness to His own perfection, even before His enemies. Who among us would stand before his most ardent opponents and put forth the challenge, "Which of you convicts Me of sin?" (John 8:46). Who among us would be bold enough to stand before the religious authorities of our day and declare, "I always do those things that please Him" (John 8:29)? Nevertheless, this was Christ's testimony about Himself, yet He was not alone in His opinion. The Father Himself bore witness of Christ's perfect obedience: "This is My beloved Son, in whom I am well pleased" (Matt. 3:17; 17:5).

Everywhere we look in the New Testament, we find testimony of the impeccable life of Jesus Christ. Even Christ's enemies acknowledge this

---

2. William Hendriksen, *New Testament Commentary: Exposition of Paul's Epistle to the Romans* (Grand Rapids: Baker, 1980), 247.

3. 2 Corinthians 5:21; Hebrews 4:15.

4. Mark 12:30.

5. 1 Corinthians 10:31.

truth. Not long after Judas betrayed Jesus, he was filled with remorse and cried out, "I have sinned by betraying innocent blood" (Matt. 27:4). Before Pilate gave his dreadful verdict, his wife warned him with these words: "Have nothing to do with that just Man, for I have suffered many things today in a dream because of Him" (Matt. 27:19). Even in the midst of his spineless compliance, which led to the execution of Christ, this ruthless and self-serving Roman official was moved to confess, "I find no fault in this Man" (Luke 23:4). Finally, the crucifixion of Christ draws to a close with the confession of a hardened Roman centurion who lifted up his voice in praise to God declaring, "Certainly this was a righteous Man!" (Luke 23:47).

The New Testament bears witness not only to Christ's sinless life but also to His positive righteousness. He preached the gospel to the poor, proclaimed release to the captives, brought recovery of sight to the blind, and set free those who were oppressed.[6] When he opened His mouth to teach, the people responded in amazement at His authority.[7] When they were hungry, He multiplied a few loaves and fishes to feed thousands.[8] He set the demon-possessed free with a word, cleansed the leper, healed the sick, and raised the dead to life.[9] It was not without reason that the people were utterly astonished at Him and bore witness saying, "He has done all things well" (Mark 7:37).

HOW CAN WE COMPARE?

In light of Jesus Christ's impeccable life and the glorious works that He accomplished, being obedient to the point of death, even death on a cross,[10] we might question the fairness or sanity of John's demand: "He who says he abides in Him ought himself also to walk just as He walked" (2:6). Why would this beloved apostle place upon us such a heavy burden that neither he nor the other apostles were able to bear?[11] How could even the most pious saint ever possess a strong assurance of salvation with such a high standard set before him? It would be easier to fulfill

---

6. Luke 4:18.
7. Matthew 7:28–29.
8. Matthew 14:16–21.
9. Matthew 8:2–3, 16; John 11:43–44.
10. Philippians 2:8.
11. Matthew 23:4.

the tedious requirements of the Pharisees or even satisfy the strenuous demands of the law itself than to emulate the perfect life of our Lord.

However, before we succumb to despair and relegate ourselves to eternal perdition, we should once again recall the context in which John is writing. He is not demanding the attainment of some impossible level of perfection, but encouraging us to examine the inclination of our lives. Are we still walking "according to the course of this world" (Eph. 2:1–3)? Or, through the sanctifying work of the Spirit, are we learning to walk as Christ walked? Is there observable, practical evidence that we are seeking to imitate Christ? Is our claim to be a disciple of Christ validated or proven false by our attitudes, actions, and words? Does our daily conduct manifest more of Christ and less of the world? Does it pain us deeply when we observe the great breach that still remains between Christ's character and our own? Do we long to be like Christ?

Imagine a little boy who loves and admires his older brother very much and seeks to imitate him in everything. Although his features are those of a child, a close examination of his face and mannerisms reveals enough of a resemblance to his older brother to prove their kinship. One snowy winter's morning the elder brother sets out to do his daily chores around the farm, and his younger brother follows closely behind. The elder brother is tall and his stride is long and sure. His footprints in the snow reveal a strength and balance far beyond the ability of the little boy. Nevertheless, undaunted by the seemingly unattainable challenge and driven by a passion to be like his elder brother, the boy lengthens his stride to match the footprints left behind. After only a few feeble attempts, it becomes obvious to the boy and any observer that the elder brother's stride is simply beyond that of the younger sibling. Though he fix his eyes upon the path marked out before him, though he set himself to the task with the greatest resolve, and though he exert himself to the point of exhaustion, the result is an extremely awkward, even comical imitation. However, in spite of his inability to match his brother's stride, the boy's perseverance proves the sincerity of his devotion to his brother. In spite of his frequent failure, it is obvious to any honest observer that the inclination of the young boy's heart and will is to be like his elder brother and to walk as he walked.

According to the Scriptures, Christ is not only our prophet, priest, and king but also our elder brother,[12] and the path that He walked provides

---

12. Hebrews 2:11–12.

both the direction and pattern for our lives. The apostle Paul writes that we were "predestined to be conformed to the image" of Christ, so that He would be the *"firstborn among many brethren"* (Rom. 8:29, emphasis added). He further exhorts us to be imitators of him just as he was of Christ.[13] The apostle Peter encourages believers in the midst of their suffering that Christ has left an example for them *to follow His steps*.[14] Finally, the author of Hebrews admonishes us to "lay aside every weight, and the sin which so easily ensnares us, and let us run with endurance the race that is set before us, looking unto Jesus, the author and finisher of our faith" (Heb. 12:1–2).

In light of these texts, it should not seem unusual to us that John has made "walking as Christ walked" a test of genuine conversion. After all, what is a disciple but someone who seeks to become like his master in all things?[15] He has devoted himself not only to learning the teachings of his master but also to imitating his manner of life. He is a student who is learning to walk as his master walked.

In most cases, the culmination of this master/disciple relationship occurs when the disciple becomes like his master and stands beside him as an equal. However, in Christianity, the master/disciple relationship never culminates. We never graduate to the level of our Master. We are always students. It is for this reason that Jesus cautioned His disciples, "But you, do not be called 'Rabbi'; for One is your Teacher, the Christ, and you are all brethren" (Matt. 23:8).

The most Christlike believer will always be a student who has yet to be fully conformed to Jesus Christ's perfections. The most mature is still learning to walk as Christ walked. The most sanctified saint will always view himself as the younger brother trying, but never able, to match his brother's stride. Even the most consistent Christian life is one that constantly stretches beyond the normal stride; thus, it is marked by imperfections and awkwardness. Even during our most Christlike moments, our resemblance to our elder Brother is slight and undeveloped. Regardless of the progress we have made in the race to catch Him, there remains a vast distance between us. Thus, the mature believer is aware that there will always be a great deal of ground to cover before he

---

13. 1 Corinthians 11:1.
14. 1 Peter 2:21.
15. Matthew 10:24–25.

gains the prize. The apostle Paul set forth this truth with amazing clarity in his letter to the church in Philippi:

> Not that I have already attained, or am already perfected; but I press on, that I may lay hold of that for which Christ Jesus has also laid hold of me. Brethren, I do not count myself to have apprehended; but one thing I do, forgetting those things which are behind and reaching forward to those things which are ahead, I press toward the goal for the prize of the upward call of God in Christ Jesus. (Phil. 3:12–14)

The great apostle Paul never made a claim to perfection. He never pretended to walk as Christ walked. However, he did demonstrate in his life a real and observable passion to be like Christ, "pressed on" toward the goal, and made progress to the point of being able to say to his fellow believers, "Imitate me, just as I also imitate Christ" (1 Cor. 11:1).

This balance in Paul's understanding of sanctification helps us approach our third test with an equally biblical balance. John is not teaching that we must attain perfection before we can assume assurance. He is not withholding assurance from all but the "wholly sanctified." However, neither does John give assurance to those who accept their lack of conformity to Christ, give no practical or observable evidence of genuinely striving for greater conformity to Him, and make no identifiable progress toward the goal of learning to walk as He walked.

EXAMINING YOUR WALK

Having properly understood this fourth test, we must now examine ourselves in light of it: Do we walk as Christ walked? What is the goal and inclination of our lives? Does our manner of living reflect a real passion to be like Christ? To the degree that we are able to answer yes, we may stand assured that a genuine work of conversion has been accomplished in our lives and that He who began a good work is perfecting it. We should simply continue proving our confession with our conduct and growing in conformity to the pattern Christ has left us. Each day that we endure will only serve to strengthen the assurance we possess.

However, to the degree that the inclinations and aspirations of our lives bear a striking resemblance to those of the unbelieving world, we should be concerned. If we share the same goals with the world, and if our thoughts, time, and resources are spent on the pursuits of this age, we have cause for fear. If we admire what the world admires and seek to mimic its ways, we should call into question the genuineness of our profession. If after we examine ourselves we find we are wanting, we should neither be apathetic or give way to paralyzing despair, but seek a resolution with the greatest urgency. However, we must recognize that the Scriptures offer no formula or step-by-step program to mend our crippled assurance; rather, they admonish us to seek the Lord in His Word and in prayer until He gives us peace. We must also remember that the Lord will validate that peace and prove it true by placing us upon the path of righteousness and teaching us to walk as He walked. All our confessions of faith and subjective feelings of assurance are only valid to the degree that they prove themselves with the practical and observable evidences of a changed and changing life.

CHAPTER SEVEN

Loving Christians

---

*Brethren, I write no new commandment to you, but an old command-
ment which you have had from the beginning. The old commandment is
the word which you heard from the beginning. Again, a new commandment I write to you, which thing is true in Him and in you, because the
darkness is passing away, and the true light is already shining.*

*He who says he is in the light, and hates his brother, is in darkness
until now. He who loves his brother abides in the light, and there is no
cause for stumbling in him. But he who hates his brother is in darkness
and walks in darkness, and does not know where he is going, because the
darkness has blinded his eyes.*

—1 John 2:7–11

Love for God's people is a recurring theme throughout both the Old and
New Testaments. Therefore, it is not surprising that John presents it as
a test of true conversion. To put it plainly, the one who demonstrates a
real and enduring love for his brother in Christ and for the church collectively gives powerful evidence of conversion. However, the one who
claims Christ and yet does not love his brother has little grounds for
such a boast.

AN ANCIENT COMMAND
John introduces this fifth test of saving faith by affirming a foundational
truth: God's command for us to love our brother has been a central theme
of His manifest will from the beginning of divine revelation. Since "God
is love" (1 John 4:8) and He has loved His people from the beginning,[1]
it is no surprise that from the beginning He has commanded them to

---

1. Jeremiah 31:3.

love one another. The command to love our brother is not something that appeared with the writing of the New Testament or even the teachings of Christ but was implicit throughout the earliest Old Testament narratives[2] and clearly revealed in the Mosaic law, demonstrated by this command from Leviticus 19:18: "You shall not take vengeance, nor bear any grudge against the children of your people, but you shall love your neighbor as yourself: I am the LORD."

In this one command we discover three important truths about the ancient duty to love. First, we learn that the law to love is an expression of who God is. In other words, the divine command takes root and springs forth from the divine character. At the beginning of Leviticus 19, in verse 2, God commands the people of Israel to be holy because He is holy. Here He commands them to love because He, their Lord, is love. John Gill writes:

> [Love was] a part of the eternal law of truth, founded upon the unalterable nature and eternal will of God, who is love itself, and requires it in all His creatures; [love] was written on Adam's heart in a state of innocence, and a branch of the divine image stamped upon him; and [love] is what was delivered in the law of Moses, for love to God and men is the sum and substance of that.[3]

Second, we learn that the love the Israelite was to show his brother was not merely emotional or something simply to talk about but real and practical. According to the law, the Israelites were to love one another by not taking vengeance or holding grudges, murdering, stealing, committing adultery, bearing false witness, or doing anything that might hinder the well-being of their brother.[4] Although love for our brother certainly involves our emotions, it is foremost a matter of the will, which manifests itself in right and selfless action.

Third, we learn that love for our neighbor is an old command—an ancient road running throughout the entirety of the Old Testament.[5] God has always been love, and love has always been His preeminent

---

2. Consider Scripture's negative view of Cain's lovelessness for Abel (Gen. 4:1–15) and Lamech's heartlessness (Gen. 4:23). We see Scripture's positive view of Joseph's love for his brothers (Gen. 45:1–15).

3. John Gill, *Exposition of the Old and New Testaments* (Paris, Ark.: Baptist Standard Bearer, 1989), 9:625.

4. Exodus 20:13–16; Leviticus 19:18.

5. Jeremiah 6:16; 18:15.

command. True piety has always manifested itself in love for God and His chosen people. To think of one without the other is an impossibility, an untenable contradiction of the worst sort.

A NEW COMMAND

If loving our brother is an old commandment, then why does John say that it is also new? We have already proven love to be an eternal attribute of an immutable God and a prevailing command that runs throughout the full course of the Old Testament. How then can it be both old and new?

We must realize that John is not contradicting himself within the same verse, but rather he is using these apparently contradictory statements to craft a beautiful presentation of the new covenant's greater revelation of God's glory. God has always revealed His love to mankind from the beginning. However, the revelation of His love through the person and work of Christ so far exceeds that of any previous revelation that it seems entirely new. Without taking anything away from the magnificent unveiling of God's love under the old covenant, we may properly say that it was a little thing in comparison to the revelation of His love through the incarnation of His Son.[6] Likewise, we may say that the love commanded, expounded, and demonstrated in Christ's teaching and sacrificial life so surpasses the demands of the Old Testament that it seems entirely new. The standard of love in the new covenant is not defined merely by propositions and precepts alone but by the example of Jesus Christ. His love toward His people is now the benchmark for the believer. His love now defines to what depths, heights, widths, and lengths the people of God are to love one another. The true essence and full revelation of the command to love has been perfectly expounded now in the person of Christ. Thus, Jesus taught His disciples: "A new commandment I give to you, that you love one another; as I have loved you, that you also love one another" (John 13:34).

Under the old covenant, the Israelite demonstrated love by obeying laws that protected fellow Israelites and by participating in a number of positive acts of charity and kindness.[7] However, under the new covenant,

---

6. I do not seek to belittle the revelation of God under the old covenant but rather to magnify it in the person of Christ, compared to whom all things are a shadow (Col. 2:17).

7. Israelites demonstrated charity by leaving a portion of the harvest in the field (Lev. 19:9–10); lending without usury (Ex. 22:25); opening their hand to the poor (Deut.15:7); defending the orphan and pleading for the widow (Isa. 1:17).

God's people are called to love as Christ loved and to lay down their lives for the benefit and well-being of one another. John fully expounds this truth later on in this epistle:

> By this we know love, because He laid down His life for us. And we also ought to lay down our lives for the brethren. But whoever has this world's goods, and sees his brother in need, and shuts up his heart from him, how does the love of God abide in him? My little children, let us not love in word or in tongue, but in deed and in truth. And by this we know that we are of the truth, and shall assure our hearts before Him. (3:16–19).

It is clear from these verses that genuine love does not remain in the realm of feelings or words but manifests itself in practical, discernible actions. The type of love produced by genuine conversion, which is the evidence of it, cannot be confined to rapturous feelings, eloquent and flamboyant language, or even the best of intentions. It must go beyond word and tongue and express itself in deed and truth. The love that Christ demands and of which John writes must act. Therefore, it finds its truest expression when we are consistently living for the benefit of others in the body of Christ by daily dying to self and doing practical works of service according to our gifts and the opportunities that providence provides. Of course, this type of love requires that we actually enter into real relationships with God's people, that we purpose to know their needs, and that we actively seek out opportunities to serve them. Consequently, it would be difficult, if not impossible, for this type of love to manifest itself consistently in a community that comes together for only one weekly show on Sunday morning. This type of love must start in the midst of individual relationships within a local body and then work its way outward to believers and believing communities throughout the world.

THE EVIDENCE OF CONVERSION

In this epistle, John clearly asserts that one of the greatest evidences of one who has been converted (if not the greatest) is love for his fellow Christian and the church as a whole. In addition, John has also shown us that true Christian love is to love as Jesus loved, to lay down our lives for the benefit of our brothers and sisters in Christ. The beauty of John's words outshines that of the greatest poets; however, he does not intend to be understood as a poet. He is not seeking to impress his readers with the aesthetics of his prose but hopes to help them obtain a sound assurance of salvation by determining whether they possess any of the evidences or accompanying virtues of a true child of God. In the Upper Room Discourse, Jesus told His disciples that all men would know they were Christians by their love for one another.[8] In 1 John 2, the apostle is telling those who claim to be Christians that they could have personal assurance of salvation only to the degree that their lives conform to the same standard: love for one another.

We are saved by grace alone through faith alone, and all the labors of love gathered from a thousand lifetimes of piety would not justify any one of us before God's judgment throne. However, the regenerating work of the Holy Spirit, which produces in us both repentance and saving faith, will also create in us a newfound and ever-increasing love for God's people. John argues this truth throughout his epistle:

> He who says he is in the light, and hates his brother, is in darkness until now. He who loves his brother abides in the light, and there is no cause for stumbling in him. (2:9–10)

> In this the children of God and the children of the devil are manifest: Whoever does not practice righteousness is not of God, nor is he who does not love his brother. (3:10)

> We know that we have passed from death to life, because we love the brethren. He who does not love his brother abides in death. (3:14)

> Beloved, let us love one another, for love is of God; and everyone who loves is born of God and knows God. He who does not love does not know God, for God is love. (4:7–8)

> God is love, and he who abides in love abides in God, and God in him. (4:16)

> If someone says, "I love God," and hates his brother, he is a liar; for he who does not love his brother whom he has seen, how can he love God whom he has not seen? (4:20)

> Whoever believes that Jesus is the Christ is born of God, and everyone who loves Him who begot also loves him who is begotten of Him. (5:1)

---

8. John 13:35.

The apostle John's inspired teaching is that the one who does not love the brethren is a child of the devil, does not know God, does not love God, and abides in death.[9] His words are bold and firm. He is not inviting debate on the matter, nor is he willing to discuss possible exceptions. The one who does not love the brethren does not know God!

It is important for us to understand that the boldness of John's language is entirely appropriate. After all, he is dealing with a matter of eternal life and death, and the souls of men are hanging in the balance. Furthermore, the truths he is communicating did not originate with him, nor were they the result of some recent revelation of the Spirit. John is simply teaching the truths he received firsthand from the Lord Jesus Christ during His earthly ministry. It was Jesus who first declared fraternal love to be one of the great evidences of true conversion. This truth is powerfully illustrated in Christ's description of the judgment of the nations in Matthew 25:31–46:

> "When the Son of Man comes in His glory, and all the holy angels with Him, then He will sit on the throne of His glory. All the nations will be gathered before Him, and He will separate them one from another, as a shepherd divides his sheep from the goats. And He will set the sheep on His right hand, but the goats on the left. Then the King will say to those on His right hand, 'Come, you blessed of My Father, inherit the kingdom prepared for you from the foundation of the world: for I was hungry and you gave Me food; I was thirsty and you gave Me drink; I was a stranger and you took Me in; I was naked and you clothed Me; I was sick and you visited Me; I was in prison and you came to Me.'
>
> "Then the righteous will answer Him, saying, 'Lord, when did we see You hungry and feed You, or thirsty and give You drink? When did we see You a stranger and take You in, or naked and clothe You? Or when did we see You sick, or in prison, and come to You?' And the King will answer and say to them, 'Assuredly, I say to you, inasmuch as you did it to one of the least of these My brethren, you did it to Me.'
>
> "Then He will also say to those on the left hand, 'Depart from Me, you cursed, into the everlasting fire prepared for the devil and his angels: for I was hungry and you gave Me no food; I was thirsty and you gave Me no drink; I was a stranger and you did not take Me

---

9. 1 John 3:10, 14; 4:7–8, 20.

in, naked and you did not clothe Me, sick and in prison and you did not visit Me.'

"Then they also will answer Him, saying, 'Lord, when did we see You hungry or thirsty or a stranger or naked or sick or in prison, and did not minister to You?' Then He will answer them, saying, 'Assuredly, I say to you, inasmuch as you did not do it to one of the least of these, you did not do it to Me.' And these will go away into everlasting punishment, but the righteous into eternal life."

Many ministers and ministries have used this passage in Matthew to validate their call to reach out to the world with practical works of charity and compassion. It has become the cornerstone text of prison ministries, hunger relief organizations, medical teams, clothing banks, and numerous other Christian ministries that seek to spread the gospel by ministering to the practical needs of a lost world. However, we should use a bit of caution in applying the text in this way. It is wrong to use a text as a pretext,[10] even for a worthy cause.

Although it is good and biblical to minister to the physical needs of others in efforts to bring them to Christ, this is not the intention of Christ's discourse. He is not teaching that our confession of faith is validated or proven true by our willingness to minister to a lost and hurting world. Instead, He is teaching that we demonstrate the reality of our confession by our willingness to identify with and minister to the needs of other Christians who are suffering imprisonment, destitution, and persecution for His sake. In this crucial text, those who are hungry, thirsty, homeless, naked, sick, and in prison are not lost people who find themselves in such dire straits because of their sin, but they are believers who are suffering for the sake of a good conscience before God and their loyalty to Christ.[11] They are children of God, brothers of Christ,[12] and so closely identified with Him through faith that to bless them or neglect them is to do the same to Christ.

When we understand the proper context of Jesus' teaching, we see that He and John are referring to the same truth: selfless love toward individual believers and the church collectively is one of the great evidences of the new birth. In His discourse on the final judgment, Jesus

---

10. We use a text of Scripture as a pretext when we use it to justify a belief or a course of action that is not being taught in the text itself.

11. 1 Peter 2:19–20.

12. Hebrews 2:11.

declares that His sheep are those who love the brethren, even at great cost to themselves. He invites them to inherit the kingdom prepared for them from before the foundation of the world.[13] In contrast, He condemns those who demonstrate their lack of love for His brethren by closing their hearts and hands to them in their time of greatest need. He culls them as goats and sends them off to eternal destruction.[14]

To understand fully the truth conveyed in this discourse, the following illustration may be helpful. Imagine a small group of second-century Christians meeting secretly in the catacombs on the far edge of the city. When their meeting is concluded, they return to their homes, each taking a different route in order to avoid suspicion. Everything seems uneventful until the next day, when news reaches the small congregation that two of the brethren were captured before they reached their home. Immediately, a meeting is called and the exact situation of the two brothers is revealed. They have been badly beaten and imprisoned without food, water, or necessary medical treatment. Their condition is grave.

In light of what they learn, the little congregation is now faced with a moral dilemma, a test of true discipleship. If they do nothing, their brothers in Christ will certainly perish (second-century prisons were not nearly as hospitable as prisons are today). However, if they seek out their brothers, they risk being identified and possibly suffering the same fate. Furthermore, the food, water, medicine, and new clothing they need will be expensive, and most in the congregation are poor laborers and slaves.

As they discuss the matter among themselves, a small division begins to appear. Most are ready to go regardless of the cost. They reason that Christ has laid down His life for them, and they ought to do the same for their brethren.[15] Furthermore, they argue that they cannot say that the love of God abides in them if they close their hearts to their brothers who are suffering for the sake of the Name.[16] In spite of the near unanimity, a small minority disagrees. In their opinion, a visit to the prison is suicidal and would accomplish nothing. Furthermore, they argue that the majority's unnecessary reaction is merely the result of an unrealistic zeal and a dangerous religious fanaticism that has been growing in the church for

---

13. Matthew 25:34.
14. Matthew 25:41.
15. 1 John 3:16.
16. 1 John 3:17.

some time. Reason dictates that they should wait until things cool down a bit. After all, the whole situation is probably not as bad as it seems.

After only a few more minutes of debate, the majority makes the decision, they gather the necessary items, and they prayerfully send an envoy from the church. They visit the prison, bandage their brothers' wounds, clothe their naked bodies, and give them food and drink. The small minority who declined to participate in such a foolish and unnecessary endeavor eventually returned to the world or left the church in search of a more reasonable fellowship.

In Jesus' discourse and in this illustration, we see that there was a prejudgment separation of the sheep and the goats, of the converted and the unconverted, in the same congregation. The majority who chose to stand with their imprisoned brothers demonstrated that they were truly born again and that the love of God abided in them.[17] The self-centered and self-preserving minority demonstrated that their profession of faith and their love for the brethren was only in "word or in tongue" and not "in deed and in truth" (1 John 3:18).

Like any good work, our love for the brethren does not lead to our salvation but is the result of it. The same regenerating work of the Spirit that results in faith leading to justification also results in a genuine love for the brethren that leads to service.

THE IMPOSSIBILITY OF LOVE

One of the greatest tests of genuine conversion is a sincere and effectual love for those who belong to Christ and are called by His name. This love is not merely poetic or theoretical, but real and practical. It is a love that dies to self and, if necessary, risks all for the sake of the Name and for those who are called by it. Such a love is evidence of regeneration and true conversion because it is an absolute impossibility apart from them.

The Scriptures teach that, prior to conversion, a man cannot come to God because he loves evil, disdains righteousness, and fears that his evil deeds will be exposed.[18] Similarly, fallen man will not seek out fellowship with a genuine disciple of Christ because he disdains the righteousness of his life and proclamation and dreads being exposed by them. To prove

---

17. 1 John 3:17.
18. John 3:19–20.

this point, the apostle John refers to one of the most infamous crimes in the Scriptures: Cain's murder of his brother, Abel. He sets forth his argument by asking and answering a simple rhetorical question: "And why did he murder him? Because his works were evil and his brother's righteous" (1 John 3:12).

Fallen men hate a righteous God and would murder Him if they could.[19] Consequently, they also hate God's righteous people and are hostile toward them. This antagonism is not a rare phenomenon; it is woven into the fabric of this fallen world. Since the first act of disobedience and the resultant curse, there has been a great and enduring enmity between the seed of the serpent (the children of disobedience) and the seed of the woman (the children of God).[20] Although the war culminated in the Messiah's victory at Calvary, the battle will continue between His people and the world until the final consummation. In his letter to the churches of Galatia, the apostle Paul illustrated this ongoing battle by appealing to history and spotlighting another set of brothers whose antagonism is nearly as infamous as that which existed between Cain and Abel. He writes: "For it is written that Abraham had two sons: the one by a bond-woman [Ishmael], the other by a freewoman [Isaac]. But he who was of the bondwoman was born according to the flesh, and he of the free-woman through promise…. But, as he who was born according to the flesh then persecuted him who was born according to the Spirit, even so it is now" (Gal. 4:22–23, 29).

The hostility of this fallen world against the children of God is an undeniable truth of Scripture and history. For this reason, John exhorts his readers not to be surprised at the world's hatred toward them.[21] We must understand as basic reality that "all who desire to live godly in Christ Jesus will suffer persecution" (2 Tim. 3:12). Jesus gave this same warning to His disciples in the Upper Room discourse the night before His crucifixion: "If the world hates you, you know that it hated Me before it hated you. If you were of the world, the world would love its own. Yet because you are not of the world, but I chose you out of the world, therefore the world hates you" (John 15:18–19).

---

19. Psalm 2:1–3; Romans 1:30.
20. Genesis 3:15.
21. 1 John 3:13.

When we see in the Scriptures the hostility of fallen man against the people of God, we can now understand more clearly why love for the brethren is such an important test of conversion. Natural man cannot love God or His people. Therefore, when a man finds himself loving both, desiring to love them more, and lamenting his lack of love for them, it should lead him to a greater assurance of salvation. When a man who once despised the people of God suddenly finds himself sharing the same desires with them and longing for their fellowship, it is a great indication that something marvelous has happened. The change is simply inexplicable apart from the Holy Spirit's work of regeneration.

As John has stated throughout his epistle, the Christian will love the people of God. However, we must understand that this love for the brethren, like all other matters of Christian virtue, will always stand in need of further growth. Our initial love for the church, which we experienced at conversion, was a result of the regenerating work of the Spirit. Correspondingly, the continued growth of our love will be the result of the Spirit's ongoing work of sanctification in us. We do not know that we are the children of God because our love is *perfect*, but because it is *being perfected* through God's enduring work in us. In 1 John 2:8, the apostle affirms that the new commandment to love was true in the Christians to whom he was writing. Yet, at the same time, he seems to indicate that it was not fully perfected in them. Their love had not yet reached the measure of the stature that belongs to the fullness of Christ,[22] but it was gradually becoming a greater and greater reality in them. The darkness of their old life was passing away, and they were being transformed by an ever-increasing revelation of the knowledge of God in Christ.

THE TEST OF LOVE

We must now examine our lives in light of these truths. Do we love the people of God and thereby demonstrate the reality of our faith? Is our love the stuff of hidden attitudes and emotions that cannot be proven, or is it demonstrated through real, practical, and discernible evidences such as words, attitudes, and actions? To help you decide where you stand in this all-important matter, the following questions are helpful.

---

22. Ephesian 4:13.

First, whose company do you most enjoy? Do you seek fellowship with other believers and delight in conversations about Christ? Or do you prefer the company of the world and rarely speak about the things of God? When was the last time you met with other believers with the sole intention of being with them and making much of Christ? We should be careful how we answer this question, realizing that much of what is called Christian fellowship has little to do with Christ.

Second, do you publicly identify yourself with Christ and His people? Or are you ashamed of the scandal that surrounds those who confess Jesus as Lord and seek to live in submission to His Word? Do your unbelieving peers indentify you as one of "those Christians"? Or are you so aligned with the world and so conformed to its image that such an accusation would rarely, if ever, be made against you? Do you stand beside the people of God as a spectacle to a world that considers itself too sophisticated to indulge in our religious delusions?[23] Or do you distance yourself from the church as a person would distance himself from a next of kin of whom he was ashamed? Can you identify with Moses, who "refused to be called the son of Pharaoh's daughter, choosing rather to suffer affliction with the people of God than to enjoy the passing pleasures of sin" (Heb. 11:24–25)?

Third, although you are aware of the church's many weaknesses and moral failures, are you committed to her improvement? Or do you align yourself with the devil and the world in their accusations against her?[24] We must always remember that the devil is the accuser of our brethren, and those who stand outside the church with similar accusations are doing the work of their father the devil.[25] In contrast, the true believer responds to his brother's failures with a love that covers a multiude of sins and gives himself to his restoration and improvement.[26] He cannot abandon the church or the fallen saint regardless of how many times they stray. He is compelled by the love of God to seek them, even as Hosea sought Gomer, and to labor for their benefit and future glory.[27]

Fourth, are you a committed and contributing member of a local, visible congregation of believers? We must remember that the kind of

---

23. 1 Corinthians 4:9–13.

24. The name "devil" comes from the Greek word *diábolos*, which may be translated "accuser." It refers to one who is prone to slander and false accusations.

25. John 8:44; Revelation 12:10.

26. 1 Peter 4:8.

27. Hosea 3:1–3.

love of which John is writing can be manifested only in the context of relationships with other believers in the body. Are you dying to self and laying down your life in service to other Christians? Are you laboring for the edification of the church through your various spiritual gifts? To put it simply, what do you actually do to build up the people of God and advance the cause of Christ among them?

These questions cannot be restricted to the clergy alone but pertain to every member of the body of Christ. In fact, one of the evidences of being a member of the body is that we are actually useful to it. Correspondingly, one of the evidences of being unconverted is that we are useless to God for any good work.[28] Love without works, like faith, is dead.[29] We would do well to remember that the sheep and the goats were divided by what they did and did not do for the people of God.

In conclusion, love is not merely one good thing among many, but it is the most excellent thing, trumping even faith and hope.[30] Therefore, it is not unusual that John would give it such an exalted place among the other tests of conversion. We must weigh our doctrinal orthodoxy against the standard of Scripture and examine our personal piety and devotional life in light of it. However, above all things we must test ourselves for love. This virtue must be found in us and manifested in our deeds before we dare assure our hearts that we have come to know Him, as John reminds us many times:

> We know that we have passed from death to life, because we love the brethren. He who does not love his brother abides in death. (1 John 3:14)

> If someone says, "I love God," and hates his brother, he is a liar; for he who does not love his brother whom he has seen, how can he love God whom he has not seen? (1 John 4:20).

---

28. Romans 3:12.
29. James 2:17.
30. 1 Corinthians 12:31; 13:13.

CHAPTER EIGHT

Rejecting the World

Do not love the world or the things in the world. If anyone loves the world, the love of the Father is not in him. For all that is in the world— the lust of the flesh, the lust of the eyes, and the pride of life—is not of the Father but is of the world. And the world is passing away, and the lust of it; but he who does the will of God abides forever.
—1 John 2:15–17

We have considered several major evidences of the Christian life: walking in conformity to the revelation of God, confessing sin, keeping the commandments, imitating Christ, and loving our brother. In this chapter, we will add one more mark to the list: the believer's enduring and increasing rejection of the world.

WHAT ON EARTH IS THE *WORLD*?

What is the *world*? Of what does it consist? The word "world" is translated from the Greek word *kósmos*. In the New Testament, it may refer to the physical universe or its human inhabitants. It may even be used to draw a distinction between the Jews and the world of the Gentiles.[1] However, in this context and many others, the word *kósmos* carries a distinct negative connotation. It refers to everything in the realm of our human existence that is contrary to the knowledge of God, stands in opposition to the will of God, and is hostile toward His person. It consists of the ideals, aspirations, philosophies, attitudes, and conduct of the great mass of fallen humanity. Though it dress itself in the finest garments of learning, sophistication, and even piety, in the end, the world is nothing more than the summation of

---

1. Romans 11:12.

three base or vile elements: the lust of the flesh, the lust of the eyes, and the boastful pride of life.

THE LUST OF THE FLESH

The word "lust" comes from the Greek word *epithumía*, denoting desire, longing, passion, or craving. The word is not necessarily negative, but it may take on a negative connotation depending upon the context. Positively, Jesus earnestly desired to eat the Passover with His disciples.[2] The apostle Paul had a great desire to see the face of the Thessalonians.[3] To the church in Philippi, he confessed his desire to depart and be with Christ.[4]

Although all these positive examples are translated from the word *epithumía*, the word is most often employed in the New Testament to denote a lust, or strong desire, that is outside the realm of God's will either in its direction or intensity.[5] In the gospel of Mark, the word is used to denote an inordinate desire for the things of this world that has the capacity to choke the progress of the gospel and make it unfruitful in a person's life.[6] The apostle Paul used the word to denote the sin of coveting or craving after that which is contrary to God's will.[7] Peter used the word to denote the corrupt desires of carnal men who despise authority and live in opposition to God.[8]

The word "flesh" comes from the Hebrew word *basar* and the Greek word *sárx*. It has a variety of meanings depending upon the context. First, it may denote the physical body of a man: his flesh, blood, and bones.[9] Second, it may refer to man as a weak and temporal creature, especially in comparison with God, who is the eternal and omnipotent Spirit.[10] Third, it may denote the fallenness of man or the moral depravity of his nature in its unregenerate state. This third option is the meaning John gives to the word in this text.

---

2. Luke 22:15.

3. 1 Thessalonians 2:17.

4. Philippians 1:23.

5. A desire may be contrary to God's will in that it is directed toward a forbidden object. It may be contrary to God's will even when directed toward a permissible object if the intensity of the desire is equal to or greater than a person's desire for God.

6. Mark 4:19.

7. Romans 7:7–8.

8. 2 Peter 2:10.

9. 2 Corinthians 10:3; Galatians 2:20; Philippians 1:22.

10. Isaiah 31:3.

Of the three things that most characterize this fallen world, the first is the lust of the flesh. In general, fallen man and his collective culture are driven, motivated, or propelled by their will to satisfy the sinful cravings of their radically depraved and morally corrupt hearts. This is the crime of all crimes—idolatry of the worst kind. A reasonable creature must have a motive for all that he does. The higher and nobler the creature, the higher and nobler the motive for his actions. Man, the pinnacle of God's creation, was made in the image of God and for His glory. Whether he eats or drinks or accomplishes any sort of task from the highest to the most menial, he is to do it all for the glory and good pleasure of God.[11] In summary, man is to be smitten with God and driven by a passion for Him. Every breath and heartbeat is to be for God's glory; every activity and accomplishment is to find its end in God's good pleasure.

Although man was made for the highest end, the Scriptures bear witness that he has sinned and fallen short of such glory,[12] he has dislocated and deformed himself. He is no longer driven by sublime affections for God but by the degraded and animal-like lusts of his morally corrupt heart. As the Scriptures see him, the natural man lives in the lusts of the flesh and indulges its desires. He is by nature a child of wrath.[13]

In this first characteristic of the world, we begin to see the difference between the regenerate and those who remain in their fallen state. It is here that we begin to draw a line between the children of God and those who do not know Him. The person who continues to be enslaved and driven by the sinful desires of his flesh is yet to know God, regardless of his profession of faith and claimed identification with Christ. However, the person who has crucified the flesh, with its passions and desires, and is walking in the liberty of the Spirit of God has great reason for hope that he has become a child of God.[14]

It is important to note that we are not saying that the genuine Christian will walk free from the flesh and its desires or that they can never overcome him. The apostle Paul makes it clear that the believer's war with the flesh is as real as it is intense. In his letter to the churches in Galatia, he describes the battle as epic: "For the flesh lusts against the Spirit, and

---

11. 1 Corinthians 10:31.
12. Romans 3:23.
13. Ephesians 2:3.
14. Galatians 5:16, 24–25.

the Spirit against the flesh; and these are contrary to one another, so that you do not do the things that you wish" (Gal. 5:17).

The proof of conversion is not the absence of warfare with the flesh, but the opposite. One of the great evidences that a person has truly been born again is that he has denounced his friendship with the flesh and has declared war against it without any intention of a truce. We must understand that there is little evidence of salvation in the person who lives at peace with sin, the flesh, and the world. Biblical assurance of salvation does not belong to the person who is wholly surrendered to his fallen flesh and driven by its corrupt desires. There is no proof of the indwelling Spirit in the person who lives at ease in Sodom, who has entered into league with the world, or who has befriended his flesh. However, there is great evidence of salvation in the person who is growing in his hatred of sin, who increases the battle against his flesh, and daily multiplies his disdain for the world. The apostle Paul is a fit example of such a man. He writes:

> And those who are Christ's have crucified the flesh with its passions and desires. (Gal. 5:24)

> The world has been crucified to me, and I to the world. (Gal. 6:14)

THE LUST OF THE EYES

John now turns to the second characteristic of which this fallen world consists: the lust of the eyes. Most commentators, ancient and contemporary, agree that this brief but difficult phrase refers to those sinful desires that are activated and fueled by what we see. It is through the eyes that we are drawn to covet the things that the love and righteousness of God prohibit.

The eyes have been an avenue of temptation since the beginning. In the garden, Eve saw that the forbidden tree was "pleasant to the eyes"; therefore, she succumbed to the deceiver's temptation (Gen. 3:6). Achan "saw" and "coveted" a beautiful mantel, shekels of silver, and bars of gold among the forbidden spoil. He took them and paid the price with his own blood and that of his kin (Josh. 7:20–21, 24–26). King David "saw" the beauty of Bathsheba, turned from the law, and took her for his own (2 Sam. 11:2–5). The result was a murdered soldier, a deceased infant, a disgraced king, and a divided kingdom. Finally, Matthew tells us that Satan took Christ to a high mountain and "showed" Him all the kingdoms of the world and their glory (Matt. 4:8–10). Even though this time-tested strategy was wasted on Christ, the tempter's use of it demonstrates that it is a frequently used armament in his arsenal.

When we consider these accounts, we may think that these people's sin was in their action, but in reality they sinned long before they committed the act. Jesus taught that a person can violate the command against adultery in his heart even when he never has performed the actual deed. He warned us that everyone who even "looks at a woman to lust for her has already committed adultery with her in his heart" (Matt. 5:27–28). To demonstrate the seriousness of sin in our hearts, Jesus goes on to teach a severe hyperbole in which He shows that we ought to prefer self-mutilation above the eternal condemnation that results from a wayward eye.[15] This is why Job declared that he had made a covenant with his eyes not to look upon a young woman.[16] And although the psalmist probably had the prohibition against idols foremost in his mind, the principle is the same when he declared that he would set no evil thing before his eyes.[17] All these Scriptures testify to what Spurgeon so clearly explained: "What fascinates the eye is very apt to gain admission into the heart, even as Eve's apple first pleased her sight and then prevailed over her mind and hand."[18]

Because of the radical nature of fallen man's corruption, the unregenerate heart is full of lust for all things that are contrary to the righteous law of a holy God. However, this lust is fanned into flame when some wicked thing is set before it in plain view and within reach. Then, to make matters worse, the flame of lust grows to even greater heights and power when the unregenerate heart is told that such a thing is prohibited. It is a well-established biblical principle that the more God declares something off limits, the more the fallen heart lusts for it![19]

In the Sermon on the Mount, Jesus drew from Jewish literature and referred to the eye as the "lamp of the body" (Matt. 6:22–23). The idea is that the focus of a person's eye reveals the content and condition of his heart. A person who has determined to turn his eyes from evil and focus on the kingdom of heaven demonstrates that his heart has been made right through the gospel and the regenerating work of the Holy Spirit.

---

15. Matthew 5:29–30.
16. Job 31:1.
17. Psalm 101:3.
18. C. H. Spurgeon, *The Treasury of David* (Grand Rapids: Zondervan, 1950), 1:240.
19. Romans 7:7–13.

However, the person who sees no beauty or benefit in the kingdom but sets his eyes upon the things of this world demonstrates that his heart remains unregenerate and the gospel has done him little good.

In order to apply this teaching properly to our contemporary circumstance, we must first be aware that we live in a culture that is mesmerized by the evil things that are dangled before it. It is not without reason that the marketers of our day rely so heavily upon the eye. They know that with one visual effect they can awaken our hearts to desires that were previously dormant and cause us to lust for things of which only the hour before we were unaware. It is as though they have taken their strategies from the playbook of the greatest of all tempters, the devil. He knew from the beginning that the eye is the greatest and widest avenue to the heart.

If we are to be biblical regarding conversion and the proofs of it, we must accept the teaching that is placed before us here: one of the great proofs of conversion is the focus of a person's life. Those who profess a place in the kingdom but who seldom have the kingdom in view should examine their profession. If we strive for the things of this world, if we pine away because of the carnal rewards we are not able to procure, and if we covet the worldly attainments of others, then we are very far from the kingdom of heaven. We should strain our ear to hear and understand the following divine correctives:

> Why do you spend money for what is not bread,
> And your wages for what does not satisfy?
> Listen carefully to Me, and eat what is good,
> And let your soul delight itself in abundance. (Isa. 55:2)

> For what profit is it to a man if he gains the whole world, and loses his own soul? Or what will a man give in exchange for his soul? (Matt. 16:26)

The proof of salvation is in its fruit. If your heart has truly been regenerated, then you are a new creature with new affections that will guide your eyes away from worldly attraction to that which is heavenly. If your heart has been truly regenerated, then the kingdom of heaven will be to you like a treasure hidden in a field, which a man finds and hides again; and from joy over it goes and sells all that he has and buys that field.[20] Again, you will be like a merchant seeking fine pearls, and upon finding

---

20. Matthew 13:44.

one pearl of great value, you will go and sell all that you have and buy it.[21] If you have truly been converted, then little by little, through the Spirit's work of progressive sanctification, you will be able to affirm the impassioned words of "When I Survey the Wondrous Cross" by Isaac Watts:

> All the vain things that charm me most,
> I sacrifice them to His blood....
>
> Then I am dead to all the globe,
> and all the globe is dead to me.

THE BOASTFUL PRIDE OF LIFE

The phrase "boastful pride of life" is translated from the Greek *alazoneía tou bíou*. The Word *alazoneía* is correctly translated "boastful pride." It refers to an empty, presumptuous, and insolent pride that leads to boasting or braggart talk. The only other place in the New Testament where this word is used is in James's strong admonition to the wealthy who boast of great plans and endeavors independently from God and without any consideration of His providence or their own frail mortality:

> Come now, you who say, "Today or tomorrow we will go to such and such a city, spend a year there, buy and sell, and make a profit"; whereas you do not know what will happen tomorrow. For what is your life? It is even a vapor that appears for a little time and then vanishes away. Instead you ought to say, "If the Lord wills, we shall live and do this or that." But now you boast in your arrogance [*alazoneías*]. All such boasting is evil. (4:13–16)

In the New Testament, two words in the Greek language are most often translated "life." The most common is *zoé*, which refers to the principle or essence of life. The other is *bíos*, from which we derive the word "biography." It tends to refer to the period or course of a person's life or to that by which a person's life is sustained: resources, wealth, property, or livelihood. In John's discussion of the believer's responsibility to the poor in a later chapter, the word is translated as "goods": "But whoever has this world's goods [*bíos*], and sees his brother in need, and shuts up his heart from him, how does the love of God abide in him?" (1 John 3:17). Combining what we know of these two words and their use in the New Testament, we can conclude that the phrase "boastful pride of life" refers

---

21. Matthew 13:45–46.

to the pride or arrogance of people who not only boast of their achievements and possessions but who also attribute them to their own wisdom and power. This is a great mark of the worldly person who sees himself as independent from God and free from His providence—a hero who has carved out his own existence, shaped his own destiny, and amassed his possessions by force of will, cleverness of mind, or sheer physical strength. He considers every gain and accolade to be a personal and private triumph, unassisted by divine grace or aid and is described by the psalmist as one who takes no thought of God in the making of his plans and renders no thanks to God when those plans succeed. David writes:

> The wicked in his proud countenance does not seek God;
> God is in none of his thoughts....
> He has said in his heart,
> "I shall not be moved;
> I shall never be in adversity." (Ps. 10:4, 6)

In describing the boastful pride of life in this way, we must be careful to understand that it does not require professed atheism or open rebellion against God. The same attitude can easily flourish among those who confess a reliance on God and even render thanksgiving to Him. A practical atheism exists in the church that is far more deadly than its bolder and more openly defiant brother. It wears the garb of Christianity and can even confess Jesus as Lord, but it rarely consults His will on a practical level. It may ask God to join in a purpose that has already been determined or to bless a plan already designed. It may even acknowledge His help in an endeavor, but it usually offers only a residual gratitude, the table scraps that remain after the glory of man has been satisfied. Those who would patronize God in this manner are the opposite of the wise man of Proverbs who trusts in the Lord with all His heart and does not lean on his own understanding, but in all his ways acknowledges Him.[22]

The boastful pride of life is the epitome of self-worship, and those who indulge in it become as pathetic as the ancient Chaldeans who gathered fish in their net and then offered sacrifices to it.[23] They worshiped a lifeless strand of string without any regard for the God who "makes His sun rise on the evil and on the good, and sends rain on the just and on

---

22. Proverbs 3:5–6.
23. Habakkuk 1:15–16.

the unjust" (Matt. 5:45). According to the Scriptures, those who worship self and glory in personal achievement worship a vapor that appears for a little while and then vanishes away, a mere breath, a passing shadow, a nose full of air.[24] Such a man makes great boasts of great things, yet he cannot make one hair of his head white or black or add one hour to his life.[25] In all his pomp, he is like the beasts that perish, and like the dew that disappears at the first hour of the dawn or the chaff that is blown away from the threshing floor.[26]

Such people fail to see that God gives to all people life, breath, and all things so that they would seek and find Him?[27] They are unaware that if He should hide His face, they would be dismayed, and if He should take away His spirit, they would expire and return to dust.[28] Such people have never wondered, "What is man that You are mindful of him?" (Ps. 8:4). They are ignorant of the truth that the nations are like a drop from a bucket before Him, and the full sum of them are regarded as a speck of dust on the scales.[29]

In this matter of the boastful pride of life we see the great distinction between the child of God and those who do not know Him. Those who have been regenerated by the Spirit and are the objects of His sanctifying work are ever growing in the knowledge that Christ is their life, and apart from Him they are "wretched, miserable, poor, blind, and naked."[30] They are learning that apart from Him they can do nothing,[31] and, being motivated by an ever-increasing knowledge of their weakness, they are driven to know God's will and keep themselves safely inside it. Furthermore, when they have done the will of God, they acknowledge that they are unworthy slaves who have done only that which they ought to have done.[32] And when something is accomplished through their feeble efforts, they sweep the ground to cover any tracks that might lead the glory of the deed back to them. They cry out with the psalmist:

---

24. Psalms 39:5; 144:4; Isaiah 2:22; James 4:14.
25. Matthew 5:36; 6:27.
26. Psalm 49:20; Hosea 13:3.
27. Acts 17:25–27.
28. Psalm 104:27–29.
29. Isaiah 40:15–17.
30. Colossians 3:4; Revelation 3:17.
31. John 15:5.
32. Luke 17:10.

> Not unto us, O LORD, not unto us,
> But to Your name give glory,
> Because of Your mercy,
> Because of Your truth. (Ps. 115:1)

The child of God is always learning the principle maxim of heaven: "He who glories, let him glory in the LORD" (1 Cor. 1:31; cf. Jer. 9:23–24). And when the believer forgets his lessons and seeks to take the glory that belongs to Christ alone, the Spirit of God is faithful to rebuke him and send him back to his proper seat in shame.[33] The Lord will not share His glory with another.[34]

In contrast, the unbeliever has no room in his heart or mind for such humility or gratitude. He is blind to his utter inability and absolute dependence upon the grace and power of God. He lives under the arrogant assumption that either there is no God, or, if there is, He does not concern Himself with human affairs. Because of this assumption, the unbeliever claims every achievement as his own, and each victory gives him one more reason to boast in self. The pathetic creature called man, who cannot make one hair of his head white or black or add one single hour to his life, stands atop all his accomplishments and declares that he is self-made.

OUR RELATIONSHIP WITH THE WORLD

In light of what we have learned as professing Christians, we must ask ourselves where we stand in relation to the world. We must not be deceived into thinking that this is a minor matter. It is crucial! Our relation to the world is one of the great litmus tests of our salvation. John warns us that love for the world and love for God are diametrically opposed. He tells us plainly that "if anyone loves the world, the love of the Father is not in him."[35] James is even bolder when he declares: "Do you not know that friendship with the world is enmity with God? Whoever therefore wants to be a friend of the world makes himself an enemy of God" (4:4).

---

33. Luke 14:7–11.
34. Isaiah 42:8; 48:11.
35. 1 John 2:15. The phrase "love of the Father" probably has a double meaning. John is stating that anyone who loves the world does not love God and is not an object of that special love God has for His people. This, of course, is the fault of sinful man, who willfully and deliberately rejects this special love of God.

According to the Scriptures, to love the world and God at the same time is a logical impossibility because the two are totally incompatible and opposing. Everything in the world—the lust of the flesh, the lust of the eyes, and the boastful pride of life—is not from the Father. It does not originate with Him, nor is it according to His will, but it is repugnant and antagonistic to Him. A person can no more love God and the world than he can "keep his cake and eat it too."

This does not mean that Christians will not have trouble with the world or that they cannot be enticed by it. The Christian will have great struggles with the world in all its various manifestations, but he will hate it, will fight against it, and will be remorseful when he gives himself to it. The difference is not merely semantic, but real and practical. The person who professes faith in Christ and yet finds beauty and joy in the things that oppose the will of God should be concerned about the validity of his profession. However, the person who professes faith in Christ and finds himself growing in his disdain for the world, living in opposition to it, and making progress in his victory over it has great cause for assurance no matter how often he may fall. The question remains: Where do we stand in our relation to the world? Following the example of the main character, Christian, in John Bunyan's famous allegory *The Pilgrim's Progress*, are we fleeing the City of Destruction? Are we determined to free ourselves from all its trappings? Or have we made a home in the city of Folly and found Vanity Fair to be a great delight?

A WORD TO SHEPHERDS

In John's day, the world was epitomized by the Roman Empire with its greed, sensuality, and lust for power. In the book of Revelation it is seen as Babylon the Great, "THE MOTHER OF HARLOTS AND OF THE ABOMINATIONS OF THE EARTH" who "made all nations drink of the wine of the wrath of her fornication" (Rev. 14:8; 17:5). Presently, the world seems more powerful and undaunted than ever. Hollywood, Madison Avenue, Wall Street, Washington, and the great majority of our academic institutions represent it. Like the Babylon of old, the world today holds out a golden cup for all to drink: a cup "full of abominations and the filthiness of her fornication" (Rev. 17:4). Also, like Babylon, the world today is armed with false prophets sent out into the four corners of the globe to lead astray humanity. Whether they are dressed in a pinstriped business suit, the latest fashion trends, or the religious garb of a prophet, their message is the same. They make no mention of the eternal but convince their hearers to lay hold of the temporal before it is gone. They care little for moral absolutes that might hamper the freedom of the individual in his plight for self-expression. They justify greed by parading it before their listeners under the guise of self-realization, self-fulfillment, and just deserts. They are always on the side of their hearers, brokering for them, looking out for their interests, telling them what they need, and making it available to them at a price. It is not difficult to discern why they have such a following. They appeal to the lust of the flesh, the lust of the eyes, and the boastful pride of life. They tickle the ears of fallen people by telling them what they desire to hear.[36] They are from the world and speak its language, and the world listens to them.[37] Though packaged in a seemingly infinite number of ways, their message is always the same. In fact, the words of these prophets are so strikingly similar that it leads us to believe that they must have a common origin: the spirit of the age, the prince of the power of the air that is now working in the sons of disobedience.[38]

All we have described thus far is to be expected. The worldliness of the world requires no great explanation, but what is beyond understanding is the bold presence of the world in the church.[39] It is one thing when the world maneuvers itself subtly and stealthily in the church as a nearly undetectable force. It is quite another when the world stands boldly in the center of the church and deforms everything in conformity to its vile image. And this is the case in much of the so-called Christianity in the West. Is the world guilty of materialism? So is the church! Is the world consumer driven? So is the church! Does the world function on a pragmatism that is unconcerned for biblical truth? So does the church! Is the world mesmerized by entertainment, distracted by amusement, and delighted with folly? So is the church! Does the world offer

---

36. 2 Timothy 4:3.

37. 1 John 4:5.

38. Ephesians 2:2.

39. An important distinction must be made here in our use of the word *church*. In this context, we are using the word *church* in the sense of professing Christianity or professing evangelicalism in the West. The true church of Jesus Christ is made up of only the regenerate, who bear the fruit of conversion, and who are to be distinguished from the great majority of professing (yet unconverted) Christians.

self-realization and self-promotion? So does the church! Is the world full of carnality, sensuality, luxury, and extravagance? So is the church! In fact, not only does the church tolerate carnality among its members, but it also defends their carnality and, like the church in Corinth, even boasts of it, turning the grace of God into licentiousness and denying our only Master and Lord, Jesus Christ.[40] In Bunyan's day, Vanity Fair was Satan's tool to amuse people and keep them in the world. Bunyan would be dumbfounded to learn that in our day, many churches use Vanity Fair to amuse seekers and keep them coming to the Sunday service.

Why and how has this happened in many churches? Primarily, it is because of the men who have been placed over the church as her shepherds.

First, we must conclude that an unsettling number of them must be unregenerate and cut off from Christ. Their flagrant and thoughtless violations of doctrine and ethics are so grotesque that they must not be converted.

Second, we must allow that some who are truly converted are not called. There is such a misunderstanding regarding the true elements of the gospel ministry. It has become so business and entertainment driven that many of the men who now stand behind pulpits would be better off as corporate heads on Wall Street or entertainers in Hollywood.

Third, we must also allow that some men are truly Christian and truly called into the gospel ministry, but they have been ensnared by the religion of the day; they lack the "iron file" of real fellowship with other men of God, and they do not know how to find their way back.[41] Like righteous Lot, their hearts are afflicted by the church's worldliness, but they have lost the moral credentials and strength to speak against it.[42] The proverb has been fulfilled in them: "A righteous man who falters before the wicked, is like a murky spring and a polluted well" (Prov. 25:26). They should be encouraged by the truth that the Lord knows how to deliver the godly from the snare of the fowler and rescue them from temptation.[43]

Fourth, many shepherds have been caught up in the trend to "do" church according to the whims of culture or the supposed effectiveness of pragmatism. Thus, many have taken on the mannerisms of an entertainer, life coach, psychoanalyst, or Madison Avenue marketing expert.

---

40. 1 Corinthians 5:6; Jude v. 4.
41. Proverbs 27:17.
42. 2 Peter 2:7–8.
43. Psalm 91:3; 2 Peter 2:9.

It seems we have forgotten that shepherds are primarily students and teachers of the Scriptures,[44] caretakers of the flock,[45] and ardent intercessors before God.[46] They are to guard the deposit that has been entrusted to them,[47] knowing that they will be held accountable on that great day.[48] They are to be exegetes, theologians, and expositors of God's Word. They are to conform to strict standards of Scripture regarding character, ethics, and duty.[49] They are to dwell alone with God like watchmen on the walls.[50] Following in the footsteps of Christ, they are to come to God on behalf of people and to people on behalf of God.

Last, we must also acknowledge that cowardliness is among us—a fear of rejection that flows from the idol of self-preservation. Thus, we have developed a distorted and convenient view of love that never upsets anyone. It is a love without truth, conviction, and the courage to teach, reprove, correct, or train.[51] It is a love that would let people walk unwarned into hell rather than confront them in their sin, wound their fragile self-esteem, or make them an enemy by telling them the truth.[52] Actually, this is not love, but the very antitype of love. If we never rebuke the sheep so as to unjustly earn their disfavor, it is not because we love them but because we want them to like us. The desire to be affirmed and appreciated is deadly venom to a man of God, yet it appears that many have been bitten. We have forgotten the warning of our Lord who said, "Woe to you when all men speak well of you, for so did their fathers to the false prophets" (Luke 6:26).

---

44. Ezra 7:10; Acts 6:2, 4; 2 Timothy 2:15.

45. Acts 20:28; 1 Peter 5:1–4.

46. Acts 6:4; Romans 1:9; Ephesians 1:15–16; Philippians 1:3–4; Colossians 1:9.

47. 1 Timothy 1:11; 6:20; 2 Timothy 2:14; Titus 1:3.

48. 1 Corinthians 3:12–15; 2 Timothy 4:8.

49. 1 Timothy 3:1–7; Titus 1:7–9.

50. Isaiah 62:6–7.

51. In 2 Timothy 3:16 the apostle Paul lays out for young Timothy the fourfold ministry of God's Word by God's minister.

52. In Galatians 4:16 Paul has confronted the error of the Galatians and asks, "Have I therefore become your enemy because I tell you the truth?"

CHAPTER NINE

Remaining in the Church

Little children, it is the last hour; and as you have heard that the Anti-christ is coming, even now many antichrists have come, by which we know that it is the last hour. They went out from us, but they were not of us; for if they had been of us, they would have continued with us; but they went out that they might be made manifest, that none of them were of us.
—1 John 2:18–19

In 1 John 2:18–19, the apostle John makes reference to a group of individu-als who had apostatized. They had rejected apostolic doctrine concerning the person and work of Christ, left the church, and become false proph-ets. John even goes so far as to refer to them as antichrists.

The infamous title "antichrist" is a conjunction of the Greek word *Christós,* or "Christ," and the preposition *anti-,* meaning "in place of," or "against." In the singular, the *Antichrist* refers to the great enemy of the Messiah who will one day attempt to usurp His place and fight against Him.[1] Its plural use refers to any number of individuals throughout the age of the church who deny the fundamental apostolic doctrines regard-ing the person and work of Christ, set themselves outside of the church and historical Christianity, and seek to lead others astray in the same regard.[2] In his epistle, John describes them as liars and deceivers who deny the Father and the Son by rejecting the incarnation and refusing to acknowledge that Jesus is the divine Christ.[3] As in John's day, our mod-ern world is filled with antichrists who either oppose Christ directly or

---

1. 2 Thessalonians 2:3–4.

2. John's phrase "in the last hour" is synomomous with "last days" (Acts 2:17; 2 Time thy 3:1; James 5:3). It refers to the age between the resurrection and exaltation of Christ and His second coming.

3. 1 John 2:22–23; 4:2; 2 John 1:7.

propagate a religion that diminishes the supremacy of His person or the essential nature of His work. Any teaching that does not hold firm to the absolute uniqueness of Christ, supplants Him, or trivializes His cross is antichrist in nature. As revealed in the Scriptures, those who are not for Christ are against Him.[4]

Although in the immediate context John is writing primarily of false teachers, he also provides us with yet another test of biblical assurance: the genuine Christian will remain within the realm of the historic doctrines of the Christian faith and in fellowship with the people of God. Those who renounce such doctrines and break fellowship with the church demonstrate that they are not—and never have been—truly converted. John writes: "They went out from us, but they were not of us; for if they had been of us, they would have continued with us; but they went out that they might be made manifest, that none of them were of us" (2:19).

This does not mean that eternal salvation is obtained or guarded in the church. A person is saved in Christ alone, by grace alone, through faith alone.[5] What it does mean is that the person who is truly converted will continue in the teachings that led to his conversion and remain within the fellowship of the Christian church. John makes a similar declaration in his second epistle: "Whoever transgresses and does not abide in the doctrine of Christ does not have God. He who abides in the doctrine of Christ has both the Father and the Son" (1:9).

ASSURANCE AND APOSTASY

A battle has raged throughout the history of the church between those who hold to the eternal security, or perseverance, of the believer and those who maintain the possibility of apostasy—the falling away of a genuine believer into eternal destruction. The matter is of such great importance that I must address it, if only briefly. I do not presume that the matter will be resolved to everyone's satisfaction. However, I do hope to put forth a few important truths with regard to the nature of conversion and demonstrate how they apply to the believer.

To begin, it is important to understand that I affirm the historical doctrine of the perseverance of the saints as held by the Reformers, Puritans,

---

4. Luke 11:23.
5. Ephesians 2:8–9.

early Presbyterians, and Particular Baptists.[6] The doctrine affirms that those who have been truly regenerated by the Holy Spirit, made new creatures in Christ, and are kept by the power of God will never ultimately fall away into apostasy and eternal destruction. The reason for this confidence is not founded upon the believer's strength of will, but upon the faithfulness and power of God. The God who saves His people also keeps them by His power. The God who justifies the believer will certainly sanctify him and ultimately bring him to glory. Like the apostle Paul, we are confident of this very thing, that He who has begun a good work will perfect it until the day of Christ Jesus.

In any discussion regarding the perseverance of the believer, four things ought to be considered. First, we must comprehend something of the nature of salvation. The superficiality of much contemporary preaching has led us to believe that the work of salvation is primarily a decision of the human will. God reveals the gospel to man and then awaits man's response. Man receives salvation by deciding for Christ and continues in that salvation by the same act of will. Thus, the man who gains salvation through a proper response to God may just as easily lose his salvation if he renounces his initial decision by a contrary act of the will.

The problem with this view is that it deals only with the will of man and fails to consider God's work upon his nature. The Scripture teaches that the man who believes unto salvation *has been* born of God.[7] Furthermore, it affirms that this new birth is "not of blood, nor of the will of the flesh, nor of the will of man, but of God" (John 1:13). Salvation does not involve just an act of the human will, but the transformation of a radically depraved human nature into a new creation.[8] It is a supernatural work of God whereby the sinner's hostile and unresponsive heart of stone is replaced by a new heart of living and responsive flesh.[9] Salvation is not the result of a wicked heart's decision to turn back to God merely through the coaxing of the preacher or even the limited promptings of

---

6. The reader is directed to chapter 17 of both the Westminster and the 1689 London Confessions, where the doctrine of the perseverance of the saints is treated at length.

7. The phrase "is born of God" is translated from the Greek verb *gegénnetai,* which is in the perfect tense and passive voice. It is rightly translated in the *English Standard Version*: "Everyone who believes that Jesus is the Christ has been born of God…" Therefore, the work of regeneration logically precedes faith, and is the cause and foundation of it.

8. 2 Corinthians 5:17.

9. Ezekiel 36:26.

the Holy Spirit, but the result of a radical new birth. Through a cataclysmic work of the Spirit of God, the sinner has become a new creature with new affections that drive him from sin and draw him to God. If salvation and its continuance were nothing more than a change of the will and a proper response to God, then it could easily be undone by a contrary change. But if salvation involves the recreation of the nature of a human, making him into a new creature, then the undoing or loss of salvation is impossible.

Second, we must comprehend something of the continued work of divine providence in the life of the truly converted. God does not merely prompt a person to believe and then leave him to his own devices. The Scriptures teach us that the God who justifies is also He who sanctifies. This truth is superbly demonstrated in Paul's epistle to the church in Ephesus. Immediately after affirming the great doctrine of justification by grace alone through faith alone in chapter 2, Paul turns his readers' attention to God's work of sanctification, which always accompanies saving faith and is a further result of grace: "For we are His workmanship, created in Christ Jesus for good works, which God prepared beforehand that we should walk in them" (2:10).

The person who has been justified by grace through faith has become the workmanship of God. He has been recreated in Christ Jesus to accomplish the good that was prepared for him before the foundation of the world by the eternal counsels of God. As Paul wrote to the believers in Philippi, God had not saved them and then set them on a course alone, but He was at work in them "both *to will and to do* for His good pleasure" (2:13, emphasis added). This powerful declaration proves that God not only has made the believer into a new creature with new affections influencing his will but also that He has worked on the believer's will so that he will live and work according to God's good pleasure. This astounding divine work was the basis of Paul's unshakable confidence regarding the ultimate salvation and future glorification of the believers in Philippi: "being confident of this very thing, that He who has begun a good work in you will complete it until the day of Jesus Christ" (1:6).

Third, in any discussion regarding the perseverance of the saints, we must comprehend something of the purpose of salvation. Although God's work of salvation is *for man,* man's well-being is not its highest good or chief end. Although it is a hard saying for modern man and even the contemporary evangelical, the chief end of all things is the glory of

God through the revelation of His character and power. In other words, God does all that He does in order that His greatness and glory might be revealed to His creation. This is the purpose of all God's works, but especially of His greatest: the salvation of men through Jesus Christ. Will God let the greatest demonstration of His character and power fail? Will He who began the work of salvation fall short in perfecting it? Will He exposes Himself to the ridicule of His enemies, who will say, "Because the LORD was not able to bring this people to the land which He swore to give them, therefore He killed them in the wilderness" (Num. 14:16)?

For His glory, God will not let salvation fail even in the weakest one who believes. Rather, He will "let the power of [the] Lord be great, just as [He has] spoken" (Num. 14:17). He will take His people from the world and bring them to Himself. He will cleanse them from all their filthiness and idols and will give them a new heart and write His laws upon it. He will put His Spirit within them and cause them walk in His statutes.[10] He will make an everlasting covenant with them that He will not turn away from them, and He will put the fear of the Lord in their hearts so that they will not turn away from Him. They shall be His people, and He will be their God. He will rejoice over them to do them good and will see to the finishing of His work in them with all His heart and soul.[11] "What then shall we say to these things? If God is for us, who [or what] can be against us?" (Rom. 8:31). Salvation will not fail, for it is not designed to prove or reveal our faithfulness and power, but God's!

Fourth, we must understand that the doctrine of perseverance has been grossly misinterpreted and wrongly expounded by many of those who claim to hold to it. Many who hold to the falling away of the true believer do so as a reaction against those who claim to hold to the doctrine of perseverance and yet teach all manner of error in its name. The historic doctrine of the perseverance of the saints does affirm the eternal security of the child of God. However, it is not a license for sin, nor does it maintain that the carnal and ungodly will be saved. Rather, it holds unwaveringly to the biblical truths that only those who endure to the end will be saved, and without sanctification leading to holiness, no one will see the Lord.[12]

---

10. Jeremiah 31: 33; Ezekiel 36:22–27.
11. Jeremiah 32:38–41.
12. Matthew 24:13; Mark 13:13; Hebrews 12:14.

Contemporary evangelicalism has been grossly affected by a "once saved always saved" teaching that argues for the possibility of salvation apart from sanctification. In the name of defending the doctrines of *sola gratia* (grace alone) and *sola fide* (faith alone), many evangelical churchmen will passionately argue for the salvation of an individual who once professed Christ but now denies Him or who continues to profess faith in Christ but remains carnal, worldly, and apathetic toward God. They claim that to require any mark of transformation or any measure of sanctification is to add works to faith and to essentially deny the Christian gospel.

The problem with this argument is that it betrays an ignorance of the nature of faith, the power of regeneration, and the divine promise of a continuing work of providence. First, we must realize that genuine faith is evidenced by works. According to the Scriptures, it is impossible to possess a saving faith that has had no observable impact upon the conduct of a person's life. James 2:17–20 asserts, "Thus also faith by itself, if it does not have works, is dead. But someone will say, 'You have faith, and I have works.' Show me your faith without your works, and I will show you my faith by my works. You believe that there is one God. You do well. Even the demons believe—and tremble! But do you want to know, O foolish man, that faith without works is dead?"

In the same way, a person who makes a saving confession of Jesus as Lord proves it by the fruit of his life.[13] The Scriptures give us the promise that if we confess with our mouths Jesus as Lord and believe in our hearts that God has raised Him from the dead, we will be saved.[14] However, Christ Himself warns us that any confession of His lordship that is not accompanied by doing the Father's will is absolutely void and powerless to save.[15] These conclusions are not based upon mere inference but upon the clear teaching of Scripture.

Second, we must realize that the whole of salvation is a gift and the result of the regenerating work of the Holy Spirit.[16] At the moment of conversion, the Spirit, who imparts saving faith to the believer, also regenerates his heart and makes him into a new creature that is alive unto God and possesses new affections for God and godliness.[17] Of necessity, this

---

13. Matthew 7:20; Luke 6:46.
14. Romans 10:9.
15. Matthew 7:21.
16. John 3:3, 5: Ephesians 2:8-9.
17. 2 Corinthians 5:17; Ephesians 2:5.

supernatural work results in a changed heart, leading to changes in the Christian's thought and conduct.

Third, we must again note that salvation comes with the accompanying promise of God's continuing work of providence, which results in the progressive sanctification of every believer.[18] God does not save and then abandon. He does not adopt and then neglect.[19] He is not a derelict Father.[20] He is not an impotent crafter who cannot finish the work He has begun.[21] We must always remember that salvation is viewed in three tenses, and God is the author and the perfecter of each.[22] He saved us from the condemnation of sin through justification, currently saves us from the power of sin through progressive sanctification, and will save from the effect and presence of sin through our future glorification. This is not merely a hopeful possibility in the believer's life, but an absolute certainty. For this reason, the apostle Paul wrote in Romans 8:28–31:

> And we know that all things work together for good to those who love God, to those who are the called according to His purpose. For whom He foreknew, He also predestined to be conformed to the image of His Son, that He might be the firstborn among many brethren. Moreover whom He predestined, these He also called; whom He called, these He also justified; and whom He justified, these He also glorified. What then shall we say to these things? If God is for us, who can be against us?

The doctrine of the perseverance of the saints is not a license for sin or a means of giving false assurance of salvation to the carnal and ungodly. Yes, the doctrine affirms that God keeps those He saves, but it also affirms that He transforms those He keeps. The genuine believer has assurance of salvation not only because of a past profession of faith but also because of the ongoing work of God in His life that continues to transform him into the image of Christ. The person who professes faith in Christ and yet bears no evidence of faith, a divine work of regeneration, or the continuing work of divine providence can have little assurance of eternal life. This is not because he has lost a salvation he

---

18. Romans 8:28–31; Philippians 1:6.
19. Romans 8:14–16; Galatians 4:4–6.
20. Hebrews 12:5–8.
21. Ephesians 2:10; Philippians 1:6.
22. Hebrews 12:2.

once possessed but because he is demonstrating that he never possessed the salvation he claims.

In 1 John 2:19, the apostle tells us of a group of individuals who had once professed faith in Christ but were now showing their lost condition by departing from the foundational doctrines of the Christian faith and the fellowship of the church. However, he makes it clear to us that they did not lose their salvation; rather, their "going out" proved that they were never truly saved. His language is precise: "They went out from us, but *they were not of us*; for if they had been of us, they would have continued with us; but they went out that they might be made manifest, that none of them were of us (emphasis added)."

This text provides us with a proper and biblical balance regarding the assurance of the believer and the possibility of apostasy. Why did these individuals fall away? John makes it clear that although they were identified with Christ and His church, they were never really *of* Christ or *of* His people. Like so many throughout the history of the church, they had assumed the garb and learned the speech of Christianity, but they had never experienced its power.[23] They were not returning to what they once were but demonstrating what they had always been. The dog that returns to its own vomit demonstrates it was never anything other than a dog, even though it might profess otherwise. The sow that returns to wallowing in the mire demonstrates that whatever washing it had received was external. Although apparently it was clean on the outside, it never possessed anything other than the nature of a swine.[24] The one who professes Christ and fellowships with His people and then permanently turns away from both has not reverted to the person he once was but has simply removed his sheep's clothing and revealed his true nature, which had never been transformed.

PERSONAL EXAMINATION

Genuine believers do not fall away. However, many who confess Christ and even identify themselves with the church are not genuine believers. They eventually fall away from a biblical church and demonstrate their true condition. However, in this matter the evangelical church has most

---

23. 2 Timothy 3:5.
24. 2 Peter 2:22.

failed its congregants. When the Word of God is not expounded so as to affect the conscience and when the church is organized to satisfy the carnal desires of the world, then the unconverted are not compelled to withdraw but can remain comfortably within the church while continuing on a course to hell. Such is the sad state of affairs in the so-called evangelical church. In the name of so many right things wrongly interpreted and applied, such as love, acceptance, and inoffensiveness, the unconverted thrive in the midst of the congregation. And all the while, the misguided prophet calls out, "'Peace, peace' when there is no peace" (Jer. 6:14; 8:11).

If there is ever to be a change, it must begin with a revival among the shepherds of God's people. They must preach the full counsel of God's Word to their hearers' consciences. They must make known the gospel in all its scandalous glory, expounding the holiness of God, exposing the depravity of man, pointing to the cross of Calvary, and commanding all men everywhere to repent and believe the gospel. They must urge the people of God to a life of holiness, disdain for the world, disinterest in self, sacrificial service, and in view of eternity. Only then will the unconverted among us be awakened from their slumber. Yes, some will awake with hatred for the preacher and his message, but still others will awake to brokenness over sin and faith unto eternal life.

Having addressed the shepherds, we must now turn our attention toward those who sit before them every Lord's Day. How would we respond if our pastor were to repent of his unfaithful discharge of his office and began to faithfully preach the Scriptures in the power of the Holy Spirit? Would we rejoice, or would we fight him until we won the case and had him expelled? Or upon not finding an ungodly majority to stand with us, would we respond like the men about whom John is writing? Would we go out from a reforming pastor and congregation and thus prove that we were never really part of the church and never really belonged to Christ?

These are hard words that many think but few will speak. What would we do if the church was no longer about us and our felt needs but about the glory of God and His Christ? How would we respond to biblical preaching aimed at our conscience? What would be our reaction if entertainment were dethroned and simple, heartfelt worship was set in its place? What would be our vote if programs were replaced by prayer meetings and family devotions? What would we do if everyone decided that being relevant and contextual were not as important as just pleasing God? If a biblical and vibrant Christianity was reborn in the midst of our congregation, where would we go? What would we do? The apostle John tells us in our text that our response would be a great indicator of the genuineness of our profession.

CHAPTER TEN

Confessing Christ

Who is a liar but he who denies that Jesus is the Christ? He is antichrist who denies the Father and the Son. Whoever denies the Son does not have the Father either; he who acknowledges the Son has the Father also. Therefore let that abide in you which you heard from the beginning. If what you heard from the beginning abides in you, you also will abide in the Son and in the Father.

—1 John 2:22–24

Beloved, do not believe every spirit, but test the spirits, whether they are of God; because many false prophets have gone out into the world. By this you know the Spirit of God: Every spirit that confesses that Jesus Christ has come in the flesh is of God, and every spirit that does not confess that Jesus Christ has come in the flesh is not of God. And this is the spirit of the Antichrist, which you have heard was coming, and is now already in the world.

—1 John 4:1–3

By this we know that we abide in Him, and He in us, because He has given us of His Spirit. And we have seen and testify that the Father has sent the Son as Savior of the world. Whoever confesses that Jesus is the Son of God, God abides in him, and he in God.

—1 John 4:13–15

The purpose of John's first epistle is to aid believers in coming to a biblical assurance regarding their relationship with God through Christ and their eternal state. However, as we read through the letter we also discover that false teachers had entered the congregation and were creating doubt with regard to some of the most foundational truths of

Christianity. From the texts at the opening of this chapter, we can discern a few of these errors that the false teachers were propagating:

They denied that Jesus was the Christ.
They denied that Jesus Christ had come in the flesh.
They denied that Jesus was the Son of God.

From these three denials and other evidences in this letter, it appears that these false teachers were Gnostics, or at least their teachings represented the early stages of the religion that eventually became known as Gnosticism. These titles are derived from the Greek word *gnosis*, which means "knowledge." Although knowledge is an essential aspect of Christianity, the Gnostics claimed a special knowledge that originated outside of the Scriptures and was contrary to them. Their central teaching was that spirit was good and matter was evil. From this unbiblical dualism resulted several deadly errors that made Gnosticism one of the most dangerous heresies to confront the early church.[1] First, according to the Gnostics, man's body was material and therefore evil. In contrast, God was pure spirit and therefore good. Second, to be saved, a person had to escape from the body, not by faith in Christ but by a special revelation to which only the Gnostics were privy. Third, since the body was evil, some Gnostics claimed that it should be deprived through an ascetic lifestyle. However, others held that the body was of no consequence, and therefore one could indulge without restraint in any form of immorality.

John addresses many of these heresies throughout this first epistle, as does the apostle Paul in the book of Colossians. Although it is beyond our study to consider each in detail, two heresies are of special interest to our study. Each pertains to the exact nature of the person of Jesus Christ and what we must believe about Him in order to be saved.

The first Gnostic heresy is called Docetism. The name is derived from the Greek verb *dokéo*, which means "to seem," or "to appear." Since the Gnostics believed that the material body was inherently evil, it was necessary for them to deny the incarnation and teach that the divine Christ only "seemed" or "appeared" to have a body. The second heresy is

---

1. Dualism is the division of something conceptually into two opposed or contrasted aspects, or the state of being so divided. In philosophy, dualism refers to any system of thought that regards reality in terms of two independent principles—material and immaterial or matter and spirit.

similar. It is called Cerinthianism, after its most prominent spokesman, Cerinthus. He taught that the spirit of the divine Christ descended from heaven upon the man Jesus of Nazareth at the moment of his baptism and that the Christ abandoned Jesus and ascended into heaven before he died on Calvary. In summary, the Gnostic teaching denied the incarnation of the eternal Son of God and held that the man Jesus and the divine Christ were two separate beings. Thus, they denied that Jesus was the Christ and the Son of God.

The contemporary application of all that we have learned is simply this: a person is not a Christian unless he believes and confesses that Jesus of Nazareth is the eternal Son of God; that He laid aside His heavenly glory and was conceived by the Holy Spirit in a virgin's womb; that He was born in Bethlehem as God incarnate; that He was fully God and fully man; that He was the Christ foretold by the Law and the Prophets; and that He is the Savior of the world. Any deviation from these essential truths regarding the person of Jesus Christ disqualifies any so-called Christian confession regardless of its apparent sincerity and zeal for good works.

WHAT THINK YOU OF CHRIST?

John Newton penned the hymn "What Think You of Christ?" while he pastored in Olney, England, and it has particular application to these passages in 1 John 4:

> What think you of Christ is the test,
> To try both your state and your scheme;
> You cannot be right in the rest
> Until you think rightly of Him.
> As Jesus appears in your view,
> As He is beloved or not,
> So God is disposed to you,
> And mercy or wrath is your lot.
>
> Some take Him a creature to be,
> A man or an angel at most,
> But these have not feelings like me,
> Nor know themselves wretched and lost.
> So guilty, so helpless am I,
> I dare not confide in His blood,

Nor on His protection rely
Unless I am sure He is God.[2]

We will begin with a declaration that might be considered somewhat radical or even avant-garde to many in the evangelical community— *Christianity is about the person and work of Jesus Christ.* If the evangelical church was in better health or at least more focused on the Scriptures, this statement would be unwarranted. However, it is necessary, and it should be the constant theme of every churchman who desires reformation and revival. It must be our dearest and most oft-repeated maxim: Christianity in its truest and most primitive form is a religion that is founded and focused upon Christ: "For no other foundation can anyone lay than that which is laid, which is Jesus Christ" (1 Cor. 3:11).

Today the church needs to heed John Newton's lyrics; they are necessary for our current malady. Newton was right in every way regarding the supremacy of Christ. He is the supreme revelation of God and the champion of His greatest work. Thus, our opinion of Christ is the test by which the validity of our Christian profession is proved. Nothing of all our confessions, identifications, or deeds has any meaning or use unless we first have a correct opinion of Christ. In fact, God's entire disposition toward us is determined by our disposition toward His Son.

In the Scriptures, two aspects of Christ's person are put forth with such clarity that to deny them is to deny the Scriptures and become antichrist. These two characteristics are more different than day and night; they are polar opposites with no link between them except in the person of Christ. In Him alone, deity and humanity dwell together and intertwine without confusing the two natures or diminishing either.

The Redeemer had to be man, for it was man who transgressed the law and who must die. If every clean animal that had ever been born were to have been sacrificed in its pristine state, the combined blood of them all could not have prevailed against our stain: "For it is not possible that the blood of bulls and goats could take away sins" (Heb. 10:4). Had all the angels in heaven been marshaled to give their lives freely and fully for our redemption, it would have been of no greater help, for

---

2. Todd Murray, "What Think You of Christ?," on *Beyond Amazing: The Forgotten Hymns of John Newton*, compact disc. Todd Murray has reproduced select songs from the *Olney Hymnal*, which John Newton published in 1779.

the Redeemer had to come from our stock—flesh of our flesh and bone of bone. For Christ to be our Kinsman Redeemer, He had to be our kin.[3]

Therefore, our Redeemer was fully man, but not just man. It was necessary that He also be God in every sense of the term, from every angle or point of view, and in every category without exception. We can't give every reason for this necessity, but we can consider at least three of them. First, God alone is Savior, and He shares this title with no one. God claimed redemption to be the prerogative of deity when He declared through the prophet Isaiah, "I, even I, am the LORD, and besides Me there is no savior" (Isa. 43:11). Therefore, if Christ is our Redeemer, then He must be God. If He is not God, then He is not our Redeemer, and we are still lost in our sin and are of all men most to be pitied.[4]

Second, the magnitude of the work of redemption demanded deity. Creation out of nothing[5] required a genius and power far beyond our wildest imagination, and yet it was a small thing in comparison to our redemption. It required no strain or sacrifice on the part of God to create a world out of nothing. He expended no energy that demanded recuperation, and He felt no weakness when the work was complete. What He did, He did effortlessly. He rested on the seventh day, not to replenish something lost but to relish something gained—a good and beautiful new world brought out of nothing by a mere word. However, on the cross, Deity made the greatest sacrifice, and on that tree the Creator wrapped in flesh was both expended and spent. Deity was strained, and heaven was bankrupted to pay the price. Who but God could render such a work? Who but God could pay such a ransom? Our lawbreaking required a payment beyond the combined worth of an infinite number of worlds and all they might contain. Even the death of a legion of seraphim would not have improved our lot before the bar of divine justice. The sacrifice of a person of infinite value was required to redeem us from the curse and penalty of the law. If Christ had not been fully divine, He could not have paid such a price.

Third, our total depravity required that our Redeemer be deity. It proves that we need more than a human remedy or moral guide. We need

---

3. Leviticus 25:25; Ruth 2:1, 20.

4. 1 Corinthians 15:19.

5. The Scriptures teach that God created the world out of nothing (Heb. 11:3). He did not borrow matter from some other source to form the world. Rather, He spoke matter into existence.

God! Anyone who thinks he can be saved by any person less than God has no understanding of the depths of his own depravity and lawbreaking. He is blind to the dark reality of his sin and deaf to what remains of his conscience. He must be awakened to a malignity that requires a cure beyond all but God, for whom nothing is impossible.[6]

If we would take an honest appraisal of ourselves—our inward thoughts, hidden deeds, and words spoken in secret—then we would be properly humbled and ashamed. If we would only realize that our crimes would not allow our acquittal even before a benign human magistrate or a jury of closest friends, then we would know gospel fear. If we would only stop either ignoring or revising history long enough to consider the sins of our fathers then we would discover that we propagate their sins in modified and more sophisticated forms. If we would only cease from our obnoxious self-flattery and the continuous celebration of each other's almost never realized potential then we would see that our optimism is built upon a foundation as ethereal as a spider's web. If we would only acknowledge that death and the grave are coming for us all then we would know that we need more than moral teaching from a human sage to save us and set our world aright. We need the God against whom we have sinned to pay the price for our redemption. The God who made us must recreate us.

Oh, that the whole world would view itself through the lens of Scripture and adopt the anthropology of Newton and the apostle Paul, who saw themselves as moral wretches apart from the saving and transforming grace of God![7] Then people would see that unless Christ is God in the fullest sense of the term, He does not possess sufficient merit or power to redeem them.

WHO DO YOU SAY THAT HE IS?

At a turning point in Jesus' ministry, He asked His disciples, "Who do men say that I am?" In response to this question, the apostle Peter declared, "You are the Christ, the Son of the living God" (Matt. 16:13–17).

---

6. Jeremiah 32:27; Luke 1:37.

7. Newton gave his opinion of himself in the famous words, "Amazing grace! How sweet the sound that saved a wretch like me!" The apostle Paul painted his self-portrait in Romans 7:24: "O wretched man that I am! Who will deliver me from this body of death?" (Romans 7:24).

From this, we understand that although it is essential that we correctly understand and believe in what Jesus did, we must also correctly understand and believe in who He was and is. This truth, combined with what we have gleaned from 1 John 4, instructs us that if we believe that the man Jesus is anything less than the Christ and God incarnate, we are not Christian.

The true church is filled with all sorts of believers: mature and immature, scholars and tradesmen, teachers and students. Admittedly, some are more educated than others in the great truths of Christ's person and more accomplished at expounding them. Nevertheless, even the most untrained among God's people will hold to the truth that Jesus is *the* unique person of history, the eternal Son of God who became flesh and dwelt among us[8] because one of the promises of the new covenant and a result of the new birth is that all of God's people, from the least to the greatest, will be taught of God and will know Him.[9]

The distinguishing mark of every religion outside of Christianity and every cult that claims identification with Christianity denies something about Christ's person. However, God will see to it that such heresies will not prevail among His people. Even those believers who are found in some of the most remote areas of the world have a primitive but sure understanding that Christ is both God and man. Although they may not be able to explain how two natures can exist within one person without confusing both or diminishing either, they know Jesus to be both divine and human in the fullest sense of the terms, and they refuse fellowship with those who teach otherwise.

To bring this study to a close, we must turn our attention to ourselves and make an appropriate application: What do you think of Christ, and what do you say about Him? You can have assurance of salvation only to the degree that you acknowledge His deity and humanity and hold Him in the highest regard.

We cannot think too highly of Christ or praise Him beyond what we ought. However, many today who profess Christ and identify themselves as Christians are betrayed by their low thoughts of Him. Although they may properly confess both His deity and humanity, they are all too nonchalant in their attitude toward Him and flippant about Him in their

---

8. John 1:14; Hebrews 2:14.
9. John 6:45; Jeremiah 31:34.

speech. We must be careful if Christ has become common to us. We must be concerned for our soul if He inspires no awe or reverence.

There is little evidence that a person has been taught of God if he thinks about Christ in a manner contrary to Scripture. There is little evidence that a person has been regenerated by the Holy Spirit if the great truths about Christ do not inspire him to greater love, reverence, and practical devotion. It is a trustworthy statement, deserving full acceptance, that regeneration will always lead to right thinking about Christ and corresponding affections for Him.

CHAPTER ELEVEN

Purifying Self

Behold what manner of love the Father has bestowed on us, that we should be called children of God! Therefore the world does not know us, because it did not know Him. Beloved, now we are children of God; and it has not yet been revealed what we shall be, but we know that when He is revealed, we shall be like Him, for we shall see Him as He is. And everyone who has this hope in Him purifies himself, just as He is pure.
—1 John 3:1–3

In 1 John 3:1–3, John turns his attention to the great importance of moral purity in the Christian life. His carefully crafted words demonstrate that purity is not a mere option for the Christian, but one of the great evidences of conversion. We know that we have truly fixed our hope on Christ for salvation if our lives are marked by striving after personal holiness—if we are seeking to purify ourselves as He is pure.

As we consider this text, we should keep in mind that the false teachers who had infiltrated the church believed the physical body was evil and of little consequence in the matter of religion. Therefore, they gave themselves to their fleshly desires and taught others to do the same without reservation. Their lives were marked by a love for the world, "the lust of the flesh, the lust of the eyes, and the pride of life" (1 John 2:15–16). They turned their supposed freedom into an opportunity for the flesh and seemed to disdain those who pursued a biblical sanctification,[1] considering them to be uninitiated, uninstructed, and bound in legalism.

It is no exaggeration to say that we find a parallel to this disdain for holiness in contemporary evangelicalism. Although we are not overrun by the Gnostics, against whom John wrote this epistle, we are inundated

---

1. Galatians 5:13; Hebrews 12:14.

with worldliness, and many of us appear to have developed distaste for any teaching that would restrict our carnality and promote moral purity. In the name of grace, some people ignore, reinterpret, or outright deny biblical mandates regarding holiness. Those who strive after a greater holiness or a more refined personal purity are often labeled as fanatical, legalistic, super-spiritual, or holier-than-thou.

In countering this heretical teaching, the apostle John points to holiness as a distinguishing characteristic of Jesus Christ and the true Christian. According to John, everyone who has truly fixed his hope on Christ "purifies himself, just as He is pure" (1 John 3:3). Although a person's personal purity is never complete on this side of glory, and although it is not a means of obtaining a right standing before God, it is nonetheless great evidence that a person has come to know God through the regenerating work of the Holy Spirit and personal faith in Christ. Those who have been saved by grace through faith have become the workmanship of God. This workmanship is manifest in a believer's conformity to God's character, of which the most distinguishing mark is holiness. As "it is written, 'Be holy, for I am holy'" (1 Peter 1:16).

Although we must avoid legalism in the church, we must regain a biblical view of moral purity. Many unbelievers have rejected the message of the gospel or have never even given it a hearing because of the blighted testimony of those who claim to have embraced it. Furthermore, the church suffers from a number of maladies that spring forth from a lack of holiness, such as estrangement from God, an absence of His manifest presence, and a dearth of spiritual life and power. Finally, and most tragically, numerous individuals who are confident of eternal life, even though they have no biblical basis for such assurance, fill our pews. The pursuit of holiness and the thought of disciplining themselves for the purpose of godliness are foreign to them.[2] They have never been warned or instructed in the truth that one of the great marks of conversion is a yearning for personal purity that leads to a genuine and repetitive striving after it. They are uninstructed and therefore unaware of the truth that without holiness, no one will see the Lord.[3]

---

2. 1 Timothy 4:7; 6:11; 2 Timothy 2:22.
3. Hebrews 12:14.

THE CHRISTIAN VIEW OF PURITY

In this text, the words "pure" and "purifies" are derived from the same Greek root. The adjective "pure" is translated from the Greek word *hagnos*, which denotes that a person or thing is pure, holy, chaste, or innocent. The verb "purify" is translated from the Greek word *hagnízo*, which means to make pure, purify, or cleanse. Although the New Testament uses the word with reference to ceremonial cleansing,[4] it also denotes a personal internal cleansing. In James's letter to the scattered believers in the early church, he calls upon sinners to cleanse their hands and purify their hearts that they might draw near to God.[5] In his first epistle, the apostle Peter describes Christians as those who have purified their souls in obedience to the truth.[6] In the text before us, the apostle John describes the genuine believer as one who purifies himself, just as Christ is pure.

Note that the Greek verb translated "purifies" is in the present tense, indicating a continuous action. Thus, the entire phrase may be properly translated, "And everyone who has this hope fixed on Him is purifying himself, just as He is pure." From this, we learn that the believer's advancement in personal purity is not necessarily or even primarily the result of some momentary experience, but a process that continues from the moment of conversion until final glorification in heaven. This is why theologians and expositors will often refer to the believer's growth in purity as *progressive sanctification*. It is true that God may use events in our lives, personal experiences in prayer, or the unusual work of revival to advance us for a time at a more rapid pace. However, the believer's growth in holiness is overwhelmingly the result of God's progressive work of providence and the believer's day-to-day striving for greater purity through the Word of God, prayer, and separation.

Also note that the verb "purifies" is followed by the reflexive pronoun "himself," indicating that the subject is acting upon himself rather than being acted upon. In other words, the one being purified is the one who is doing the work of purification. This is not a negation of God's participation in our sanctification, but proof that our sanctification is synergistic, which means that there is an interaction or cooperation between two or more working agents to produce a combined effect. Although our

4. John 11:55; Acts 21:24, 26.
5. James 4:8.
6. 1 Peter 1:22.

regeneration is monergistic, or the work of God alone, our sanctification is synergistic, the result of God's work and the believer's cooperation. This truth is beautifully set forth in Paul's encouragement and exhortation to the church in Philippi: "Therefore, my beloved, as you have always obeyed, not as in my presence only, but now much more in my absence, *work out your own salvation* with fear and trembling; for it is God *who works in you* both to will and to do for *His* good pleasure" (Phil. 1:6, emphasis added).

Purification, or sanctification, is a synergistic work in which both God and the believer are actively participating to achieve the desired goal: the believer's conformity to the image of Christ. God has predestined and is leading the way in this work through His indwelling Spirit and multiform acts of providence. His divine initiative and participation ensure the believer's advancement in holiness and is the basis for Paul's bold confidence that He who began a good work in the believer will perfect it until the day of Christ Jesus. At the same time, the Scriptures also recognize that the believer's sanctification is also dependent upon his own personal participation. While God is working to cleanse the believer of all his filthiness and idolatry, the believer is called upon to purify himself as Christ is pure and to cleanse himself from all defilement of flesh and spirit, perfecting holiness in the fear of God.[7]

Recognizing the human element in our sanctification, the contemporary reader may ask, "Is this not proof that some genuine believers may go unsanctified or that some may remain carnal with little progress in holiness?" Again, this question betrays an ignorance of the nature of salvation. First, the believer's desire for holiness is the result of the new birth. He has become a child of God, a new creature with new affections set on righteousness. Although there will be great struggles against the flesh, the world, and the adversary, these new affections for God will lead every believer to a greater disdain for the world and a greater attraction to holiness. Second, we must never forget that God is at work in every believer, "both to will and to do for His good pleasure" (Phil. 2:12–13). He both conforms the believer's will to His own and strengthens the believer to do that will. He provides both the inclination and the power; He leads and enlivens. Finally, we must never forget that God has promised to be ever vigilant over His children. He will not abandon them to ungodliness

---

7. Ezekiel 36:25; 2 Corinthians 7:1.

or be slack in loving, purposeful discipline. For this reason, the author of Hebrews writes:

> "For whom the LORD loves He chastens, and scourges every son whom He receives."
>
> If you endure chastening, God deals with you as with sons; for what son is there whom a father does not chasten? But if you are without chastening, of which all have become partakers, then you are illegitimate and not sons. Furthermore, we have had human fathers who corrected us, and we paid them respect. Shall we not much more readily be in subjection to the Father of spirits and live? For they indeed for a few days chastened us as seemed best to them, but He for our profit, that we may be partakers of His holiness. (12:6–10)

Progressive sanctification is a characteristic to be found in the life of everyone who has been truly converted. We will discuss this at length in the conclusion of this chapter, but the reader should even now keep in mind that the genuine Christian will not only be marked by submission to God's work of sanctification in his life but he will also actively participate in this work through the means provided him in the Scriptures.

THE CHRISTIAN MEANS OF PURITY

God's lead and participation in the believer's sanctification is not grounds for slackness or idleness, but a call and encouragement to duty. Since God is at work in us, we have the assurance that our striving will not be in vain. We have no excuse for passivity, but every cause for a zealous pursuit of purity. We are to be passionate, serious, and focused in our striving after holiness. As the apostle Paul encouraged Timothy, we must discipline and strenuously exercise ourselves for the purpose of godliness.[8]

According to the Scriptures, God has provided the believer with several means by which he may purify himself. Although it is beyond the boundaries of this study to consider them at length, the mention of four of the most prominent is necessary. First, we may properly say that purity begins with separation from sin. Cleansing is an impossibility if we have not first cut ourselves away from that which contaminates. It does little good to scrub ourselves with soap unless we first come out from under

---

8. 1 Timothy 4:7.

the shower of filth. It is of little use to put on clean clothes while standing in a cesspool or wallowing in the mire. It is for this reason that the apostle Paul exhorted the believers in Corinth:

> "Come out from among them
> And be separate, says the Lord.
> Do not touch what is unclean,
> And I will receive you." (2 Cor. 6:17)

Second, God has given the Scriptures as a foundational discipline for a godly life. According to the psalmist, a young man can keep his way pure only by heeding God's Word, and he is to treasure that Word in his heart that he might not sin against Him.[9] The apostle Paul taught that the believer must renew his mind if he is to escape the godless imprint of this world and be transformed in conformity to the good, acceptable, and perfect will of God.[10] The apostle Peter, in the context of his exhortation regarding holiness, encouraged believers to long for the pure milk of the Word, so that by it they might grow in respect to salvation.[11]

Third, a powerful and yet greatly neglected means of purification is the discipline of prayer. The Lord commanded us to pray that we might not be led into temptation, but be delivered from evil.[12] In the garden of Gethsemane, the night He was betrayed, Jesus gave a similar command to His inner circle: "Pray that you may not enter into temptation" (Luke 22:40). In his letter to the church at Ephesus, the apostle Paul, after addressing the matter of spiritual warfare, exhorted the believers to pray at all times with all kinds of prayer and to be on the alert with all perseverance and petition for all the saints.[13]

Fourth, the Scriptures teach us that the believer may grow in purity and holiness to the degree that he catches greater and greater glimpses of Christ and His gospel. Although this fourth means is inseparable from the study of Scripture and prayer, it needs to be treated separately so that we understand that we are not changed merely by the application of propositional truth or the mimicking of biblical principles, but we are changed by ever-increasing revelations of Christ through the Word.

---

9. Psalm 119:9, 11.
10. Romans 12:2.
11. 1 Peter 2:2.
12. Matthew 6:13.
13. Ephesians 6:18.

Nothing is more purifying than to be acquainted with a person who is truly godly or Christlike. The more time we pass in such a person's presence and the more intimate our fellowship, the greater the effect wrought on our life. If this maxim holds true for fellowship with other people, then how much greater is the effect when we spend time with Christ? His teaching is life and spirit,[14] His example is impeccable, and the glory of His person is transforming. For this reason, the apostle Paul writes: "But we all, with unveiled face, beholding as in a mirror the glory of the Lord, are being transformed into the same image from glory to glory, just as by the Spirit of the Lord" (2 Cor. 3:18).

Although during our earthly pilgrimage we may see Christ only dimly at best, the smallest glimpse is capable of working the greatest transformation, even in the least of all the saints.[15] The more we see, experience, and commune with Christ in the Scriptures and prayer, the more we will be transformed by His glory and take on His image—an image that is free from even the most miniscule particle of moral contamination. As the writer of Hebrews assures us, He is holy, innocent, undefiled, separated from sinners, and exalted above the heavens.[16]

Although the use of these spiritual disciplines are not explicitly recorded in Scripture as evidence of conversion, they may serve as something of a litmus test to the true spirituality of the person who professes faith in Christ. The most mature and devoted believers are sometimes painfully neglectful of the spiritual disciplines that promote moral purity and conformity to Christ. However, we would be hard pressed to prove the conversion of a person whose life was void of the use of such means—who cared so little for his own advancement in purity that he remained apathetic in heart and passive in action.

PURITY AS EVIDENCE OF CONVERSION

The ending of this text is powerful and filled with truth. We must not be deceived by its brevity for it contains a maxim that would heal many of the maladies that face contemporary evangelicalism: "And everyone who has this hope in Him purifies himself, just as He is pure" (1 John 3:3).

---

14. John 6:63.
15. Ephesians 3:8.
16. Hebrews 7:26.

The first thing we should notice is John's reference to "everyone," so as to include all who truly believe in the Lord Jesus Christ unto salvation. John's meaning is clear: Everyone who is truly Christian will be marked by a personal and practical striving for holiness. The pursuit of purity is not a thing confined to a handful of super-spiritual saints, but is a characteristic of all who have truly fixed their hope in Christ. An erroneous three-tiered ranking of individuals within the evangelical community has existed for far too long: the unbeliever, the carnal Christian, and the spiritual Christian. Such a ranking has allowed the church to be filled with men, women, and youth who have a form of godliness, but deny its power; who profess God, but deny Him with their deeds; and who emphatically confess Christ's lordship, but do not do the will of the Father.[7] While it is true that Christians still struggle with sin, and even the strongest of saints must fight against the ever-present threat of apathy, no grounds exist for what is now popularly called the carnal Christian. There is no such thing as a Christian who lives in a continuous or lifelong state of carnality; there is no such thing as a Christian in whom God is not working effectually.

The Scriptures testify that God is at work in the life of every believer without exception both to will and to work for His good pleasure.[18] We are His workmanship, created in Christ Jesus for good works.[19] He is the God who works all things after the counsel of His will and who does whatever He pleases in the heavens, the earth, the seas, and in all the deeps.[20] Is it possible that the God who rules creation cannot establish His purpose or accomplish His good pleasure in His children?[21] The Scriptures teach that the names of God's children are inscribed upon the palms of His hands.[22] Have they somehow escaped His notice or run beyond His paternal care? Would the God who commands men to raise up their children in the fear and admonition of the Lord leave His own in a neglected state?[23] Would He require elders to manage their own household well while His house is in disarray?[24] We know the answer from

---

17. Matthew 7:21; 2 Timothy 3:5; Titus 1:16.
18. Philippians 2:13.
19. Ephesians 2:10.
20. Psalms 115:3; 135:6; Ephesians 1:11.
21. Isaiah 46:9–10.
22. Isaiah 49:15–16.
23. Ephesians 6:4.
24. 1 Timothy 3:4–5.

having considered Hebrews 12:6–8: God deals with His people as sons and chastens those He loves.

God is relentless in His care and discipline of His children. That so many people within the evangelical community run wild is not a denial of God's promises but proof of their illegitimacy. God has not neglected them. The terrifying fact is that they are simply not His children. If they were, Hebrews tells us, He would chasten them, and they would endure.

We find a great truth in these passages from 1 John and Hebrews: our sanctification is both the work of the believer and the God who has called him. The believer who has truly fixed his hope upon Christ for salvation purifies himself as He is pure, and the One who has adopted him as a son takes the greatest care to conform him to His will. He will not relent, even though the greatest scourging[25] of discipline may be required.

Again, the believer will continue to struggle with sin, the flesh, and the world. He will fail. Furthermore, there will be apparent lulls in God's sanctifying work and times when it seems that little is being accomplished in the believer's life. Often the greatest pruning and preparation is being accomplished when there is the greatest absence of visible fruit. What this means is that those who profess to hope in Christ for salvation and future glorification at His coming will evidence such a hope by the pursuit of purity, a striving after holiness, and a genuine and observable desire for conformity to the image of Christ. To the degree that these things are evident and growing, we may increase in assurance that we have truly come to know Him. To the degree that they are absent in our lives, we should be concerned.

The Scriptures teach with the greatest clarity that without sanctification no one will see the Lord.[26] This does not mean that we must be striving to be pure enough to enter the kingdom, for that would be a salvation of works and not of grace: "If it is of works, it is no longer grace" (Rom. 6:11). Personal holiness does not achieve for us a right standing before God or eternal salvation, but it is the evidence that we have received such by grace through faith. This truth held a prominent place in gospel preaching until the present age, but now it is all but unknown to many contemporary Christians. It is often not properly expounded or

---

25. It is difficult to overemphasize the severity of the verb "scourges" in Hebrews 12:6. It is translated from the Greek verb *mastigóo*, meaning "to beat with a whip."

26. Hebrews 12:14.

pressed upon the consciences of those who profess faith in Christ. Thus, some true believers are not as assured as they ought to be, and some false converts are confident although they have no reason to be.

Christians do not merely wait to be made pure at the coming of Christ, but they seek to purify themselves through the faithful employment of separation, the study of God's Word, and prayer. The true believer has an inner yearning to be like His Savior that manifests itself in seeking first God's kingdom and righteousness and in disciplining himself for the purpose of godliness.[27] If these things are foreign to us, we should exercise all diligence in examining ourselves to see if we are in the faith and in making our calling and election sure.[28]

ENCOURAGEMENT FOR THE CHRISTIAN

We have not been called to embark alone upon a journey with an uncertain end. We have been promised that God will work in us, and He who began a good work will perfect it. Although John tells us that we do not know what we will be like when the work of God is complete in us, we do know that we will be like Him.[29] We do not lack knowledge about what we will be like because the outcome is uncertain but because of the greatness of the outcome. The believer's end is so illustrious that we may say that no eye has seen and no ear has heard, nor has all that God has prepared for those who love Him entered into the heart of the most discerning of men.[30] Though the best of Christians must now still mourn over sin and failure and weakness and doubt, future grace awaits even the most frail and pitiful among us. Though it delay, it will come with Christ and His great appearance to the world. Then, not only will Christ be vindicated and glorified but also His now belittled and berated people will be vindicated, transformed, and glorified with Him. It will be the final and unequivocal confirmation of our sonship. This great hope founded upon divine decree and confirmed by the blood of Calvary fills the believer with "joy inexpressible and full of glory" and drives him to purity, desiring to "be holy, for [He is] holy" (1 Peter 1:7–8, 16).

---

27. Matthew 6:33; 1 Timothy 4:7.
28. 2 Corinthians 13:5; 2 Peter 1:10.
29. 1 John 3:2.
30. 1 Corinthians 2:9.

CHAPTER TWELVE

Practicing Righteousness

And now, little children, abide in Him, that when He appears, we may have confidence and not be ashamed before Him at His coming. If you know that He is righteous, you know that everyone who practices righteousness is born of Him.

—1 John 2:28–29

Whoever commits sin also commits lawlessness, and sin is lawlessness. And you know that He was manifested to take away our sins, and in Him there is no sin. Whoever abides in Him does not sin. Whoever sins has neither seen Him nor known Him.

Little children, let no one deceive you. He who practices righteousness is righteous, just as He is righteous. He who sins is of the devil, for the devil has sinned from the beginning. For this purpose the Son of God was manifested, that He might destroy the works of the devil. Whoever has been born of God does not sin, for His seed remains in him; and he cannot sin, because he has been born of God.

In this the children of God and the children of the devil are manifest: Whoever does not practice righteousness is not of God, nor is he who does not love his brother.

—1 John 3:4–10

In the preceding chapter, we learned that the mark of a true believer is a growing conformity to Christ in regard to holiness. John wrote, "And everyone who has this hope in Him purifies himself, just as He is pure" (1 John 3:3). In the two passages before us, we learn that the mark of a true believer will be conformity to Christ in regard to the practice of righteousness. The similarities between the two tests are apparent:

The believer purifies himself as Christ is pure.[1]
The believer practices righteousness as Christ is righteous.[2]

There is a sense in which these two characteristics of a genuine Christian are mirror images. Although distinctions can and should be drawn between holiness and righteousness, neither exists without the other in the same person. A person who is marked by one will be equally marked by the other. To the degree we purify ourselves, we will also grow in righteousness.

In another sense the term *righteousness* adds clarity to what it means to be pure or holy. It proves to us that true holiness or moral purity is not validated by a feeling or some ecstatic spiritual state but by the practice of righteousness. "Righteousness" is translated from the Greek word *dikaiosúne* and denotes the state of something or someone who is right before God or approved of God. When the term is used with regard to a believer's positional righteousness, it refers to his legal, or forensic, right standing before God through faith in the person and work of Christ. When the term is used with regard to the believer's personal righteousness, it refers to his conformity to the nature and will of God as revealed in the entirety of Scripture and foremost in the person of Jesus Christ. It is important to note that even though there is no contradiction between Christ and the law, Christ is the greater revelation of all things concerning God and His will. We would do well to recognize that John ranks Christ as the ultimate standard for both purity and righteousness.[3] This is a powerful and transforming truth that allows the believer's morality and ethic to be truly christocentric.

The word "practice" comes from the Greek verb *poiéo*, which means to make, do, cause, act, accomplish, perform, practice, keep, and work. The reason for this long list of terms is to demonstrate that the word *poiéo* denotes activity and that the righteousness of which John writes is active, practical, and observable. It is not the righteousness of those who are merely hearers of the word, but of those who actually do it: "But be doers of the word, and not hearers only, deceiving yourselves" (James 1:22). Neither is it the righteousness of mere mystics or those who exceed in knowledge but fail in action; rather, it is the righteousness of simple obedience, observable conformity to the law of God, and the imitation of Christ.

---

1. 1 John 3:3.
2. 1 John 2:29.
3. 1 John 3:3, 7.

It is important to note that the verb *poiéo* is in present tense, denoting a continuous action, style of life, or settled practice. Although the Christian life will include great struggles with sin and recurring failures, it will be marked by striving after conformity to God's will, growth in submission to it, and greater personal brokenness when it is violated.

A MUCH-NEEDED WARNING

We should not be surprised that practical and discernible obedience is a test of conversion. We have already encountered this truth twice. In the first test in 1 John 1:5–7, we learned that the genuine Christian walks in the light—his style of life conforms to God's revelation of His person and will. In the third test in 1 John 2:3–5, we discovered that those who are genuinely converted keep God's commands. Now, in 1 John 2:29, we are told that everyone who practices righteousness, conforming his life and deeds to the standard of God's law, is truly born of Him. These texts stand with many others throughout the New Testament that demonstrate that salvation by grace through faith is evidenced by works;[4] that justification is proven by sanctification;[5] that positional righteousness is validated by personal righteousness;[6] that a person's confession of Christ as Lord is tested by practical obedience;[7] and that if anyone is in Christ, he is a new creature for whom old things have passed and new things have come.[8]

Although these statements are thoroughly biblical and held by prominent men and confessions of church history, they are nearly forgotten among contemporary evangelicals. To even suggest that salvation might have practical proofs or that those who are grossly given over to the world are not truly converted causes great offense and results in a harsh reproach from the majority of the evangelical community. It is for this reason that we desperately need to pay attention to John's warning:

> Little children, let no one deceive you. He who practices righteousness is righteous, just as He is righteous. (3:7)

---

4. James 2:14–26.
5. Philippians 1:6; 2:12–13; Hebrews 12:14.
6. Titus 1:16.
7. Matthew 7:21.
8. 2 Corinthians 5:17.

In this the children of God and the children of the devil are manifest: Whoever does not practice righteousness is not of God, nor is he who does not love his brother. (3:10)

We should note that we are not reading the words of a legalistic man filled with bitterness and criticism. The elder John addresses his readers as children for a twofold purpose: first, to communicate his paternal love for them as an apostle and shepherd of Christ's flock; and second, to remind them that, like little children, they are prone to deception and to being "tossed to and fro and carried about with every wind of doctrine" (Eph. 4:14). This is especially true with regard to Christian ethics or morality.

The Christian church walks a narrow road with deadly pitfalls on both sides. To one side is legalism: a religion of rules and rewards, the exaltation of man's performance, and consequently the diminishing of the person and work of Christ. Man triumphs, and God becomes a debtor bound to reward him for his piety and noble achievements. It makes for Pharisees who love rules rather than God and who consider grace to be the need of lesser folk.[9] Such a religion points out specks and ignores beams, strains gnats, and swallows camels.[10] It is constantly measuring, comparing, and competing.[11] It is all about rankings, pecking orders, and submission.[12] It usually ends in a feeding frenzy of biting, devouring, and consuming.[13]

On the other side of Christianity's perilously narrow path is the pitfall of antinomianism,[14] or lawlessness. Though as deadly as legalism, it is more prominent in contemporary Christianity and therefore deserves our attention in greater detail. Antinomianism is a poisonous doctrine that turns the grace of God into licentiousness[15] and boasts a terrible motto—"Shall we continue in sin that grace may abound?" (Rom. 6:1; cf. 3:8). In its most extreme form, it is easily recognized and rejected.

---

9. Luke 18:11.

10. Matthew 7:3–5; 23:24.

11. Matthew 7:1–2; 2 Corinthians 10:12.

12. Matthew 23:5–7; Mark 12:38–39; Luke 11:43; 20:45.

13. Galatians 5:15.

14. Antinomianism is the doctrine that grace frees the Christian from the moral restraints of the law, resulting in the uncensored practice of immorality.

15. Jude v. 4. "Licentiousness" is translated from the Greek word *asélgeia* and denotes unbridled lust, excess, wantonness, sensuality, shamelessness, insolence.

However when it camouflages itself in the cloak of open-mindedness, compassion, and Christian charity, it becomes deceptive and deadly.

We must recognize that we live in an age of relativism in which moral absolutes are denied. This malady has entered the church, and the results have been devastating. It has torn down the righteous standard of God's law, denied that there is a specifically Christian way of living, and made it impossible to define the narrow way. Thus, many of us view as suspect any preaching that would lay upon us a moral absolute. The moment that any law or truth is pressed upon our conscience, we decry the preacher as a legalist and his teaching as bondage. Since we have become convinced that truth regarding our behavior can no longer be known, we are left to the only other possible option: self-government, in which every person does what is right in his own eyes.[16] This has been tried many times before but always with the same devastating consequences, for where there is no vision or revelation of the law, the people are unrestrained and finally perish: "Where there is no revelation, the people cast off restraint; but happy is he who keeps the law" (Prov. 29:18).[17]

We live in an age of humanism and individualism in which man is the center and end of all things, and the lone individual demands unrestrained autonomy to express himself without the least hint of censure. Since there is no longer a divine standard to be known and obeyed, we are left with one another's opinions. Therefore, if one man censures another he can be dismissed as ignorant and arrogant, simply seeking to exalt his opinions over everyone else's. Since we no longer believe that what God has said can be specifically discerned and applied, we can now justify turning a deaf ear to the most accurate exposition of Scripture and denounce as a dangerous fanatic any one who says, "Thus saith the Lord!" We fail to realize that we are in the very clutches of the evil one whenever we speak his mantra—"Has God indeed said?" (Gen. 3:1).

Finally, we live in the midst of a twisted romanticism where piety has been redefined as an open-mindedness to everything, and tolerance is the supreme manifestation of love. Thus, any form of rebuke is considered the greatest act of immorality. Because of this, much of the terminology of Christianity has been either redefined or removed entirely. To say "I

---

16. Judges 17:6; 21:25.

17. The second phrase of this verse defines the first, making it clear that the vision is a revelation of God's law.

am wrong" is self-destructive; to say "You are wrong" is criminal. Thus, prophets are exiled and spiritual life coaches are raised up in their place; biblical teaching, reproof, correction, and training in righteousness are exchanged for motivational principles leading to self-realization;[18] iron sharpening iron becomes an exercise in mutual affirmation;[19] and church discipline is denounced as a monstrosity equal to the Salem witch trials. It seems that our love has become so refined and elevated that we can no longer stomach the primitive commands of Christ.

Thus, in the name of our self-imposed ignorance, supposed esteem for the individual, open-mindedness, and tolerance we have effectively torn down every standard and become practical antinomians, a lawless people without wisdom or principle. We live in the world and look like the world. We either ignore or bury under rhetoric every biblical marker to direct us in the narrow way. We have been told that we cannot know the truth, and, believing a lie, we have condemned ourselves to walk in darkness.

If contemporary Christianity is ever to regain its health and strength, it must put an end to the deception that has fallen upon it. We must realize that saving faith and genuine conversion are demonstrated by a gradual, practical, and observable growth in holiness and righteousness. We must return to the simple, commonsense instruction the apostle John put forth. The truth put forth in 1 John 3:7 and 10 is that a person who confesses Christ may have assurance of salvation only to the degree that he possesses a desire for righteousness, actually practices it, and is broken over his shortcomings.

The animal kingdom is segregated according to genus and species, based upon observable characteristics and behavior. Man is differentiated from lower animals by what he is and does. We would never confuse a horse for a fish or a primate for a beetle because of their observable traits. However, in the confused menagerie of contemporary Christianity, not only have we found it impossible to discern distinctions between the children of God and the children of the devil, but we have found it incomprehensible to think that there even are distinctions.

We do not possess the power ultimately to confirm or deny the conversion of another, and we must be careful even in judging ourselves. Balance is necessary, and we must strive to avoid the twin pitfalls of

---

18. 2 Timothy 3:16.
19. Proverbs 27:17.

leniency on one side and severity on the other. However, although we cannot pronounce assurance or withdraw it from anyone, we can and should warn people to examine themselves with regard to purity and the doing of righteousness.[20] If, in the light of Scripture, they find themselves to be apathetic to righteousness, a practitioner of sin without remorse or improvement, lawless, immoral, and worldly, they should be warned that these are the marks of the unconverted. They should be called to "seek the LORD while He may be found," and "call upon Him while He is near" (Isa. 55:6). If, however, in the light of Scripture, they find themselves to be seeking first the kingdom of God and His righteousness,[21] making progress in conformity to Christ, lamenting what remains unchanged,[22] and being contrite of spirit when their sins are made known to them,[23] they should be encouraged that these are the marks of the children of God.

DISCERNING FAMILY TRAITS

In the first several verses of chapter 3, the apostle John presents a lengthy contrast between the children of God and the children of the devil. Although such divisions of mankind may be disturbing to our hypersensitive culture, we should remember that it is the common practice of the Scripture, which often divides the world into mutually exclusive categories: Jew and Gentile, believer and unbeliever, the church and the world.

However offensive one might believe these classifications to be, none of them is as radical or abrasive as the two that are in this text. Can the world really be divided up into the children of God and the children of the devil? Is there no middle category for those in the unbelieving world who have not made league with Satan or committed the atrocities of Hitler? The language seems all too offensive, and yet it is the language of the New Testament. According to John—and to Christ—the world is divided between the Christian, whose spiritual parentage is from God through Christ, and the unbeliever, who is identified with the devil through Adam and his own disobedience.

In light of these biblical truths, we can begin to understand why John would end this section of his first letter (3:10) with the affirmation that

---

20. 2 Corinthians 13:5.
21. Matthew 6:33.
22. Matthew 5:4.
23. Psalm 51:17; Isaiah 66:2.

there are discernible differences between the believer and the unbeliever; that a person's confession of faith can and should be tested; that assurance of salvation is not merely based upon what a person says or feels but upon the practical evidences of a changed and changing life.[24] In this verse, John says that the differences between the believer and unbeliever are "manifest," or obvious. The word is translated from the Greek adjective *phanerós*, which means to be apparent, manifest, evident, plainly recognized, or known. Mark uses the same root and word in his record of Jesus' teachings when He declares, "For there is nothing hidden which will not be *revealed*, nor has anything been kept secret but that it should come to light" (4:22, emphasis added).

The evidence of our conversion is not a mysterious or indiscernible secret, but it is revealed through our manner of living. The differences between the believer and the unbeliever are obvious and easily recognized. John summarizes them with amazing clarity:

The unbeliever practices sins and does not practice righteousness. (3:8–10)

The believer practices righteousness and does not practice sin. (3:7–9)

According to John, the unbeliever is distinguished by two ominous realities: what he does and does not do. He practices sin and does not practice righteousness. Although these two characteristics are mentioned separately, they basically refer to the same thing—disobedience, to miss the mark of God's will or to deviate from its standard. Thus, the unbeliever is exposed by his ongoing neglect to practice the righteousness of God as it is revealed in the commandments and by his ongoing participation in the very things that God has prohibited. He is proven to be aligned with the devil in that he participates in the works of the devil that Christ came to destroy, and he practices the sins that Christ died to take away.[25]

---

24. The phrase "a changed and changing life" is important in that it demonstrates both the initial power of regeneration and the continuing work of sanctification in the believer's life. These two realities must be held in tension. In a real sense the believer has been changed through regeneration, but in another sense equally as real, the believer continues to be changed through the progressive work of sanctification, a work that continues until the believer's final glorification in heaven.

25. 1 John 3:5, 8.

As we have already explained in brief, for a person to align himself with the devil does not require that he be involved in some dark cult such as witchcraft or satanism. Neither does it require that he be a "great" sinner who openly expresses his hostility toward God and is given over to every form of immorality. In fact, many who indentify themselves with Christianity and the evangelical faith are equally guilty. Even though they claim allegiance to Christ, the entire course of their life proves their allegiance to be false. They have prayed the sinner's prayer, attend a weekly service, and exhibit a morality that is a step up from the vice of this present age. Nevertheless, they are engrossed in the pursuits and affairs of this world. They demonstrate little interest in understanding the Scriptures and are unaware of God's will. Consequently, they display a startling lack of biblical discernment and are able to freely participate in sin without the least offense to their conscience. In the words of the apostle Paul, they are "having a form of godliness but denying its power" (2 Tim. 3:5).

We must not be deceived into thinking that apathy toward godliness and neglect of God's law is a lesser crime than outright rebellion. According to 1 John 3:4, all sin is lawlessness, an act of treachery against God and a declaration of war upon His throne. Those who identify themselves with Christ but exhibit an ongoing disinterest in His Word are in as great danger as those who live in open defiance and shake a clenched fist in the face of God. This is the gist of Christ's warning to professing disciples at the end of the Sermon on the Mount: "And then I will declare to them, 'I never knew you; depart from Me, you who practice lawlessness!'" (Matt. 7:23).

In this warning, Christ employs the same word that John uses in our text: lawlessness. Like John, He is telling us that those who address Him as Lord and yet continue to live as a law unto themselves will be condemned on the day of judgment. Again, neither Christ nor John is teaching justification through the law or perseverance through works. We are saved by grace alone through faith alone and not of ourselves lest any man should boast. However, true grace never leads to antinomianism or lawlessness, but godliness, conformity to Christ, and true piety. The apostle Paul confirms this truth in his letter to Titus: "For the grace of God that brings salvation has appeared to all men, *teaching us that, denying ungodliness and worldly lusts, we should live soberly, righteously, and godly in the present age*" (2:11–12, emphasis added).

Grace does not free us from the righteousness of God so that we might present the members of our body to sin as instruments of unrighteousness.[26] It does not make void the eternal truths of the Old Testament that were written for our instruction,[27] nor does it dethrone Christ and make Him a mere figurehead without sovereign will or command.[28] The depreciation of righteousness and the promotion of lawlessness was never the intention of grace, and yet this seems to be the prevalent opinion of our day. Within the evangelical community, few seem to care for ordering their lives according to the dictates of Scripture, and any mention of a certain and specific morality defined by the Scriptures is immediately labeled as legalistic. Far too many evangelicals seem content to be ignorant of Scripture's teaching, free from its reproof, untouched by its correction, and unshaped by its training.[29] Far too many act as if no king was in Israel and as if everyone has been left to do what is right in his own eyes. Thus, the church is inundated with individuals who claim Christ as Savior and hold to the hope of eternal life, and yet they are marked by an apathy to God's revealed will, leading to a life of lawlessness. This is tragic because it leads to a false assurance culminating in final and irrevocable judgment.

Like the unbeliever, the genuine Christian is also distinguished by two realities: what he does and does not do. However, this is where the similarities between the believer and unbeliever end and the great contrast begins, for the Christian practices the righteousness that is shunned by the unbeliever and shuns the sin the unbeliever continues to practice.[30] For John, the reason for this unmistakable contrast in behavior is clear: those who have been genuinely converted cannot give themselves to the habitual practice of sin because they have been born of God and God's seed abides in them.[31]

The word "seed" is translated from the Greek word *spérma*. It may refer literally to the seed from which a plant germinates or the semen that results in the conception of human life. Here it seems best to understand the word metaphorically as the Holy Spirit's divine life operating within the believer's soul by which he is regenerated and progressively

---

26. Romans 6:12–13.
27. Romans 15:4.
28. Luke 6:46.
29. 2 Timothy 3:16.
30. 1 John 3:7, 9–10.
31. 1 John 3:9.

sanctified. John's reference to the divine seed and the new birth are intended to emphasize that conversion is a supernatural work of God and the Christian is a new creation with a new nature remade in the likeness of God in righteousness and holiness.[32] As the apostle Peter writes, the Christian has become a partaker of the divine nature and an object of divine power resulting in both life and godliness.[33]

It is because of this extraordinary work of God in the life of every believer that John is able to write with the greatest confidence that "whoever has been born of God does not sin" or is even able to do so (3:9). This does not mean that a believer is without sin, immune to temptation, free from struggles with the flesh, or beyond the possibility of moral failings. What it does mean is that the person who has been regenerated by the Spirit of God cannot live in habitual sin any more than a fish can live for long out of water. This inability is not due to the believer's strength of will but to the work of God that has been and is being accomplished in him. God has made him into a new creature who simply cannot tolerate the sin and unrighteousness in which he once delighted. He cannot practice sin without experiencing the greatest affliction of conscience and the nausea of its defilement. This, coupled with God's ongoing work of providence manifested in discipline, ensures that the believer who falls into sin will soon withdraw in repentance and seek cleansing and restoration.[34]

The New Testament leaves no room for the popular evangelical opinion that a person may be truly born again who is apathetic toward righteousness and lives a life of open sin and rebellion. Those who profess faith in Christ and live in this way should be greatly concerned for their eternal welfare. They should not be deceived but give heed to John's simple test: "He who practices righteousness is righteous," but "whoever does not practice righteousness is not of God."[35]

---

32. 2 Corinthians 5:17; Ephesians 4:24.
33. 2 Peter 1:3–4.
34. 1 John 1:8–10.
35. 1 John 3:7, 10.

CHAPTER THIRTEEN

Overcoming the World

For whatever is born of God overcomes the world. And this is the victory
that has overcome the world—our faith. Who is he who overcomes the
world, but he who believes that Jesus is the Son of God?

—1 John 5:4–5

You are of God, little children, and have overcome them, because He who
is in you is greater than he who is in the world. They are of the world.
Therefore they speak as of the world, and the world hears them. We are
of God. He who knows God hears us; he who is not of God does not hear
us. By this we know the spirit of truth and the spirit of error.

—1 John 4:4–6

In a sense, humans have only two problems: the condemnation of sin
and the power of sin,[1] both of which are resolved in the person and
work of Jesus Christ. Through faith in Him, we are justified, so the condemnation of sin is cancelled: "There is therefore now no condemnation
to those who are in Christ Jesus" (Rom. 8:1). Through the regenerating
work of the Holy Spirit, we are born again and strengthened to walk in
newness of life, so the power of sin is broken.[2] The believer is not victorious by his strength of will or personal devotion but overcomes by what
has been done for him on the cross and by what has been and is being
accomplished in him through the Spirit and the faithful workings of
God's providence.

In New Testament teaching, the child of God faces many struggles
from within and without. He is at times defeated and even dejected.

---

1. Pastor Charles Leiter, conversation with the author regarding Romans 6.
2. Romans 6:4–6.

However, an air and aura of real victory runs through the course of his life. Though he falls seven times, he rises again and again.[3] Though he walks through many dark valleys, his pilgrimage leads him to greater and greater heights. Though he experiences intermittent failure, failure does not have the final word. Though he endures defeats, the Christian is not ultimately defeated. Such is the nature of salvation, for the God who began a good work will finish it. The 1689 London Baptist Confession, chapter 17, states it this way:

> Those whom God hath accepted in the beloved, effectually called and sanctified by his Spirit, and given the precious faith of his elect unto, can neither totally nor finally fall from the state of grace, but shall certainly persevere therein to the end, and be eternally saved, seeing the gifts and callings of God are without repentance, whence he still begets and nourisheth in them faith, repentance, love, joy, hope, and all the graces of the Spirit unto immortality; and though many storms and floods arise and beat against them, yet they shall never be able to take them off that foundation and rock which by faith they are fastened upon; notwithstanding, through unbelief and the temptations of Satan, the sensible sight of the light and love of God may for a time be clouded and obscured from them, yet he is still the same, and they shall be sure to be kept by the power of God unto salvation, where they shall enjoy their purchased possession, they being engraven upon the palm of his hands, and their names having been written in the book of life from all eternity.

In this test of salvation, we learn that one of the great marks of true conversion is that the world will not overcome the Christian so that he denies Christ and returns to it. Neither will the world prove successful in hindering God's work in the believer's life so that he becomes fruitless. We know that we know God and are truly born again because, through countless battles that rage within and without and frequent failures and falls, God sustains us and continues working in us for our good and His glory.

THE WORLD VERSUS THE CHRISTIAN

As we learned in an earlier chapter, the world represents all that is hostile to God and stands in opposition to the Christian as he seeks to walk

---

3. Proverbs 24:16.

in the narrow way according to Christ's commands. John Bunyan illustrates this epic battle well in *The Pilgrim's Progress*, which traces the events in Christian's life as he travels the long road from the City of Destruction to the Celestial City. He meets all that the world can throw at him on his journey: temptations without number, deceitful men and devils, discouraging events, vicious slander, merciless accusations, afflictions, persecutions, and countless opportunities to return to the world. However, in spite of all his stumbling through adversity and failure, Christian overcomes by the "blood of the Lamb" (Rev. 12:11), the "word of God" (1 John 2:14), and the providence of the One who said, "I will never leave you nor forsake you" (Heb. 13:5).

As Christians, we should never be astounded or shaken at the hostility of the world toward us or the extent to which it will labor to thwart our progress in Christ. For this reason, the apostle Paul informs us that "all who desire to live godly in Christ Jesus will suffer persecution" (2 Tim. 3:12). And the apostle Peter admonishes us never to be surprised at the fiery ordeals through which we must pass as though some strange thing were happening to us.[4] The believer and the world are as different as righteousness and lawlessness, daylight and dark, Christ and Belial, the living God and dumb idols.[5] Therefore, opposition and antagonism will always exist between the two without the slightest possibility of a truce. Since the battle between the Christian and the world will never be resolved, he must hope in God, look to Christ, and fight the good fight of faith. He must be strong in the Lord and in the strength of His might and put on the full armor of God so that he will be able to stand firm against the schemes of both devils and men.[6]

Never has a war been waged upon this earth that required more fortitude and perseverance than that which is waged against the Christian every day. Never has an army been marshaled upon this earth that can compare in strength and cunning to that which faces the believer on a daily basis. We are behind enemy lines in an alien world that opposes our doctrine and our morality. We are surrounded by both human and demonic deceivers. We are berated for our religious fanaticism and encouraged to consider the benefits of compromise. We are engulfed in

---

4. 1 Peter 4:12.
5. 2 Corintians 6:14–16.
6. Ephesians 6:10–11.

voices that tempt us to deny our Lord, abandon the call, and return to the City of Destruction.

THE CERTAINTY OF VICTORY

In light of such unrelenting opposition from the world, we might ask how we can have any degree of assurance that the Christian will overcome and not fall away. The answer is simple: our hope is not founded upon our moral fortitude, religious devotion, or personal piety but upon the greatness of our Savior and the nature of the salvation that is ours in Him. In the words of the apostle Paul, "We are more than conquerors through Him who loved us" (Rom. 8:37).

In 1 John 5:4–5, the Christian's certain victory is attributed to three important realities. He overcomes by the new birth, by faith in the person and work of Christ, and by the greatness of the One who indwells him. [7] In other words, our victory is sure because it is His victory, wrought in His strength, and accomplished for His good pleasure and glory. The Christian's battle is real. He is called to strive,[8] hold fast,[9] and fight[10] with the greatest diligence and zeal.[11] Nevertheless, when the dust has settled and every foe has been conquered, the Christian admits that the battle and the victory were the Lord's.[12] If we believed, victory was by the faith He gave us.[13] If we did not fall to temptation, it was because He delivered us.[14] If we made our way through the dark labyrinths of doubt and despondency, it was because He was our guide.[15] If in battle we showed the greatest character, it was the character He created in us.[16] If we stood, He made us stand.[17] If we labored with the greatest diligence and sacrifice, it was by His grace alone.[18] No Christian who has ever known such

---

7. 1 John 4:4; 5:4–5.

8. Luke 13:24; Romans 15:30.

9. 1 Corinthians 15:2; 1 Thessalonians 5:21; Hebrews 3:6, 14; 4:14; 10:23; Revelation 2:25; 3:11.

10. Ephesians 6:12; 1 Timothy 1:18; 6:12.

11. Romans 12:11; Hebrews 6:11; 2 Peter 1:5.

12. 1 Samuel 17:47; 2 Chronicles 20:15; Zechariah 4:6.

13. Mark 9:24.

14. Matthew 6:13; 1 Corinthians 10:13; 2 Peter 2:9.

15. Psalms 5:8; 31:3; 43:3; 48:14; 139:10.

16. Ezekiel 36:26; 2 Corinthians 5:17.

17. Psalms 18:33; 66:9; Ezekiel 37:10; Romans 14:4.

18. 1 Corinthians 15:10; Ephesians 3:7.

grace would ever argue against it. None would think that God had been given too much credit or lobby for greater credit for self. Rather, they would exclaim with King David and the apostle Paul:

> Not unto us, O LORD, not unto us,
> But to Your name give glory,
> Because of Your mercy,
> Because of Your truth. (Ps. 115:1)

"He who glories, let him glory in the LORD." (1 Corinthians 1:31)

According to John, the first reality that assures the Christian's victory is the new birth: "For whatever is born of God overcomes the world" (1 John 5:4). Throughout this work, we have returned to this doctrine many times. The doctrine of regeneration is a magnificent work of God whereby a radically depraved human being who is hostile toward God and cannot submit to His will[19] is transformed into a new creature that loves Him, delights in His will, and seeks His glory. It explains how those who were dead in their trespasses and sins are made alive unto God.[20] It answers the longstanding question, "Can these bones live?" (Ezek. 37:3).

The doctrine of regeneration could be called the lost doctrine of contemporary evangelicalism. Failure to understand or preach it has resulted in several consequences. The glory of conversion has been diminished to nothing more than a human decision to follow Christ, with almost nothing said about the miracle that is required for such a thing to occur. The Christian is seen as nothing more than a person who has made a decision. Whether he grows, bears fruit, or continues is dependent upon further personal decisions. Thus, he has gained eternal life by a right decision for Christ but may continue in a life of carnality, worldliness, and immorality if he decides to go no further. This opinion reveals ignorance of the nature of conversion and makes the full course[21] of salvation dependent upon the volition of a person whose nature has undergone little or no transformation.

However, in regeneration and conversion rightly understood, a person repents and believes as a result of a supernatural work of God that transforms his nature, affections, and will. He is a new creature who loves God, desires to please Him, and longs to be conformed to His image. He

---

19. Romans 8:7.

20. Ephesians 2:1–5.

21. The full course of salvation refers to salvation in its totality, or three tenses—past justification, present sanctification, and future glorification.

now makes the right decision because he possesses right affections—his nature has been renewed in the likeness of God in true righteousness and holiness. Thus, he overcomes by virtue of what he has become through the miraculous divine work of regeneration.

Second, 1 John 5:4 attributes the Christian's certain victory to faith in the person and work of Christ. The believer's positional righteousness before God by faith alone is the bedrock of Christianity. Apart from the reality of this truth in the believer's life, there is no sure foundation to build upon and there can be no peace or strength to resist the onslaught from within and without. Apart from the doctrine of justification by faith, victory is impossible.

To be converted, a person must possess at least some knowledge of the severity of God's righteous standard and his failure to conform to it. As he grows in his knowledge of the Scriptures, he becomes even more convinced of the great distinction between God's character and his, between what God requires and what he is able to perform. Such knowledge would lead a believer to the brink of despair and defeat if he were not assured of the certain, impeccable, and immutable righteousness that has been imputed to him through faith in Christ. He is able to overcome every temptation to fall into despair only because he knows that he has been justified by faith; that he is clothed in the righteousness of Christ; and that his right standing before God is not founded upon his own virtue and merit but upon the virtue and merit of One who is both flawless and infallible. He stands victorious even in the midst of his weakness and failure because he trusts in the sure word of the gospel:

> Therefore, having been justified by faith, we have peace with God through our Lord Jesus Christ. (Rom. 5:1)

> There is therefore now no condemnation to those who are in Christ Jesus. (Rom. 8:1)

The believer's obstacles include his failings and the doubt and despair that arise from within. He is also confronted with the gross accusations of the accuser of the brethren, the serpent of old who is called the devil and Satan, who deceives the whole world, who is filled with fury because he knows his time is short, and who prowls around like a roaring lion seeking someone to devour.[22] He is a cruel and merciless enemy who

---

22. 1 Peter 5:8; Rev. 12:9–10, 12.

hates the people of God with an unimaginable hatred. He seeks their destruction with a passion inflamed by hell.

Although the devil has a great arsenal from which to draw, one of his greatest tactics is to point to the believer's failure and argue that he is beyond God's grace. With one edge of the sword he wounds the believer, and with the other edge he cuts off hope for cure. He does this by exaggerating the believer's failure and by diminishing the unconditional nature of God's love toward His children.

If Christianity were a religion of works or propagated some form of complementary doctrine that required even the most minimal personal righteousness on our part, we would be driven to despair. We would walk away from the Christian faith condemned and treat its teaching as a divine ruse that demanded something far beyond what we could ever deliver. It would be crueler than the worst prose of Greek mythology in which the gods played with the fates of mankind and delighted in their anguish. And this is exactly what the devil would have us believe!

But Christianity stands at the farthest possible distance from a works religion. In fact, it is grace undiminished and unmingled. A person is not justified by the combined strength of faith and works but by grace through faith alone. The believer's works do not complement or add to Christ's perfect work but flow from it. Those who have been justified by faith have also been regenerated by the Spirit; they have been made new creatures, with new affections set on doing the will of God. Where Christianity is found in its purest form, salvation is declared to be by faith, but works flow from salvation and are evidence of it.

The devil would have us twist the order of this beautiful doctrine by combining works with faith and making us believe that works are a means rather than the result of the saving work of God. Such a mingling of species is a perversion of the Scriptures, which always treat grace and works as mutually exclusive in terms of the cause of salvation. As Paul writes to the church in Rome, "And if by grace, then it is no longer of works; otherwise grace is no longer grace" (Rom. 11:6). Again, this is not a contradiction of James, who writes that faith without works is dead. We are justified by grace alone through faith alone, but the evidence of justification and regeneration is works.

Faith is the means by which the believer overcomes the world and does not yield to its inviting temptations or brutal attacks. In the midst of battles within and without, in the face of foes and failures, the

Christian rests upon the unshakeable foundation of Christ alone. He glories in Christ Jesus and puts "no confidence in the flesh" (Phil. 3:3). When doubts arise and the onslaught of the enemy is at a fever pitch, the believer does not look inward to find personal virtue or strength; rather, he rebuffs the enemy's brutal accusations by turning his eyes from self, pointing to God in Christ, and crying out victoriously: "Who shall bring a charge against God's elect? It is God who justifies. Who is he who condemns? It is Christ who died, and furthermore is also risen, who is even at the right hand of God, who also makes intercession for us" (Rom. 8:33–34).

By faith, the believer overcomes the accusations of his own heart and those of the enemy. Even the reality of his personal failure has no power to enslave him in fear or to hold him captive in despair. He continues with an unassailable confidence in his right standing before God because it is founded upon the person and work of Christ his Savior. The hymn writer Horatio Spafford beautifully summarizes this truth:

> Though Satan should buffet, though trials should come,
> let this blest assurance control:
> that Christ has regarded my helpless estate,
> and has shed His own blood for my soul.
>
> My sin, oh, the bliss of this glorious thought!
> my sin, not in part, but the whole,
> is nailed to the cross, and I bear it no more,
> praise the Lord, praise the Lord, O my soul![23]

Last, the Christian's certain victory is attributed to the greatness of the One who indwells him. John writes, "He who is in you is greater than he who is in the world" (4:4). A great truth to learn is that God is not only with us but He also indwells us through the Holy Spirit. Even the most godly among us have not fully fathomed the intimate fellowship that is communicated by this truth.[24] Because we are sons, God has sent forth the Spirit of His Son into our hearts, crying, "Abba, Father!" He is the seal and proof that we are no longer slaves, but sons and heirs of God.[25] He assures us of our adoption by testifying with our spirit that we are the

---

23. Horatio Spafford, "It Is Well with My Soul."
24. 2 Corinthians 13:14; Philippians 2:1.
25. Galatians 4:6–7.

children of God.[26] He is the deposit guaranteeing our inheritance until our future redemption is complete.[27]

According to our need, the indwelling Spirit ministers to us so that God's great purpose might be fulfilled in us. He enables us to comprehend something of what God has done for us and given to us in Christ.[28] He aids us in guarding the doctrines of the gospel that have been entrusted to us so that we do not depart from its truths or mislead others with another gospel.[29] He wars with our flesh and aids us in the great conflict against it.[30] He strengthens us with power in the inner man that we might be able to know the love of Christ and be filled with all the fullness of God.[31] He protects us from deception, bears His fruit in our lives, leads us, and empowers us for ministry.[32] He also "helps us in our weakness. For we do not know what we should pray for as we ought," but He Himself intercedes for us with groans that words cannot express (Rom. 8:26). How can we not triumph over the world, the flesh, and even all of hell when such a Paraclete[33] is freely given to us in Christ?

Another great truth we learn from this text is that the God who indwells us is infinitely greater than all our foes combined. The entire universe of men and demons making a collective assault upon the throne of God would have less effect than a tiny gnat beating its head against a world of granite. The nations are like a drop from a bucket before Him. God regards their combined strength as less than nothing and meaningless. He stretches out the heavens like a curtain, reduces rulers to nothing, and makes the judges of the earth as meaningless.[34] He "does according to His will in the army of heaven and among the inhabitants of earth," and no one can ward off His hand or question Him regarding what He has done (Dan. 4:35). Against Him there is no wisdom, understanding, or counsel.[35]

---

26. Romans 8:16.
27. 2 Corinthians 1:22; 5:5; Ephesians 1:13–14; 4:30.
28. 1 Corinthians 2:12; 1 John 2:20, 27.
29. 1 Timothy 6:20; 2 Timothy 1:14; Galatians 1:6–7.
30. Galatians 5:17.
31. Ephesians 3:16–19.
32. Acts 1:8; Romans 8:14; Galatians 5:18, 22–23; 1 John 2:26–27.
33. The title "Paraclete" is from the Greek word *paraklétos*. It refers to one who is called alongside for aid; a counselor or advocate. John frequently uses the title in reference to the Holy Spirit (John 14:16, 26; 15:26; 1 John 2:1).
34. Isaiah 40:15–23.
35. Proverbs 21:30.

This is the God who indwells the Christian. He is not a faithful God who is unable or an able God who is faithless. Rather, He is the faithful God who keeps His promises, and what He has promised He is able to perform.[36] He who began a good work in us will perfect it. He is able to keep us from stumbling and to make us stand in the presence of His glory, blameless and with great joy.[37] Therefore, the smallest and weakest among us is able to cry out with the apostle Paul: "Yet in all these things we are more than conquerors through Him who loved us. For I am persuaded that neither death nor life, nor angels nor principalities nor powers, nor things present nor things to come, nor height nor depth, nor any other created thing, shall be able to separate us from the love of God which is in Christ Jesus our Lord" (Rom. 8:37–39).

THE QUESTION OF OVERCOMING

The Christian overcomes the world by virtue of the new birth, by faith in the person and work of Christ, and by the greatness of the One who indwells him.[38] However, we must be sure that we have a proper notion regarding what it means for the Christian to overcome. First, it does not mean that he will overcome the flesh once for all and never be bothered with it again. The struggle with the flesh will sometimes be titanic, even in the life of the most mature and sanctified believer.[39] Second, it does not mean that the true believer will overcome sin in this life and walk in an uninterrupted course of sinless perfection. James, who was noted for his godliness among the apostles, included himself when he wrote, "For we all stumble in many things" (3:2). And the beloved apostle John is even more severe when he writes, "If we say that we have no sin, we deceive ourselves, and the truth is not in us" (1 John 1:8).

The victorious Christian life does not mean that we are raised above all conflict or even loss in battle. The victorious Christian life is found in perseverance and endurance. To overcome means that in spite of our failure, we continue. Our journey may be a constant series of two steps forward and one step back, but we continue believing, repenting, and following. We cannot deny Christ anymore than we can deny our own

---

36. Deuteronomy 7:9; Romans 4:21.
37. Jude v. 24.
38. 1 John 5:4–5.
39. Galatians 5:17.

reality.[40] We cannot return to the world because we know that He alone has the words of eternal life.[41] We hold on tenaciously to the gospel and force our way into the kingdom,[42] not because of some inner strength of will or even some exceptional piety but out of sheer desperation. We are utterly convinced of our own inability and cling to Christ like a drowning man clings to a lifeline or a tottering mountaineer clings to his pitons[43] and rope. Overcoming means that we simply go on with Christ and persevere in the faith until the end.[44]

However, if we find ourselves in a fixed state of unbelief, compromise, and worldliness, we have reason to fear. If we are continually beset with sin with no evidence of sanctification, we have grounds for doubt.[45] If we stray from God's commands and do not receive discipline, we are right at least to question the legitimacy of our birth.[46] If we find ourselves in a never-ending sleep of apathy toward God, His Christ, and His gospel, we should examine ourselves in light of Scripture to see if we are in the faith.[47] As in the parable of the sower, the matter of our salvation is not so much decided by how we begin with the gospel, but how we end.[48] Those who seem to have a good start but are finally overcome fall away and become unfruitful, giving strong evidence that their faith was false from the outset of the race.

---

40. Pastor Charles Leiter, conversation with the author.
41. John 6:68.
42. Luke 16:16.
43. A *piton* is the peg driven into the rock face to support the climber.
44. Matthew 24:13.
45. Hebrews 12:14.
46. Hebrews 12:8.
47. 2 Corinthians 13:5.
48. Matthew 13:3–9, 18–23.

CHAPTER FOURTEEN

Believing in Jesus

If we receive the witness of men, the witness of God is greater; for this is the witness of God which He has testified of His Son. He who believes in the Son of God has the witness in himself; he who does not believe God has made Him a liar, because he has not believed the testimony that God has given of His Son. And this is the testimony: that God has given us eternal life, and this life is in His Son. He who has the Son has life; he who does not have the Son of God does not have life.
—1 John 5:9–12

Often the best item in a series is left for last. This is the case before us now as we concern ourselves with the final test of conversion: personal faith in the testimony of God concerning His Son. According to John, we know that we have become the children of God because we believe the things that God has revealed concerning His Son, Jesus Christ of Nazareth. Taking a word from the apostle Paul, we are marked as Christians because we glory in Christ alone and put no hope in the flesh![1]

A DEPRECIATION AND MISDIRECTION OF FAITH
Before we address the text before us, we must confront two popular but erroneous opinions regarding saving faith. The first error has to with the nature of faith and our appreciation of it. In much of modern-day evangelism, saving faith has been reduced to nothing more than a mental and often superficial assent to a few spiritual principles or laws. In the minds of many, it has become a one-time decision of the will to accept Christ through praying a prayer by rote. Although the one who claims to be

---

1. Philippians 3:3.

converted may live the rest of his life with little thought of Christ, he is assured of his salvation by looking back to that one moment in time when he made the right decision and did the right thing. Thus, saving faith is not viewed as a lifetime of looking unto Christ or a persevering trust in the promises of God but as a decision made once and often forgotten.

The Scriptures and the great confessions of the church rank saving faith among the "deep things" of God, a doctrine of unfathomable profundity that should be examined and contemplated with the greatest concern and care. However, in our attempts to simplify the gospel, we have diminished saving faith to little more than ritual and stripped it of its significance and grandeur. We have reduced this universe of glory into a small parcel of land that can be traversed in a few moments. In its redefined and reduced state, it is now treated as milk for babes in Christ to be quickly comprehended and left behind en route to the meatier matters of Christian doctrine. Again, this modern-day depreciation of saving faith is contrary to the Scripture, which places the greatest importance upon it and goes to the greatest lengths to both define and explain it.[2] If we are ever to restore the gospel to its original splendor and power, we must regain a biblical understanding of what it means to believe God's testimony concerning His dear Son. We must renounce the present-day methodologies that lead people to trust in a sinner's prayer and bring them to a persevering "looking unto Christ" in faith.

The second erroneous opinion regarding faith has to do with its direction or chief end. Contemporary evangelicalism abounds with faith churches, faith movements, faith conferences, and books about faith. However, this intense preoccupation is chiefly concerned with the kind of faith that gains from God temporal blessings and shows little interest in the kind of faith that leads to eternal justification. Christian bookstores are overrun with instruction on faith for victory, prosperity, and power, yet they are practically barren regarding biblical exposition on

---

2. The writer of Hebrews identifies "faith toward God" as a part of the "elementary" teachings about Christ (6:1). At first glance, one might think that he is classifying saving faith among the more rudimentary doctrines of the Christian faith. However, this is not the case. The word "elementary" is translated from the Greek word *arché*, which means beginning, origin, or the first in a series. Thus, the idea being conveyed is that saving faith is among the primary and foundational doctrines of Christianity. Although it may rightly be called the beginning step of the Christian life, it is also the last. In fact, the entire Christian life may be properly described as a walk of faith. For the righteousness of God is revealed through the gospel from faith to faith.

the nature and evidence of genuine saving faith. If this emphasis on temporal materialism over eternal redemption and personal prosperity over the knowledge of God is any indication of the heart and soul of evangelicalism, then we are in a frightening state.

If we are to restore the gospel to its original splendor and power, we must renounce this disturbing preoccupation with the temporal and turn our attention toward the eternal. We must readjust our scales to give an honest reading so that when the eternal and temporal are placed on opposite sides of the balance, the scales tip in eternity's favor. The apostle Peter is quick to remind us that the goal of our faith is the salvation of our souls, and not our temporal gain: "the end [outcome, or *telós* in Greek] of your faith—the salvation of your souls" (1 Peter 1:9). Thus, the *telós*, or great end of our faith, looks beyond this mortal life and concerns itself with the rescue of our souls from eternal damnation, setting its eye upon a restored relationship with God and the future hope of glory. Although we are to believe God for both the temporal and the eternal, to set the former above the latter is to gather dross and leave behind the gold.

THE NATURE OF FAITH

Our text is primarily concerned with faith in the testimony of God concerning His Son. The theme seems simple enough, yet the amount of confusion surrounding the exact nature of faith is overwhelming. Many evangelicals claim to possess a faith that saves and yet that faith has little real impact upon their daily lives. This malady leads us to some very important questions: What does it mean to believe God's testimony concerning His Son? What does it mean to possess faith? The writer of Hebrews tells us: "Now faith is the substance of things hoped for, the evidence of things not seen" (11:1).

According to the writer of Hebrews, faith is the conviction that a person possesses regarding the reality of something that he hopes for but has not yet realized or seen. This definition leads us to some very important questions: How can a reasonable person do this? How is faith any different from wishful thinking or the insane pursuit of personal delusion? The answer is found in the integrity of God's person and the trustworthiness of His revelation. A person can be assured of what he hopes for and convinced of what he has not seen only because God has given testimony of it. The life of Noah clearly illustrates this truth, and the writer of

Hebrews states regarding him: "By faith Noah, being divinely warned of things not yet seen, moved with godly fear, prepared an ark for the saving of his household, by which he condemned the world and became heir of the righteousness which is according to faith" (11:17).

Noah built an ark because he believed that the world was soon to be destroyed by a deluge. No historical accounts of previous global floods upon which to base his conviction existed, nor was there present evidence that such an event was soon to happen. He had assurance of an oncoming flood and dedicated his entire life to building an ark simply because he had been "warned by God about things not yet seen." Noah believed in a global flood and acted upon his belief because God had given testimony concerning a coming flood.

The life of Abraham presents another illustration of faith. Concerning him, the apostle Paul writes the following commentary: "And not being weak in faith, he did not consider his own body, already dead (since he was about a hundred years old), and the deadness of Sarah's womb. He did not waver at the promise of God through unbelief, but was strengthened in faith, giving glory to God, and being fully convinced that what He had promised He was also able to perform" (Rom. 4:19–21).

According to this, Abraham was "fully convinced" that he was going to sire a son through his wife, Sarah. However, his great assurance was not founded upon anything that he could see since both he and Sarah were far beyond the years of childbearing. He hoped against hope and did not waver in unbelief but was fully assured of a son who was yet to be conceived simply because of God's testimony concerning the matter. His assurance was founded upon the fact that what God had promised, He was able also to perform.

In light of these verses, we may conclude that genuine faith is the personal assurance of what we hope for and the conviction of what we have not seen simply because God has given testimony of it. This is especially true with regard to God's Son, about whom He has given His greatest testimony.

THE TESTIMONY OF GOD

The main theme of 1 John 5:9–12 is the testimony of God concerning His Son, Jesus Christ of Nazareth. The word "testimony," which is translated from the Greek word *marturía*, is used 113 times in the New Testament.

Of these occurrences, sixty-four are in John's writings. In the gospel of John, testimony concerning Jesus is given by John the Baptist,[3] the apostle John,[4] God the Father,[5] the Holy Spirit,[6] the Scriptures,[7] the works of Jesus,[8] and Jesus Himself.[9] In John's first epistle, testimony is given by the apostle John;[10] the Spirit, the water, and the blood;[11] and finally by God the Father.[12] In the gospel of John, the purpose of the witness is that all might believe that Jesus is the Christ, the Son of God, and that believing, they might be saved.[13] In John's first epistle, the purpose of the witness is to confirm the truth about Jesus Christ and His gospel and to give assurance to the true believers who had been shaken in their faith by false teachers.[14]

John begins by putting forth a powerful argument regarding the trustworthiness of God and the reasonableness of believing Him. He draws a contrast between men and God and then reasons from the lesser to the greater. If we receive the lesser testimony of men, how much more should we be inclined to receive the greater testimony of God?[15] In this world, all of us are called upon to trust many sorts of testimonies ranging from the reasonably credible to the most fallacious. In fact, if we did not trust someone, we would soon find it impossible to function as individuals or societies. Thus, we believe people in spite of everything we know about them, especially their tendency to distort the truth.[16] If, then, we consider it reasonable to believe men who are prone to lie, how much more should we believe the God of truth, of whom the Scriptures testify

---

3. John 1:6–8, 15; 3:26, 32–33; 5:32–34.
4. John 19:35; 21:24.
5. John 5:37; 8:18.
6. John 15:26.
7. John 5:39.
8. John 5:36; 10:25.
9. John 3:11, 32–33; 8:14, 18; 18:37.
10. 1 John 1:2; 4:14.
11. 1 John 5:6–8. The reference to "water and blood" is probably a reference to the baptism and crucifixion of Jesus. Both His baptism and bloody crucifixion testify that He is the Christ, the Son of God and the Savior of the world.
12. 1 John 5:9–11.
13. John 20:31.
14. For a fuller explanation of this text, the reader is directed to *Letters of John*, by Colin G. Kruse, 179–84.
15. 1 John 5:9.
16. Psalm 116:11; Romans 3:4.

that He cannot lie?[17] In fact, the perfections of His nature make it impossible for Him to do so.[18] The prophet Samuel declared, "The Strength of Israel will not lie nor relent" (1 Sam. 15:29). And even the wayward Balaam was forced to render the following commendation:

> "God is not a man, that He should lie,
> Nor a son of man, that He should repent.
> Has He said, and will He not do?
> Or has He spoken, and will He not make it good?" (Num. 23:19)

To believe the lesser (men) and to dismiss the testimony of the greater (God) is not only unreasonable but also betrays a mistrust in the character of God. Even within the context of human relations, to doubt a person's word is to denigrate his character, and what we do with another's words reveals what we think about him as a person. If this is true regarding people, it is even more so with regard to God, whose character is so closely tied to His Word.[19] For this reason, the Scriptures view man's unbelief in God's Word to be a heinous crime, an inexcusable attack upon His character, and an offense to be reckoned with. In the words of John in this text, "He who does not believe God has made Him a liar" (5:10).

Having argued for the truthfulness of God and the trustworthiness of His testimony, John now reveals the subject of God's testimony: His Son. In verse 9, John declares that God "has testified of His Son." John's use of the perfect tense denotes God's irrevocable and immutable position regarding His Son. He has given testimony concerning Him and will not change. D. Edmund Hiebert asserts, "God has placed Himself permanently on record as bearing witness to His Son."[20] He has done so through the Old Testament prophets,[21] John the Baptist,[22] the works of the Spirit,[23] His audible voice,[24] the supernatural and cataclysmic events

---

17. Psalm 31:5; Isaiah 65:16; Titus 1:2.
18. Hebrews 6:18.
19. Psalm 138:2.
20. Hiebert, *Epistles of John*, 241.
21. Luke 24:44–47; John 5:39.
22. John 1:6–8, 15; 3:26, 32–33; 5:32–34.
23. John 5:36; 10:25.
24. God spoke audibly from heaven at Christ's baptism (Matt. 3:16–17; Mark 1:10–11); at His transfiguration (Matt. 17:5; Mark 9:7; Luke 9:35); and before the crowd during the Passover (John 12:27–39).

surrounding the crucifixion,[25] the resurrection,[26] the outpouring of the Spirit on the Day of Pentecost,[27] and the ongoing witness of the Spirit through the church.

In light of such overwhelming divine testimony concerning the Son, unbelief is not an option. The Scriptures never coddle the unbeliever or cater to his demands for more information or proof. Unbelief is never condoned or excused; rather, it is the result of the sinner's obstinate denial of the facts simply because he refuses to submit to the righteousness of God. The serious and dreadful nature of unbelief is revealed in Christ's warning: "He who believes in Him is not condemned; but he who does not believe is condemned already, because he has not believed in the name of the only begotten Son of God" (John 3:18).

THE MEANING OF ETERNAL LIFE

Up to this point, John has labored to prove that God has given a clear and sure testimony concerning Jesus of Nazareth as the incarnate Son of God who was crucified for the sins of His people. He has also argued the reasonableness of believing this testimony and the crime of rejecting it: "He who does not believe God has made Him a liar" (5:10). Therefore, having established his argument, John now tells us the exact nature of God's testimony concerning His Son: "that God has given us eternal life, and this life is in His Son" (5:11). It is not an exaggeration to say that in these few words are found the sum and substance of the gospel. However, to understand this text fully, we must concern ourselves with two important questions: What is eternal life? What are the meaning and implications of the phrase "in the Son"?

A great deal of confusion stems from a misunderstanding of both the time and nature of eternal life. Regarding the time, many seem to view eternal life exclusively as a future hope and regard it as synonymous with glorification or a future life in heaven. Such a view is contrary to the Scriptures, which teach that eternal life begins at the moment of regeneration and then lasts throughout eternity. From John's gospel we understand that "he who believes in the Son has everlasting life" (3:36). The verb "has" is translated from a present-tense Greek verb, demonstrating that

---

25. Matthew 27:50–53.
26. Romans 1:4; 4:25.
27. Acts 2:1–36.

eternal life is a present reality for those who truly believe. In 1 John 5:11, John declares that "God has given us eternal life." The phrase "has given" is translated from an aorist tense Greek verb, demonstrating that eternal life had already been given to those who have believed in the Son. From this we gather that although eternal life is a future hope, it is also a present reality. It begins at the moment of first faith in Christ, and it will never end throughout the countless ages of eternity.

The first, most common error is to regard eternal life as merely a quantity of time rather than a quality of life and ignore the nature of it. Although eternal life is never ending, the great emphasis is on the *new kind* of life that the believer has received in Christ. In the Upper Room Discourse, the Lord Jesus Christ described eternal life in this way: "And this is eternal life, that they may know You, the only true God, and Jesus Christ whom You have sent" (John 17:3).

Here, Jesus does not regard eternal life as a quantity of time but as a quality of life in fellowship with God and His Son. To grasp the significance of this truth, we must understand the meaning ascribed to the word "know." It is translated from the Greek verb *ginósko* and is often used to communicate the Hebrew idea of knowledge within the context of a personal relationship. In the Scriptures, it is often used to describe the personal and even physical intimacy between a man and a woman. Here it is used to describe eternal life as a life of intimate fellowship with God. John further confirms this understanding of the text by his closing remarks at the end of his first epistle: "And we know that the Son of God has come and has given us an understanding, that we may know Him who is true; and we are in Him who is true, in His Son Jesus Christ. This is the true God and eternal life" (5:20).

Here again, eternal life is equated with the knowledge of God through the Son in the context of a personal and intimate relationship. The logical order is as follows: Through the preaching of the gospel and the regenerating and illuminating work of the indwelling Spirit, God gives life, understanding, and a willing heart to His people. As a result, they enter into a new life of faith, communion, praise, and service to God. This is eternal life—not merely the lengthening of days or the future hope of heaven, but a new life in Christ. Eternal life is not an undetectable positional standing before God or a theological conjecture. It is a present, experimental, and discernible reality in the earthly pilgrimage of the believer. It is as real to him as the recovery of sight to the blind, the gift of hearing to the deaf, and the restoration of life to the dead. Although the experimental reality of this life may vary by degrees from believer to believer and from day to day, it is nonetheless real.

LIFE IN THE SON

We will now direct our attention to the inexhaustible truth that this life is "in His Son" (1 John 5:11). These three words are translated from the Greek phrase *en to huio*, and they reveal one of the most beautiful truths in all the Scriptures. In the Greek the preposition helps us to understand that the noun is in a case that indicates the sphere in which eternal life is found. It is found exclusively *in the Son!* This is proof that Jesus is not merely all that we need, but He is all that we have! Apart from Him we have no part with God. In Him, we possess every blessing of God to man. Outside of Him we have nothing. We are "wretched, miserable, poor, blind, and naked" (Rev. 3:17). Christ alone is the foundation upon which anything that can be built is built. He is the hinge upon which everything swings. He is the great determining factor in everything that has to do with a right standing and right relationship with God. This inexhaustible truth and its implications cannot be comprehended fully, nor can they ever be exaggerated.

Among the greatest, most foundational truths of Christianity is that eternal life and every other spiritual blessing are exclusively in the Son. Jesus testified of Himself, "I am the way, the truth, and the life. No one comes to the Father except through Me" (John 14:6). Peter stood before the rulers of Israel and declared, "Nor is there salvation in any other, for there is no other name under heaven given among men by which we must be saved" (Acts 4:12). The apostle Paul wrote to young Timothy, "For there is one God and one Mediator between God and men, the Man Christ Jesus" (1 Tim. 2:5). The truth that eternal life is exclusively *in the Son* cannot be overstated. In fact, Christianity is found in its pristine state when it acknowledges that apart from the Son we are "aliens from the commonwealth of Israel and strangers from the covenants of promise, having no hope and without God in the world" (Eph. 2:12).

In Ephesians 1, the uniqueness, essentialness, and exclusiveness of Christ is set forth unmistakably. In the first fourteen verses, Paul uses the phrase "in Christ" or its equivalent eleven times. *In the Son,* we are blessed with every spiritual blessing. *In the Son,* we were chosen before the foundation of the world. *In the Son,* God freely bestowed His grace upon us. *In the Son,* we have redemption and the forgiveness of trespasses. *In the Son,* God made known to us the mystery of His will. *In the Son,* God has united all things in heaven and earth. *In the Son,* we were sealed with the Holy Spirit of promise.[28] Every spiritual blessing that we possess, including eternal life, is because of God's beloved Son and His work on our behalf! It is for this reason that John concludes with one of the most powerful declarations in the Scriptures regarding the uniqueness, supremacy, and centrality of Christ in salvation: "He who has the Son has life; he who does not have the Son of God does not have life" (1 John 5:12).

To the Christian, this truth is beyond precious because it lays every hope of heaven upon Christ and acknowledges the infinite worth of His person and work. The human heart that has truly been regenerated by the Holy Spirit and justified by faith in Christ's blood will not take offense when every accolade is lavished upon the Son. On the contrary, he will revel at any thought or word that brings Christ glory and sets Him in the highest place. Furthermore, the Christian delights in knowing and proclaiming that Christ is the whole of his salvation. He glories in a redemption that was gained without his contribution and a justification that was granted apart from his own virtue and merit. He will even exult in having his own sin painted across the sky if upon such darkness the Morning Star[29] might appear more glorious. If we are truly Christian, we will delight in ascribing all credit for our salvation to the Son, and we would be dismayed if even the smallest measure of credit were assigned to us.

In the Scriptures, the portrayal of Christ as the lone Savior and only Mediator between God and man is a precious truth to the Christian. However, to the unbeliever it is the greatest scandal, a stone of stumbling and a rock of offense.[30] Unbelievers decry it as arrogant bigotry because it sets Christianity apart as an exclusive religion that refuses to entertain any hope for salvation outside of Christ. To the postmodern man, whose unrighteousness coerces his own mind to bend to the absurd hypothesis that all religions are equally true, this is the only unpardonable sin. It is the reason early Christians were labeled atheists and burned on crosses,

---

28. Ephesians 1:3–4, 6–7, 9–10, 13.
29. A reference to the Messiah. Numbers 24:17; 2 Peter 1:19; Revelation 22:16.
30. Romans 9:32–33; 1 Peter 2:8.

and it is the reason any form of biblical and historical Christianity is disdained in our present day. If the church would only relinquish or even temper this declaration, it could make peace with the world and reunite itself with the rest of humanity. However, in doing so it would betray Christ and forfeit its peace and union with God.

THE INWARD WITNESS

According to the apostle John, the testimony of God is this: He has given us eternal life, and this life is in His Son. Furthermore, John states that everyone who truly believes in the Son has this testimony in himself.[31]

This remarkable truth is far more difficult to interpret than one might first think. Even among scholars within the conservative and Reformed tradition, several views have been put forward. Is John saying that the one who believes has accepted and internalized the testimony that God has given concerning His Son? Is John alluding to the inward testimony of the Spirit, who is dwelling within the believer? Or, is he referring to the experimental testimony of eternal life that the believer now possesses, the reality of a new kind of life centering upon an intimate fellowship with the Father and the Son? It may be that the meaning is broad enough to include all of these.

A first mark that we have been truly converted is that we have accepted the testimony of God that was first communicated through eyewitnesses such as the apostles[32] and since then has been conveyed to each successive generation through faithful gospel preaching. We know that we are Christian because we hold to and rely upon the gospel of Jesus Christ that was "once for all delivered to the saints" (Jude v. 3). We stand upon the Scriptures and within the current of historic evangelical Christianity. We have not moved away from the hope of the gospel but continue in the faith firmly established and steadfast.[33]

It is important to note that a genuine acceptance of God's testimony resulting in salvation is not superficial or trite; as a result, we gradually assimilate it into every aspect of our lives. To the true convert, Christ becomes both our meat and drink: Jesus said to them, "Most assuredly, I say to you, unless you eat the flesh of the Son of Man and drink His blood,

---

31. 1 John 1:10.
32. 1 John 1:1–4.
33. Colossians 1:23.

you have no life in you" (John 6:53).[34] His words become the foundation, pattern, and goal of life. The gospel becomes a part of us and the distin - guishing mark of who we are; it both defines us and sets our course. It is within us and part of our very being. We could no more separate our- selves from the gospel than we could divide our person and scatter it to the four corners of the globe. From the depths of our innermost man, we agree with the gospel, delight in its beauty, and desire to be conformed to its precepts. Every faithful proclamation of the gospel that we hear or read is a further confirmation to our hearts that Christ is everything and that eternal life is only *in the Son*!

A second mark that we have truly become Christian is the inward testimony of the Spirit who dwells within us. From John's gospel, we learn that the Holy Spirit has been sent forth to testify of Christ, indwell the believer, and guide him into all truth.[35] From John's first epistle, we learn that the Spirit also labors within the believer to both confirm and strengthen his assurance of sonship. We know that we are the children of God and that we have an abiding relationship with Christ by means of the Spirit, whom He has given us.[36] The Spirit of God bears witness to the incarnation and atoning work of Christ and confirms their reality within our hearts.[37]

Note that this teaching on the inward witness of the Holy Spirit not only occurs in John's writings but is essential to Paul's view of the Chris- tian life also. The Holy Spirit and the life that flows from Him have been given to every believer as a kind of firstfruits and pledge of the life to be revealed at our final glorification.[38] Through the Holy Spirit, the love of God is poured out within our hearts in a real and discernible expe- rience.[39] The Holy Spirit removes our slavish fear of condemnation and

---

34. The phrase "our meat and drink" comes from *Olney Hymns*, by John Newton, "What Think Ye of Christ," no. 89:

> If asked what of Jesus I think?
> Though still my best thoughts are but poor;
> I say, he's my meat and my drink,
> My life, and my strength, and my store.

35. John 14:16; 15:26; 16:13.
36. 1 John 3:24; 4:13.
37. 1 John 4:2; 5:6–8.
38. Romans 8:23; Ephesians 1:13–14
39. Romans 5:5. The reader should not conclude that such manifestations of divine love are to be experienced continually or always with the same intensity. Though the love of God

replaces it with a strong assurance of sonship, which leads us to cry out, "Abba Father."[40] The Spirit also leads us according to the will of God and supports us in the midst of our weakness.[41] Finally, the Holy Spirit bears witness that we are the children of God through His ongoing work of sanctification, conforming us to the image of Christ and producing the fruitful life of Christ within us.[42]

According to John and Paul, this inward work of the Spirit will be a reality in the life of every child of God. Its manifestations will vary from believer to believer. And even in the most mature saint, there will be times of pruning, apparent barrenness, and a lessening or loss of God's manifest presence.[43] Nevertheless, every believer's life will exhibit practical and discernible manifestations of the Spirit's work. This is the birthright of the children of God and one of the means by which we are assured that we know Him.

A third mark that we have truly believed unto salvation is the witness of the reality of eternal life within us. To understand this statement requires that we remember the true nature of eternal life. It is not merely an infinite length of days but a quality of life founded upon and flowing from an intimate knowledge and communion with God and His Christ.[44] If eternal life refers to nothing more than an unending life or a future reality in heaven, then even the most carnal and worldly person may claim to possess it, and no one will be able to refute him. However, if eternal life is a new kind of life that manifests itself in a real knowledge of God and fellowship with Him, then the confidence of the carnal and worldly person is exposed as tenuous at best and utterly false at worst.

---

is a constant reality in the believer's life, discernible manifestation of that love may increase or diminish according to the believer's need, his devotion, or the wise providence of God.

40. Romans 8:15; Galatians 4:6. Again, it should be recognized that the believer's assurance of sonship may vary in strength and intensity. Though our strong assurance of salvation is the Father's will, even the most mature saint may struggle with doubt as he fights against the foes arrayed against him—the flesh, the world, and the devil.

41. Romans 8:14, 26.

42. Romans 8:16; 15:13; Galatians 5:22–23. The Spirit's witness is certainly not limited to the emotions or the mystical. He also bears witness to our sonship through the practical and discernible evidences of a godly and Christlike life.

43. Although God is omnipresent, He does not always manifest His presence, nor is it always discernible to the believer. Even the most mature and godly believer may pass through times when there is little sense of God's presence in his life. Such times serve to teach the believer to walk by faith and to trust God even in the darkness.

44. John 17:3.

A maxim that is both popular and biblical exists within evangelical Christianity: "We know that we have eternal life because we believe." However, we can also reverse the order of the words and create a new maxim that is equally as biblical: "We know we have believed because we have eternal life." In other words, we know that we have truly believed in Christ and are justified by that faith because of the discernible and ongoing reality of a new kind of life within us that began at conversion. We know that we have believed unto salvation because we have entered into a real, vital, and abiding fellowship with the only true God and Jesus Christ whom He has sent.[45] This is eternal life! Is this true in us?

SUMMARY

To conclude our study, we will consider briefly the characteristics of a true child of God that are presented to us in 1 John. It is our hope that the believer might grow in his assurance of salvation and that the unconverted might come to the realization that he has yet to know Christ.

Test 1: We know that we are Christian because we walk in the light (1 John 1:4–7). Our style of life is being gradually conformed to what God has revealed to us about His nature and will.

Test 2: We know that we are Christian because our lives are marked by sensitivity to sin, repentance, and confession (1 John 1:8–10).

Test 3: We know that we are Christian because we keep God's commands (1 John 2:3–4). We desire to know God's will, strive to obey it, and mourn our disobedience.

Test 4: We know that we are Christian because we walk as Christ walked (1 John 2:5–6). We desire to imitate Christ and grow in conformity to Him.

Test 5: We know that we are Christian because we love other Christians, desire their fellowship, and seek to serve them in deed and truth (1 John 2:7–11).

---

45. John 17:3; 1 John 5:20.

Test 6: We know that we are Christian because of our increasing disdain for the world and because of our rejection of all that contradicts and opposes God's nature and will (1 John 2:15–17).

Test 7: We know that we are Christian because we continue in the historic doctrines and practices of the Christian faith and remain within the fellowship of others who do the same (1 John 2:18–19).

Test 8: We know that we are Christian because we profess Christ to be God and hold Him in the highest esteem (1 John 2:22–24; 4:1–3, 13–15).

Test 9: We know that we are Christian because our lives are marked by a longing and practical pursuit of personal holiness (1 John 3:1–3).

Test 10: We know that we are Christian because we are practicing righteousness (1 John 2:28–29; 3:4–10). We are doing those things that conform to God's righteous standard.

Test 11: We know that we are Christian because we overcome the world (1 John 4:4–6; 5:4–5). Although we are often hard pressed and weary, we press on in faith. We continue following Christ and do not turn back.

Test 12: We know that we are Christian because we believe the things that God has revealed concerning His Son, Jesus Christ. We have eternal life in Him alone (1 John 5:9–12).

If we have these qualities, and they are increasing in us, we have evidence that we have come to know God and bear the fruit of a child of God. However, if these qualities are absent from our lives, we should have the greatest concern for our souls. We should be diligent to seek God regarding our salvation. We should reexamine ourselves to see if we are in the faith. We should be diligent to make our calling and election sure.[46]

---

46. 2 Corinthians 13:5; 2 Peter 1:8–11.

PART TWO

Gospel Warnings, or Warnings to Empty Confessors

You believe that there is one God. You do well. Even the demons believe—and tremble!

—James 2:19

Enter by the narrow gate; for wide is the gate and broad is the way that leads to destruction, and there are many who go in by it. Because narrow is the gate and difficult is the way which leads to life, and there are few who find it.

—Matthew 7:13–14

CHAPTER FIFTEEN

Gospel Reductionism

*You believe that there is one God. You do well. Even the demons believe—
and tremble!*
—James 2:19

Two things viewed separately may seem almost identical until they are set side by side. What seemed to be only apparent differences or minor departures become glaring contrasts. Making comparisons and contrasts, which has proven beneficial in nearly every discipline of discovery, is also a great aid in the study of Scripture and the formation of systematic theology. The church and individual believers have always benefited from comparing and contrasting their beliefs and practices with the great standard of Scripture and with the lesser but still useful standard of church history. Presently, the evangelical community would do well to follow this course no matter how painful the process or what it might reveal. The discovery of even the most dreadful malady is not bad news if there is still time for healing.

The slightest overview of historical Christian thought from the Reformers to the present reveals that there is a great contrast between the gospel of contemporary Christianity and that of our fathers. This contrast is not confined to the liberal fellowships that deny the major tenets of orthodoxy but is found even in the most conservative and evangelical churches. Arm in arm, we have taken the "glorious gospel of the blessed God" and reduced it to a shallow creed (1 Tim. 1:11). Anyone who professes this creed is declared to be born again and thoroughly Christian.

RIGHT ANSWERS TO WRONG QUESTIONS

The apostle James seemed to be moved by one great concern: the setting forth of "pure and undefiled religion" in the sight of God (1:27). For this reason, his general letter is extremely straightforward and often sharp. He paints in broad strokes and has little use for nuance. He tells us clearly that he is unimpressed by our professions of faith and claims to piety. He demands greater evidences and wants to see our faith proven by action.

In the text we are considering, James strikes at the heart of his fellow Jews who had professed faith in Christ in word alone. They had fallen into the deadly pit of empty creedalism. They had given some form of mental assent to the great doctrines of the Christian faith but were yet unconverted. To remedy the situation, James recalls Israel's greatest doctrinal confession, the Shema: "Hear, O Israel: The LORD our God, the LORD is one!" (Deut. 6:4).[1] Then, with cutting sarcasm, he argues that an agreement with and confession of the greatest of all creeds is worthless if it is not accompanied by genuine faith that results in corresponding behavior. A person who believes there is only one true God has done well. However, if his belief results in nothing more than a verbal confession, he is worse off than demons, for these malignant and condemned creatures also believe the same truth yet by their shuddering demonstrate greater reverence toward God than the one who confesses faith and remains unmoved by it.

From James, we learn that our public confession of faith in Christ and our verbal assent to pristine doctrinal statements are not conclusive evidence of salvation. Demons believe all sorts of right things about God, and the Scriptures even record them making correct public declarations about Christ: "And the unclean spirits, whenever they saw Him, fell down before Him and cried out, saying, 'You are the Son of God'" (Mark 3:11). Nevertheless, these demons were not redeemed. Although they believed great truths, demonstrated insight into great doctrines, and professed great things, they were still demonic spirits prone to evil, opposed to righteousness, and at enmity with God. In the same way, though a person believes right things about God and professes them publicly, he may be no better off than a demon.

What James was combating nearly two thousand years ago is alive and well in contemporary Christianity. The Jews had reduced the ancient faith of Israel to a public profession of faith in monotheism. We have reduced the Christian faith to nothing more than a positive response to a few simple questions. A modern-day gospel presentation often begins with this

---

1. *Shema* is derived from the Hebrew word for "hear."

question: Do you know that you are a sinner? If the person answers positively, then a second question is asked: Do you want to go to heaven? If the person gives a second positive response, he is then encouraged to pray and ask Jesus into his heart. If he prays and is convinced of his sincerity, he is assured of his salvation and welcomed into the family of God.

In this chapter, we will take a closer look at this popular method of evangelism and discover that it is not only inadequate but extremely dangerous. Millions of people sit in church pews who are unconverted yet assured of their salvation because at one time they gave right answers to wrong questions.

ARE YOU A SINNER?

Ours is a fallen world, and we are a fallen race. According to the Scriptures, the image of God in man has been seriously disfigured, and moral corruption has polluted his entire being: body,[2] reason,[3] emotions,[4] and will.[5] How then can a person, apart from the Scriptures and the work of the Spirit, even understand when he is asked if he is a sinner? If he simply says yes, what does it mean? What have we learned about him? Our culture "drinks iniquity like water" (Job 15:16). Sin is relished, esteemed, promoted, and propagated. We not only sin but we also boast in the extent of our sin and our lack of shame. Therefore, when a person merely agrees that he is a sinner, it means very little. The devil would tell us that he is a great sinner, but his profession would not bring him any closer to God nor would it prove that God was working in his heart. We may say the same of a man.

Knowing this, we would do well to recognize that the proper question is not if a person knows he is a sinner but rather if God has so worked in his heart through the hearing of the gospel that his view of sin and disposition toward it have changed. Is he beginning to see sin as God sees it and as the Scriptures speak of it? Does he now consider himself to be utterly destitute of merit and worthy of God's judgment? Has his love for self and sin been replaced with disgust and shame? Does he long to be forgiven, freed, and cleansed?

---

2. Romans 6:6, 12; 7:24; 8:10, 13.
3. Romans 1:21; 2 Corinthians 3:14–15; 4:4; Ephesians 4:17–19.
4. Romans 1:26–27; Galatians 5:24; 2 Timothy 3:2–4.
5. Romans 6:17; 7:14–15.

It is one thing for a person to say he is a sinner or even to make an outcry against sin, but it is quite another thing for a person to come to hate his sin and be ashamed of it. According to the Scriptures, it is not a public declaration of sin but an inward change of heart toward sin that proves that God has accomplished a work of salvation in a person's heart.

Bunyan's *Pilgrim's Progress* provides us with an excellent example of the difference between a person who merely acknowledges that he is a sinner and one whose disposition has turned against his sin. We see this in a conversation between the true believer Faithful and the false convert Talkative:

> *Talkative:* I see that our talk must be about the power of things. Well, it is a very good question, and I am willing to answer you. First, and in brief, when the grace of God is in the heart, it cries out against sin....
>
> *Faithful:* Wait! Hold on! Let's consider one thing at a time. I think you should say instead that grace evidences itself by causing the soul to abhor its own sin.
>
> *Talkative:* Why, what difference is there between crying out against and abhorring sin?
>
> *Faithful:* Oh, a great deal. A man may cry out against sin, as a general policy, but he cannot abhor it unless he has a godly hatred of it.[6]

Poor, self-deceived Talkative knew all the right things to say, but none of them was a reality in his heart. He knew that it was proper for a person to acknowledge sin in his life and even to speak against it, yet in his heart there was no true hatred of sin and no shame for his participation in it.

From this brief interchange between Talkative and Faithful, we learn that we must be careful not to deal superficially with sin in either preaching the gospel or counseling seekers. It is not enough to ask them if they are sinners based upon their definitions of the term or their opinions of themselves. We must exhaust every resource in the Scriptures until seekers gain a biblical understanding of sin, comprehend something of their own sinfulness, and show evidence of a new disposition toward it. Only then can we leave behind the discussion of sin and advance to other matters of the gospel.

---

6. John Bunyan, *The New Pilgrim's Progress: John Bunyan's Classic Revised for Today with Notes by Warren Wiersbe* (Grand Rapids: Discovery House Publishers, 1989), 99.

DO YOU WANT TO GO TO HEAVEN?

Often with contemporary evangelistic methods, if a person responds positively to the first question regarding his sin, he is then confronted with the second: Do you want to go to heaven? At this point we must again ask ourselves a very important question: If the person responds negatively or positively, does his response tell us anything about the true condition of his heart? If a person did choose hell over heaven, it would simply mean that either he does not comprehend the terrors of hell or he is a lunatic. However, if he declares his preference for heaven, does it prove that God is working, that there is repentance, or that he has saving faith? People can and do desire heaven for an almost infinite number of reasons, most of them selfish.

First, people may desire heaven for heaven's sake. Secular humanism and its social reforms have taught us that all men have an innate desire for a utopia, an ideally perfect place. Who but the mad or criminally insane would choose chaos over paradise? All people want a perfect world where everything is beautiful, fear is eliminated, death is vanquished, and every dream comes true. However, does such a desire indicate a work of conversion in a person's heart? A desire for heaven "for heaven's sake" means nothing.

Second, people may desire heaven because the only alternative is hell. At certain times a year in the northern jungles of Peru, the farmers set fire to their rice fields in order to burn off the chaff. The flames are intense, and the world seems engulfed in smoke and ash. If you look closely, you will see every sort of viper and vermin fleeing the flames. Though driven only by instinct, they have a sense of self-preservation. They slither and crawl out of the field as quickly as possible, but when they reach a safe haven, they are still vipers and vermin. They are not new creatures. Their desires have not changed. They still long for the dark and murky marsh they have left and have no desire for the high ground to which they have fled. Their only desire for leaving the one and fleeing to the other is self-preservation.

In a similar manner, a desire for heaven born out of a fear for hell tells us nothing about whether God has wrought any change in his heart. While it is true that the fear of hell is a biblical motivation for salvation, it is never the exclusive or primary motivation. John the Baptist warned men to flee the wrath to come.[7] Jesus told people to fear Him who is able

7. Matthew 3:7.

to destroy body and soul in hell.[8] On the Day of Pentecost, the apostle Peter cried out for his listeners to be saved from a perverse generation.[9] Even in *Pilgrim's Progress*, Christian fled to the Celestial City because he saw destruction coming upon his present dwelling. However, in true conversion, a person's fear of hell and sense of self-preservation are soon overshadowed by his love for God and a desire for righteousness. In true conversion, people do not simply run from something they fear, but they run to something they desire: a pearl of great price,[10] the kingdom of God and His righteousness.[11] They fear being lost because they fear missing Jesus![12] However, a person's singular and sincere desire to save his own skin does not prove a work of conversion in his heart.

Third, people may desire a heaven without God. As we have already stated, most people want a heaven, but they disagree about what it should look like and how it should be governed. Many people believe that heaven is a place where everyone gets exactly what they want. However, with so many conflicting ideas and desires among its inhabitants, how could such a place exist? It would require that every individual be given a private heaven where he or she made all the rules and governed with absolute sovereignty. Would the God of Scripture fit into such a scheme? We must recognize that when the great majority affirm their desire for heaven, they are not really thinking of a place where God is the epicenter of every thought, delight, and worship. A kingdom where God alone is the absolute sovereign and His will is the only rule is not just foreign to their thoughts but distasteful.

A film titled "What Dreams May Come" is about an agnostic doctor who died and went to heaven. As he is standing there, dumbfounded at the reality of life after death, an angel approaches him. In the interchange that takes place, the good doctor reasons, "If there is a heaven, is there also a God?" The angel responds in the affirmative, and the good doctor asks, "Where is He?" The angel points upward and responds, "He's up there."

This simple interchange tells us volumes about man and his enmity against God. Finding it impossible to deny the existence of God, man has done everything in his power to suppress what he knows to be true about

---

8. Matthew 10:28.
9. Acts 2:40.
10. Matthew 13:45–46.
11. Matthew 6:33.
12. Thought from Pastor Charles Leiter.

Him.[13] In past decades, man has sought to remove God from every aspect of life on earth (culture, government, education, even religion) and conveniently relegate Him to heaven, where He remains unseen and uninvolved. Now it seems that man has made a monumental breakthrough in his war on God by removing Him from heaven and relegating Him to an even higher plane. Like a teacher who graduates a bothersome student just to get him out of his class, mankind has placed God on a higher plane simply to be rid of Him. All this demonstrates one powerful and irrefutable truth: everyone wants to go to heaven, but most do not want God to be there.

Further proof that most people desire a heaven without God is that the desires and ambitions of most here on earth are totally contrary to those of heaven. Why would a person who has no desire for worship on earth desire to go to heaven where everything is worship? Why would those who love sin desire a place where sin cannot be found? Why would one who is apathetic about righteousness desire a place where perfect righteousness dwells? Why would one who is unconcerned with the will of God desire a place where the will of God is everything?

All men want to go to heaven, but the heaven they want is different from the one revealed in the Scriptures. Therefore, the question of whether a person wants to go to heaven would be better restated in this way: Has God so worked in your heart through the hearing of the gospel that there is now a real and definite longing for Him? Has the God in whom you once took no interest and felt no desire become the object of your desire? Has love for God been awakened in your heart? Are there new affections drawing you irresistibly to Him? The question is not whether a person wants to go to heaven but if he wants God. As Jesus declared: "And this is eternal life, that they may know You, the only true God, and Jesus Christ whom You have sent" (John 17:3).

DO YOU WANT TO PRAY?

In much of modern-day evangelism, if a person responds positively to the first question regarding his sin and to the second question regarding heaven, he is then confronted with a third and final question: Do you want to pray and ask Jesus into your heart? If the person is hesitant about praying on his own, he may be led to repeat the sinner's prayer, which

---

13. Romans 1:18.

often appears at the conclusion of evangelistic tracts. After the prayer, the person is assured that if he prayed sincerely then God has saved him and Jesus has come into his heart.

Although this has become *the* evangelistic method of contemporary Christianity, we must still ask ourselves the following questions: Is there biblical precedent for such a method? Is it found in the teachings and example of Christ or His apostles? Although the Scriptures teach that men must receive Christ as Savior and Lord,[14] it would be wrong to think that this biblical requirement is fulfilled merely because someone has made a decision for Christ or prayed the sinner's prayer, especially because Christ and His apostles never gave such an invitation. In fact, their manner of inviting people to be saved was quite different from the invitations given today:

> Now after John was put in prison, Jesus came to Galilee, preaching the gospel of the kingdom of God, and saying, "The time is fulfilled, and the kingdom of God is at hand. Repent, and believe in the gospel." (Mark 1:14–15)

> I kept back nothing that was helpful, but proclaimed it to you, and taught you publicly and from house to house, testifying to Jews, and also to Greeks, repentance toward God and faith toward our Lord Jesus Christ. (Acts 20:20–21)

It is noteworthy that nowhere in Scripture do we see Christ, the apostles, or anyone else calling for people to repeat a sinner's prayer or to open up their heart and ask Jesus in. Rather, we see over and over a call to repentance and genuine faith in Jesus Christ. The question then is not whether a person wants to pray and ask Jesus into his heart but if God has so worked in his heart through the preaching of the gospel that he is now repenting of sin and believing in Jesus Christ for the salvation of his soul.

If a person makes a profession of faith in Christ, it is appropriate to rejoice with him, but not without further admonition and warning. He must be encouraged by the truth that if he has genuinely repented and believed, he is saved. However, he must also be instructed that if his conversion is genuine, it will be further validated by his continuation in the things of God. He must know that salvation is not a one-time vaccination that no longer requires attention. If a person has truly repented unto salvation, he will continue repenting and growing in an ever-deepening

---

14. John 1:12.

repentance throughout his life. If he has truly believed unto salvation, he will continue believing and growing in dependence upon God. In other words, the evidence that God has truly begun a work in a person's life through conversion is that He continues working in him throughout the entirety of his life. If after a supposed conversion experience a person returns to apathy in the things of God, makes no progress in godliness, and abandons the community of faith, he has no biblical grounds for confidence that his conversion experience was genuine or that he was ever a child of God. It is a great and dangerous error to send new converts away without such a warning.

WRONG QUESTIONS AND MISPLACED TRUST

No one will argue that numerous individuals in the street and pew have acknowledged their sin, made a decision, and prayed to receive Christ but show little or no fruit of genuine conversion. Although the Scriptures teach that there will be false professions of faith, even under the best of preaching,[15] the sheer number of continuously carnal professing Christians is absolutely overwhelming. What could be the reason for this malady?

As we survey the vast expanse of evangelical Christianity and scrutinize the most popular methodologies of personal and mass evangelism, we must conclude that we are simply reaping the harvest of a superficial gospel and an even more superficial invitation of sinners to Christ. As a result, the majority of those who have raised hands, walked aisles, made decisions, and prayed sinner's prayers were never truly converted. They simply gave the right answers to all the wrong questions and were granted false assurance by stewards of the gospel who should have known better. Their foundation is sand, and their end will be destruction. We must tell them that people are not saved by merely making decisions and praying prayers but by looking to Christ. We must warn them that the evidence of past conversion is the continuation of that work of conversion into the present: the God who saves also sanctifies. If their past decision does not continue to impact their present life, it is likely that their hope is in vain!

---

15. Matthew 13:3–23.

CHAPTER SIXTEEN

The Small Gate

Enter by the narrow gate; for wide is the gate and broad is the way that leads to destruction, and there are many who go in by it. Because narrow is the gate and difficult is the way which leads to life, and there are few who find it.

—Matthew 7:13–14

Many consider the Sermon on the Mount to be the Christian manifesto. In it is found some of the most beautiful teachings of Christ, the loftiest virtues of the Christian faith, and the most radical demands of Christian discipleship. It is a singular sermon of more weight than any of us could ever comprehend in a Christian lifetime.

Matthew 7:13–14 marks the beginning of the end of this magnificent sermon. It is a fitting conclusion—a straightforward, even pungent warning regarding the seriousness of Christ's words and their eternal implications. It proves to us that this sermon is not dealing in trivialities, but with the weightiest matters of human existence. Eternity is stamped on every word as Christ comes to the podium and deals with the issues of heaven and hell, everlasting life and everlasting destruction. He speaks with a terrible solemnity, as one having the greatest authority to deal with such eternal matters.[1] As we read it, we are astonished[2] and convinced that never was there a greater time for us to heed the testimony of the Father concerning His Son: "This is My beloved Son. Hear Him!" (Mark 9:7).

In this text and those to follow in Matthew 7, we will be confronted with a series of contrasts. We will discover that there are two gates and

---

1. Matthew 7:29.
2. Matthew 7:28.

two ways: one leads to life and the other to destruction. We will meet two kinds of preachers: one who feeds the sheep, and the other who ravishes them (v. 15). We will come upon two kinds of trees: a good tree that bears good fruit and receives pruning, and a bad tree that bears bad fruit and is cut down and thrown into the fire (vv. 16–20). We will be introduced to two kinds of professing Christians: one who acknowledges the lordship of Christ and enters into the kingdom of heaven, and one who confesses the same Lord but is barred from entrance and cast into hell (vv. 21–23). Finally, we will encounter two builders: one who builds upon the rock and is saved from the raging deluge of God's wrath, and another who builds upon the sand and is engulfed in final and irrevocable judgment.

THE GATE IS CHRIST

Our text begins with the solemn and firm exhortation to "enter by the narrow gate." There are only five words in this command, but they are weighty beyond measure and demand our full attention. On hearing them, we find ourselves in the spotlight with no opportunity of escape. We are at a crossroad, a deciding point. We cannot pretend that we have not heard, nor can we delay the choice or relegate it to the authority of another. We must make a great determination between life and death, heaven and hell, Christ and every other supposed door back to God. As we stand in that "valley of decision," we are surrounded by countless gates, each with its own hawkers vying for our attention, yet through the noise we hear the one great voice of Christ (Joel 3:14). He is directing us to Himself, the only true gate, the only breach in the prison wall through which we might pass to freedom. He made the breach; He is the breach, the door through which one might enter and be saved.[3] We must make a decision. Whom will we hear? Whom will we believe? Again, the words of God the Father ring in our ears, "Hear Him!" (Matt. 17:5).

If there is one undeniable truth that stands above all debate in the New Testament, it is that Jesus Christ of Nazareth is "the way, the truth, and the life," and "no one comes to the Father except through Him" (John 14:6). "There is one God and one Mediator between God and men, the Man Christ Jesus" (1 Tim. 2:5). "There is no other name under heaven given among men by which we must be saved" (Acts 4:12). This is the

---

3. John 10:9.

great truth and scandal of Christ and Christianity. Jesus of Nazareth stands before the entire world and cries out, "I, even I, am the LORD, and besides Me there is no savior" (Isa. 43:11). It matters little that the world covers its ears, rends it clothing, and gnashes its teeth. God settled the matter long ago in the eternal and secret counsels of God.

Christianity needs only to move a few inches toward a more ecumenical position to become one of the most beloved religions on the face of the earth. Only one tiny alteration is required to end the war between Christianity and the modern mind and to usher in an era of blessed coexistence and mutual affirmation: we must change the definite article *the* for the indefinite article *a* and proclaim Christ as a savior of the world rather than the Savior to the exclusion of all others. If we would compromise on this one matter, Christ would have a greater hearing, and we would become the delight of those who now oppose us and berate us as narrow-minded bigots and public enemies of the global community. If we made this one, seemingly small concession, we might even suppose that the world would allow Jesus to sit at the head of its pantheon of saviors and to make us important members in its cabinet. Why then will Christians not concede on this one, seemingly trite matter? Why will they choose social alienation, persecution, and death rather than move away from their exclusivity? It is enough to bewilder and enrage the most tolerant of postmodern minds.

However, the answer is simple: Christianity is an all-or-nothing religion. The man Jesus of Nazareth was either the Son of God or a blasphemer; the greatest revelation of truth, or the most heinous liar who ever walked the planet; the Savior of the world or a shameless charlatan. Unlike other religions, Christianity is not primarily a religion revolving around teachings or ethical codes that disciples can follow in part or in whole. Instead it is a religion that is founded upon a person who either is or is not who He says He is. In the now famous trilemma of C. S. Lewis, Jesus of Nazareth is lunatic, liar, or Lord. No room is allowed for the patronizing of His person or finding some middle ground between what the Scriptures claim Him to be and any other view, no matter how small the deviation.[4]

---

4. C. S. Lewis wrote: "I am trying here to prevent anyone saying the really foolish thing that people often say about Him: 'I'm ready to accept Jesus as a great moral teacher, but I don't accept His claim to be God.' That is the one thing we must not say. A man who was merely a man and said the sort of things Jesus said would not be a great moral teacher. He would either be a lunatic—on a level with the man who says he is a poached egg—or else he would be the Devil of Hell. You must make your choice. Either this man

To be Christian, we must stand firm on this point. Neither Christ's person nor His teachings allow for concessions or compromises. If we long for the approval of the world, then we must lose the approval of Christ. If we seek to gain our life in this age, we must forfeit it in the next.[5]

If we have truly become Christians, we recognize the danger of giving in to any demand that the world might make upon us regarding the uniqueness of Christ's person and work. Furthermore, we recognize that there is no compelling reason to do so apart from our own self-preservation or to make ourselves more acceptable to this evil age.[6] The Christ we know and serve has no need to make a bargain with this world or to lobby for position among the other so-called saviors and lords. He is the Savior of the world and the Lord of all.[7] From the Scriptures, we know that God has made this Jesus, whom we crucified, to be both Lord and Christ; that He has seated Him at His right hand, far above all rule, authority, power, dominion, and every name that is named, not only in this age but also in the one to come; that He has declared that every knee will bow and every tongue will confess that Jesus of Nazareth is Lord.[8] Though all the world rage against this truth, God's decree remains unaltered. God has declared Christ's sonship through word and power.[9] He has installed Him as Savior and king in Zion, and He has given Him the nations as His inheritance and the ends of the earth as His possession.[10]

The evangelical community still has much reason to rejoice about the proclamation of Christ as the narrow gate of salvation. The majority of confessing evangelicals holds fast to one of the greatest and most essential columns of the Christian faith: *solus Christus*, or Christ alone. Although evangelicals are often at odds with one another about so many things, some trivial and some of excruciating importance, we can rejoice that most are convinced and willing to suffer for this one great truth: the

---

was, and is, the Son of God: or else a madman or something worse.... You can shut Him up for a fool, you can spit at Him and kill Him as a demon; or you can fall at His feet and call Him Lord and God. But let us not come up with any patronising nonsense about His being a great human teacher. He has not left that open to us. He did not intend to." *Mere Christianity* (Westwood, N.J.: Barbour and Company, 1943), 45.

5. Matthew 10:33, 39; 2 Timothy 2:12.
6. Galatians 1:4.
7. John 4:42; Acts 10:36; Romans 10:12.
8. Acts 2:36; Ephesians 1:20–22; Philippians 2:10–11.
9. Psalm 2:7; Matthew 3:17; 17:5; Romans 1:4.
10. Psalm 2:6, 8.

uniqueness of Christ's person and office. Christ is Lord, and there is no savior besides Him.[11]

However, we must always be vigilant, for some marks of erosion indicate compromise even among confessing evangelicals. To the contemporary postmodern mind, nothing is more brutally scandalous than to make a claim of truth to the exclusion of others. Every realm of culture, education, politics, economics, and even most religions have now come to believe that a peaceful coexistence is only possible in a society where everyone agrees or at least no one is wrong. Therefore, any individual or community that holds to an absolute standard of truth and seeks to point others to that standard is bigoted, discriminatory, deserving of ridicule, and requiring censure. We should not underestimate the power of this new spirit of the age. As it grows it will not only seek to misrepresent and marginalize those who preach Christ alone, but it will also seek to coerce and censure them to the point of silence.

As Christians, we must realize that the kingdom of heaven has to do with the mind, the heart, and the conscience. We must never oppose the hostile culture that surrounds us with anything other than the truth of the gospel, the power of prayer, and the influence of a righteous life. At the same time, we must not give way to the increasing opposition or the temptation of self-preservation. Furthermore, we must not believe the lie that has become prevalent among evangelicals that we can repackage the gospel to make it less offensive without losing its essential content. This is a great deception put forth by people whose weak theology does not teach them to fear God or the admonition that warns, "But even if we, or an angel from heaven, preach any other gospel to you than what we have preached to you, let him be accursed" (Gal. 1:8). Although our position is intolerable to a culture that prides itself on its tolerance, although it creates for us the greatest hardships, and although it exposes us to the reproach of the majority, we must advance against the current. Like the faithful saints who have gone before us, we cannot submit our proclamation to the counsel of a godless culture. We must stand upon Scripture. We must stand for Christ. We cannot and must not retract.[12] To diminish the supremacy and uniqueness of Christ is to deny Him.

---

11. Isaiah 43:11.

12. From Martin Luther's famous declaration at the Diet of Worms in 1521: "I cannot submit my faith either to the Pope or to the Councils, because it is clear as day they have

A VIOLENT ENTRY

Christ is the narrow gate that alone leads to salvation, and we must consider our response to this truth. We are commanded to enter through Him. The command is translated from the Greek word *eisérchomai*, which denotes the act of entering into something. The verb is a command and requires obedience on the part of the hearer. It is also found in the aorist tense, denoting a singular rather than continuous action. The idea is that the hearers are to make a decision or to act decisively in response to Christ's teaching. We would do well to remember that Christ is not a philosopher to be pondered, but the Lord incarnate who demands to be heard and obeyed. Only one door leading to salvation has opened for mankind for a limited time. People are therefore admonished to enter into it with the greatest sense of urgency and diligence. If we can imagine the diligence—even violence—with which people would have fought to enter into the ark had they believed Noah's report, then we have some idea of the urgency with which people should seek to enter into the narrow gate!

The sense of urgency and diligence in our text becomes even more apparent in light of a similar admonition given by Jesus in the gospel of Luke. The Scriptures tell us that while Jesus was teaching throughout the villages, someone said to Him, "Lord, are there few who are saved?" (Luke 13:22). He responded with an indirect but unmistakable affirmation through the following admonition: "Strive to enter through the narrow gate, for many, I say to you, will seek to enter and will not be able" (Luke 13:24).

Jesus' words have both an admonition and a warning. First, He admonishes us to "strive to enter through the narrow gate." "Strive" is translated from the Greek verb *agonízomai*, from which we derive the English word *agonize*, and it means to struggle, fight, labor fervently, or endeavor to do something with strenuous zeal. It originally meant to enter a contest or to contend in the gymnastic games, and was often used in regard to fighting against adversaries or struggling against difficulties and dangers. A related term, *agonía*, is used to describe Christ's struggle in Gethsemane.[13] From this we may properly conclude that entering into

---

frequently erred and contradicted each other. Unless therefore, I am convinced by the testimony of Scripture...I can and will not retract.... Here I stand.... I can do no other. So help me God, amen!"

13. Luke 22:44.

the kingdom through the narrow door, which is Christ, will be anything but easy. Though we enter by repentance and faith, it will be a struggle and involve striving.

Second, Jesus not only admonishes us to enter in with the greatest striving but He also warns us that many "will seek to enter and will not be able." This is an important truth that has often been grossly misunderstood. Jesus is not teaching that many will want to be saved but are not good enough. Rather, He is explaining that although many will desire the promises and benefits of the kingdom, they will be deterred from responding to the call of salvation because of their apathy, hardness of heart, desire for self-preservation, and love for the world. The self-denial that is required and the trials, persecutions, and difficulties associated with the kingdom will deter all but the most desperate from truly entering in. John MacArthur grasps something of the meaning of Christ's words when he writes:

> Christ is not suggesting that anyone could merit heaven by striving for it. No matter how rigorously they labored, sinners could never save themselves. Salvation is solely by grace, not by works. But entering the narrow gate is nonetheless difficult because it costs in terms of human pride, because of the sinner's natural love for sin, and because of the world's and Satan's opposition to the truth.[14]

The idea that it is easy to be saved is totally foreign to the Scriptures and to most respected theologians and ministers of church history. William Hendriksen writes,

> It is clear, therefore, that our Lord does not follow the method that is used by certain self-styled revivalists, who speak as if "getting saved" is one of the easiest things in the world. Jesus, on the contrary, pictures entrance into the kingdom as being, on the one hand, most desirable; yet, on the other, not at all easy. The entrance-gate is narrow. It must be "found." And the road with which it is linked is "constricted." ...Is it not true that the really great evangelists—think of Whitefield, Spurgeon, and their worthy present day followers— stressed and are stressing this same truth?[15]

---

14. John MacArthur, *MacArthur Study Bible*, 1542.
15. William Hendriksen, *New Testament Commentary: Exposition of the Gospel According to Matthew* (Grand Rapids: Baker, 1973), 367.

Not only is it *not* easy to be saved but it is an absolute impossibility apart from the power of God. In fact, it is easier for a camel to pass through the eye of a needle than it is for a man to be converted.[16] Although all conversion experiences are distinct and vary in degrees of personal struggle, the Scriptures portray conversion as a difficult thing that requires a great determination and decisiveness on the seeker's part. The following texts are particularly helpful in illustrating this truth:

> "And from the days of John the Baptist until now the kingdom of heaven suffers violence, and the violent take it by force." (Matt. 11:12)[17]

> "The law and the prophets were until John. Since that time the kingdom of God has been preached, and everyone is pressing into it." (Luke 16:16)

As the kingdom of heaven advances throughout the world and in each successive generation, some people seek to suppress it violently, and others seek to enter into it with equal, if not greater violence. The truth we should glean is that the kingdom of heaven does not belong to the passive, apathetic, or unconcerned but to those who earnestly and decisively will and act to enter into it by faith. This does not mean that people gain the kingdom by strength of will or the stamina of self-discipline and determination. Jesus is not teaching that His kingdom belongs only to the strong; in fact, He is teaching just the opposite.

The urgency, earnestness, and even violence by which people enter into the kingdom is the result of a twofold work of the Spirit of God. First, the Spirit awakens a person to his total inability to save himself, thus creating in him a violent desperation to gain the only one who can save him: Jesus Christ. Under normal circumstances, a slightly built and physically weak man presents little danger to three strong and highly trained athletes. However, if the man were drowning in the sea and going down for the third time, he would present the greatest danger to all three. Out of sheer desperation, in light of his impending doom, the weakling would have the strength and determination to lay hold of any who came within arm's length. Driven by fear, he would cling

---

16. Matthew 19:24; Mark 10:25; Luke 18:25.

17. Debate continues with regard to Christ's exact meaning in this text and Luke 16:16. Although a variety of interpretations has been put forth, the most prevalent is the one applied here: that those who truly enter into the kingdom are marked by earnestness, determination, and zeal born out of desperation to be saved.

with a violence that the strongest man could not overcome. His relentless tenacity would not be the result of some physical trait or virtue in his character but the result of need. In the midst of certain drowning and death, he has found one hope of salvation from which he cannot be pried, even with the greatest violence.[18] In the same way, it is a person's recognition of his weakness or total inability to save himself that makes him fight any and all who would oppose him on his way to entering through the narrow gate.

Second, the Spirit of God regenerates a person's heart and mind so that he sees Christ as precious beyond all things combined, thus creating in him a violent desperation to have Him above all else. By new and holy affections, a person is driven to possess what has become for him the irresistible beauty of Christ. He must have Christ and Christ alone! Though he were given life without end in a perfect state and granted every created beauty for his eternal pleasure, if Christ is absent he will see himself as doomed to the misery of eternal hell. By the recreating and regenerating work of the Spirit of God, he has been awakened to the excellency of Christ, and nothing else, even in the highest heavens, can now satisfy him. All is twisted, shadowed, and soiled in comparison to Christ. In the words of John Flavel:

> O fair sun, and fair moon, and fair stars, and fair flowers, and fair roses, and fair lilies, and fair creatures! But, O ten thousand, thousand times fairer Lord Jesus! Alas, I wronged Him in making the comparison this way. O black sun and moon; but O fair Lord Jesus! O black flowers, and black lilies and roses; but O fair, fair, ever fair Lord Jesus! O all fair things, black, deformed, and without beauty, when Ye are set beside the fairest Lord Jesus! O black heaven, but O fair Christ! O black angels, but O surpassingly fair Lord Jesus.[19]

By the Spirit's doing, a person is made violent, even recklessly violent, by twin motivations that could not be more completely opposite: one is a repugnant terror and the other an irresistible beauty. Yet, in the end, the person would prefer the terrors of hell if he could only look upon the face of Christ rather than have the glories of heaven without a glimpse of that face.

---

18. Pastor Charles Leiter, conversation with the author.
19. "The Life of John Flavel," in *The Works of John Flavel* (London: Banner of Truth, 1968), 1: ixx–xx.

Before God dealt with us, we were all apathetic regarding the great realities of religion. Then, through circumstances or preaching or both, we were awakened to our sin and the emptiness of our lives. We saw ourselves as incapable of fulfilling the law's demands and without any power to free ourselves from certain judgment. At that point, the Spirit of God revealed Christ to us, and we saw Him as a pearl of great price that we had to possess at any cost. We did not think of bargaining to lower the price but were willing to lose all, even to forsake all, in order that we might have Him.[20] Now that we are His and He is ours and we have tasted and seen that the Lord is good, we cannot—will not—let Him go.[21] The reality of our utter inability to save ourselves combined with the knowledge that He alone has the words of eternal life causes us to cling to Him with an unwavering violence.[22] We would sooner release our grasp and plummet to our death in a rocky chasm than let go of Christ. We would rather be adrift without aid in the midst of the North Atlantic than be for one moment without Him. We know that the sharpest stones and the most violent seas are nothing compared to the wrath of God that awaits those without Christ. Furthermore, now that we have tasted and seen that the Lord is good, now that we have beheld His beauty, it is no longer the fear of wrath that causes us to cling to Him, but the magnificence and excellency of His person.[23] Our regenerated heart and newfound holy affections must have Him. We simply cannot live without Him except in the greatest of misery. Thus, our violence comes from desperation, and our desperation from our need and want of Him.

CUTTING OUR WAY THROUGH

So far we have considered that which creates a holy violence, earnestness, and urgency in the hearts of those who are truly seeking salvation, but now we must consider why these things are so necessary. The answer is that there are formidable foes and daunting obstacles that stand between the awakened sinner and the small gate through which he must pass.

This truth is beautifully and powerfully illustrated in *Pilgrim's Progress*. Christian, the main character, is awakened to the doom that is to fall

---

20. Matthew 13:45–46.
21. Psalm 34:8.
22. John 6:68.
23. Psalm 27:4.

upon the City of Destruction. In the midst of his despair, he is directed by Evangelist to the house of the Interpreter, where he is shown many marvelous scenes, one of which sheds important light upon the truths we are now considering. Bunyan writes:

> Then the Interpreter took Christian, and led him up towards the door of the palace. At the door stood a great company of men who desired to go in, but dared not; while at a little distance from the door, at a table, with a book and pen before him, sat a man taking down the name of any who should enter there. He saw also that in the doorway stood many men in armor to protect it, ready to do what hurt and mischief they could to the men that would enter. Now Christian was amazed.
>
> At last, when every man stayed back for fear of the armed men, Christian saw a strong and determined-looking man come up to the man that sat there to write, saying, "Set down my name, sir." And when he had done this, the man drew his sword and put a helmet upon his head and rushed toward the armed men, who attacked him with deadly force; but the man, not at all discouraged, cut and hacked fiercely. So after he had received and given many wounds to those that attempted to keep him out, he cut his way through them all and pressed forward into the palace, at which there was a pleasant voice heard from those who walked upon the top of the palace, saying "Come in, come in, eternal glory thou shalt win."[24]

In this scene from the Interpreter's house, Bunyan gives us a vivid picture of the resoluteness that is required to enter into the kingdom. Driven by a desperate need of salvation and by an unquenchable desire for Christ, the awakened sinner must strive against that which opposes him and take hold of Christ by faith. This is Christ's meaning when He admonishes people who would be saved to strive to enter through the narrow door and to press into it with violence.[25]

This idea of pressing into the kingdom was in the common speech of Reformers, Puritans, and early evangelicals. However, such language is now foreign to contemporary Christianity. Salvation and conversion are now described only in terms of those metaphors most palatable to the carnal mind, those that present salvation as a gift to be received as easily as taking an apple from a low-hanging branch or unwrapping a

---

24. Bunyan, *New Pilgrim's Progress*, 43–44.
25. Matthew 11:12; Luke 13:24; 16:16.

gift at Christmas. Although we must adamantly defend and boldly proclaim that salvation is a free gift to be received by all, such metaphors are incomplete if they stand alone. A coin must have both sides if it is to be of any value. In the same way, the free offer of the gospel must also be accompanied by certain and specific admonitions that call for people to press into the kingdom by faith until they know with utmost certainty that they have passed through the gate and obtained the prize. Regarding this matter, Charles Spurgeon writes:

> Now, our Saviour, when He witnessed all this struggling round about to get near Him, said, "This is just a picture of what is done spiritually by those who will be saved. As you press and throng about Me, and thrust one another with arm and elbow to get within reach of My voice, even so must it be if ye would be saved. For the kingdom of heaven suffereth violence, and the violent take it by force." …Christ pictured to Himself a crowd of souls desiring to get to the living Saviour. He saw them press, and crowd, and throng, and thrust, and tread on one another, in their anxious desire to get at Him. He warned His hearers, that unless they had this earnestness in their souls, they would never reach Him savingly…. Someone may say to me, "Do you want us to understand, that if a man is to be saved he must use violence and vehement earnestness in order to obtain salvation?" I do, most assuredly, for that is the doctrine of the text. Again someone may respond, "I thought it was all the work of God." So it is, from first to last. But when God has begun the work in the soul, the constant effect of God's work in us is to set us working; and where God's Spirit is really striving with us, we shall begin to strive too. This is just a test whereby we may distinguish the men who have received the Spirit of God, from those who have not received it. Those who have received the Spirit in truth are violent men. They have a violent anxiety to be saved, and they violently strive that they may enter in at the strait gate.[26]

Those who would be saved must be marked by the earnestness and resoluteness both Bunyan and Spurgeon depict because even though salvation is free, it is not easy. Many obstacles within and foes without deter sinners from coming to Christ. They must be confronted and overcome

---

26. C. H. Spurgeon, *The New Park Street Pulpit* (Pasadena, Tex.: Pilgrim Publications, 1981), 1:217–18.

with a holy violence. Although these obstacles are almost innumerable, we will consider a few of the most common.

First, those who would come to Christ must strive against the great bane of salvation: their self-righteousness. Salvation is granted only to those who acknowledge their total destitution of saving merit and utter inability to gain a right standing before God. Works and grace, and self-righteousness and a humble saving faith, are diametrically opposed. Those who would come only halfway and seek Christ's aid as a complement to their own merit are as far from salvation as the Pharisee who claims he needs no help at all. In this matter there can be no wavering. The old saints were fond of saying that a person may enter the kingdom in spite of many shortcomings and misdeeds; however, he will not enter in with even one shred of self-righteousness upon his back. To enter in, a person must oppose every attempt to whitewash his tomb. He must strive against and cut through the deception of his own heart, the flesh, the devil, and even the contemporary evangelical community that would tell him that he is not as bad as antiquated Puritan preaching would tell him.

Second, those who would come to Christ must strive against the desire for autonomy. The Scriptures know nothing of a salvation that does not confess Jesus as Lord[27] or acknowledge a genuine confession that does not prove itself in a new, progressive submission to God's will.[28] Those who come to Christ must grapple with both His claim to absolute lordship and His radical demands of discipleship. Those who would be saved must fight their way through some devastating choices. Luke tells us that when Jesus saw the large crowds that were going along with them, He said, "If anyone comes to Me and does not hate his father and mother, wife and children, brothers and sisters, yes, and his own life also, he cannot be My disciple. And whoever does not bear his cross and come after Me cannot be My disciple."[29] Placing such demands on would-be followers was a common practice in Jesus' evangelistic methodology.[30] It was His method of culling the crowd and revealing the violently desperate who had to have Him at all cost. Since modern-day evangelism seems to ignore these demands, the hearers have no reason to grapple with these titanic choices.

---

27. Romans 10:9.
28. Matthew 7:21.
29. Luke 14:26–27.
30. Matthew 10:39; 16:24–26; Mark 8:34–38; Luke 9:23–26.

Thus, multitudes confess Christ and claim salvation without ever having to count the cost and without any real sense of surrendering themselves to His absolute lordship. For this reason, the modern-day gospel proclaims a salvation that is not so much free as it is cheap.

Third, those who would come to Christ must strive against the desire to hold on to certain cherished sins. Matthew tells us of a rich young ruler who was sincere in his religion and moral to a fault. He honestly desired eternal life, but our Lord's unerring discernment saw that he desired one thing more than even the saving of his soul: his riches. One singular sin that he would not acknowledge and denounce kept him from heaven and condemned his soul to hell. Like the eagle who drowns in the depths of the lake because he will not let go of the great fish he covets yet cannot lift, so the sinner will drown in hell because of the sin he will not denounce! It is important to note that Christ was not requiring perfection from the young man. He does not demand that the sinner eradicate his sin before he might be saved but that he recognize his sin, hate it, strive against it, violently cut away at its entanglements, and run to Christ. Abraham had his Isaac to sacrifice, and the rich young ruler had his wealth to surrender. All who would enter through the narrow gate must violently denounce even their most cherished vice, and, in doing so, their earnestness is revealed.

Fourth, those who would come to Christ must strive against the lure of this world. In physical science, the greater an object's mass, the greater its gravitational pull. We may also apply this truth to the spiritual realm. The great mass of fallen humanity, with its ideas, attitudes, and deeds, exercises a great influence upon the seeker. If he is to come to Christ, he must wrench himself away from everything in the world that would oppose him. He must swim against the current while those drifting in the opposite direction reach out to pull him back. Bunyan marvelously illustrates this truth in *Pilgrim's Progress*. No sooner had Christian determined to flee the City of Destruction than his family, friends, and fellow citizens sought to deter him with lengthy and clever arguments. As he journeyed toward the narrow gate he was met by several personalities who sought to draw him back to the world and turn him from the path that led to the cross. Christian would have been utterly defeated if it had not been for God's providence and the coming of Evangelist, who warned him not to listen and scolded him when he did.

In the same way, those who would seek to be saved through faith in Christ must cut their way through the deceitful temptations and coercions of this present age. They must break league with the world if they are to lay hold of Christ, for the two things are mutually exclusive and greatly opposed. The Scriptures warn us clearly that friendship with the world is hostility to God, and whoever wishes to be a friend of the world makes himself an enemy of God.[31] Thus, the oft-repeated saying for those who desire salvation is, "For what will it profit a man if he gains the whole world, and loses his own soul?"[32]

Fifth, those who would come to Christ must strive against the lies of the enemy, the devil. According to the Scriptures, every person is born entangled in his snares and held captive by him to do his will.[33] When, by God's grace, a person comes to his senses and seeks escape, the devil comes after him like a roaring lion, seeking whom he may devour.[34] If anyone thinks that the devil's chase is only show, he should realize that the devil's den is littered with the dried bones and withered carcasses of countless seekers who gave ear to his lies and perished forever.[35] He was a murderer from the beginning, and his death toll increases every day. He is a liar and the father of lies and the accuser of God and of any who would be reconciled to Him.[36] He has an almost unlimited store of venom prepared for all who set out to find Christ. His arrows drip with poison and are set aflame by the very fires of hell.[37] How could anyone entertain the idea that salvation would be easy with such an enemy of souls lurking about? Like the corrupt religious leaders of Jesus' day, he works to shut the kingdom of heaven in people's faces and opposes all those who try to enter into it.[38] To overcome such violent opposition requires the grace of God, the Word of God, and a holy violence to press in and press through.[39]

Finally, those who would come to Christ must strive against the temptation to give up seeking because of the difficulty of the gospel. This truth is almost unheard of today, so it must be explained carefully. The way of God's providence in the salvation of sinners will remain a

---

31. James 4:4.
32. Mark 8:36.
33. 2 Timothy 2:26.
34. 2 Timothy 2:25–26; 1 Peter 5:8.
35. Matthew 13:19; Mark 4:15.
36. Genesis 3:1, 4–5; John 8:44; Revelation 12:10.
37. Ephesians 6:16.
38. Matthew 23:13.
39. 2 Timothy 2:25–26;1 John 2:14.

mystery until eternity, when He chooses to reveal it. Some people hear the gospel and understand it almost immediately. They take it as their own with full assurance from the first day they hear it. However, others find a much more difficult road. They hear the gospel and are drawn to it with great sincerity. Nevertheless, they struggle to understand it and are unnerved by its demands. They seek genuine repentance and faith and wonder whether they possess either. They study the Scriptures, cry out to God, and examine themselves to see if they are in the faith. They wear themselves out to the point of exhaustion with little or no breakthrough. Like Bunyan's pilgrim, they may often find themselves in the Slough of Despond, overcome with doubt and despair. In this case, they must be counseled carefully and patiently. The evangelist must know when to draw near with a word and when to leave them alone with God. He dare not seek to alleviate their struggle by giving them something to do, such as pray the sinner's prayer, and then pronounce them saved because they have done it.[40] He must encourage them to pore over the promises and seek God in prayer until Christ has opened their minds to understand the Scriptures;[41] until the Father has shed abroad His love into their hearts and declared their adoption;[42] until the Spirit bears witness with their spirit that they are the children of God.[43] Thus, he must encourage them to strive to enter by faith alone through the narrow gate; to strive to enter into their rest in Christ, as the author of the book of Hebrews testifies:

> Therefore, since a promise remains of entering His rest, let us fear lest any of you seem to have come short of it. For indeed the gospel was preached to us as well as to them; but the word which they heard did not profit them, not being mixed with faith in those who heard it. For we who have believed do enter that rest, as He has said:
>
> "So I swore in My wrath,
> 'They shall not enter My rest,'"
> although the works were finished from the foundation
> of the world.[44]

---

40. The practice of leading seekers in the sinner's prayer and pronouncing them saved is based upon a faulty interpretation of texts such as John 1:12, Romans 10:8–9, and Revelation 3:20.

41. Luke 24:45.

42. Romans 5:5; 8:15; Galatians 4:6.

43. Romans 8:16; 1 John 5:10.

44. See also Hebrews 3:18–19; 4:10–11.

The evangelist must maintain a delicate balance. On one hand, some people treat salvation superficially and live their entire life with a false assurance that will result in their final condemnation. They show little evidence of genuine repentance in their conversion experience, and their faith is shallow and misplaced. Furthermore, they show no ongoing evidence of sanctification or any noticeable growth in grace. They simply continue in their evangelical religion with little real concern for eternity and piety and are oblivious to their need to examine themselves to see if they are in the faith.[45]

On the other hand, some people have an equally dangerous imbalance in their theology, and they bolt the doors to heaven and shut themselves out with their severity. They have a high view of salvation and take it as a matter of utmost seriousness. They willingly submit to the biblical admonitions to examine themselves and make their calling and election sure.[46] However, they have set a standard that is beyond the Scriptures. They believe that before they can possess even the slightest degree of assurance they must bear the marks of the most mature Christian. They compare their initial repentance and faith to the Scripture's portrayal of these two doctrines in their most perfect and mature form, and they find themselves wanting. They compare their ongoing sanctification to that which is not obtained by even the most mature Christian, and, again, they find themselves wanting. They labor and strive to reach a moral standard by which they might have some assurance of salvation, and in the process they have turned Christianity into a religion of works. They are no longer looking to Christ but have turned their eyes inward to focus on self and performance. It is a deadly focus!

Obviously, different remedies are required to cure these ailments. The person caught in the first extreme must be confronted with the superficiality of his religion, but the person caught in the second must be confronted with the severity of his. Although the first is more prevalent in our day and age, the second, though appearing more pious, is just as deadly. Over and over evangelists must be faithful to proclaim with a clarion call that salvation is gained when a person recognizes his total inability and looks to Christ alone. They must clearly explain that although our assurance can be weakened or fortified by an appropriate

---

45. 2 Corinthians 13:5.
46. 2 Corinthians 13:5; 2 Peter 1:10.

examination of our present life style, the foundational questions that we must first ask are these: Do we glory in Christ Jesus and put no confidence in the flesh?[47] Have we lost all hope in self? Are we looking to Christ alone? Has Christ become precious to us?

Those who examine themselves with an unbiblical severity need further counsel in the nature of salvation. Although it is popular to say that conversion results in a changed life, it may be more accurate to say that it results in a changing life. Although conversion leads to the immediate change in our standing before God, the transformation of our nature, and the infusion of spiritual life, the outward working of this transformation as a visible reality will take time and be achieved only through many struggles.[48] Although repentance and faith resulting in salvation must be genuine, we should not expect the same depth of brokenness and belief in a new believer that we find in a Christian of forty years. Repentance and faith, like all other Christian virtues, are subject to sanctification. Furthermore, even though the new believer will witness some radical changes in his lifestyle from the beginning, we should not expect the same sanctification from him that we might find in a mature believer. Our assurance of salvation should not be founded upon a comparison of our sanctification with that of other believers, but upon our relying on the merits of Christ alone and our recognition of God's providential and sanctifying work in our lives.[49] We have become His workmanship.

Modern evangelism has a remedy for people who are struggling with assurance. These doubters need only pray the sinner's prayer and stand on the promises. Afterward, if their doubt continues, they should reject it as the false condemnation of the devil. This, however, is a false balm that will bring no lasting cure, and the ministers who apply it are among those who heal the brokenness of God's people superficially. The sinner's conversion should not be treated in such a trite fashion. Much is at stake, and the minister must work with as much earnestness in counseling as the seeker must exhibit in pressing in.

---

47. Philippians 3:3.
48. Romans 5:1; 2 Corinthians 5:17; Ephesians 2:4–5.
49. Philippians 2:12–13; Hebrews 12:5–11.

CONTEMPORARY APPLICATION FOR EVANGELISTS

After the evangelist preaches the gospel, he must make a passionate call for all to come to Christ. However, he must give this call in accordance with the Scriptures. He must not compromise or tone down the demands that Christ places upon those who would enter the kingdom, nor should he set before his listeners a method of salvation and assurance that is unknown to Scripture and foreign to church history. Either of these represents a dangerous tampering with the gospel and will result in an "easy-believism," or what the German martyr Dietrich Bonhoeffer referred to as "cheap grace":

> Cheap grace means grace sold on the market like a cheapjack's[50] wares. The sacraments, the forgiveness of sin, and the consolations of religion are thrown away at cut-rate prices. Grace is represented as the Church's inexhaustible treasury, from which she showers blessings with generous hands, without asking questions or fixing limits. Grace without price; grace without cost! And the essence of grace, we suppose, is that the account has been paid in advance; and, because it has been paid, everything can be had for nothing. Since the cost was infinite, the possibilities of using and spending it are infinite. What would grace be, if it were not cheap?... In such a Church the world finds a cheap covering for its sins; no contrition is required, still less any real desire to be delivered from sin.... Cheap grace means the justification of sin without the justification of the sinner. Grace alone does everything, they say, and so everything can remain as it was before.... Cheap grace is the preaching of forgiveness without requiring repentance, baptism without church discipline, communion without confession, absolution without personal confession. Cheap grace is grace without discipleship, grace without the cross, grace without Jesus Christ, living and incarnate.[51]

In light of Christ's admonitions and warnings, we must ask ourselves, "Why does the grace of modern-day evangelicalism so painfully fit Bonhoeffer's description of cheap grace? Why is the idea of striving and struggling to enter the kingdom so foreign to us? How is it that so many seem to enter the kingdom with ease? The answer is twofold. First, the cost of truly being Christian is rarely mentioned in gospel preaching; therefore, the seeker has no reason to struggle. The hearer has no inward

---

50. A seller of cheap or inferior goods; a hawker at a market or fair.
51. Dietrich Bonhoeffer, *The Cost of Discipleship* (New York: Collier Books, 1963), 45–47.

battle regarding Christ's call because he has not been confronted with the realities of biblical Christianity. The radical demands of Christian discipleship are now replaced with "God loves you and has a wonderful plan for your life." Christianity has been redesigned into a broad way, where nothing need be ventured but everything is gained; where an individual's autonomy is tenaciously defended and biblical commands are mere guidelines subject to culture and conscience; where friendship with the world is not only permitted but encouraged; where the Christian may have dual citizenship and the godly are no longer persecuted.

When the gospel is truly presented, a person comes face-to-face with the battle of the ages: autonomy versus surrendering his will to another; self-preservation versus the danger of opposing the majority; reputation and the approval of men versus being marginalized at best and martyred at worst; holding on to a world that is seen versus setting out in search of a city that has foundations, whose architect and builder is God;[52] and enjoying the passing pleasures of sin versus considering the reproach of Christ greater riches than the treasures of this world.[53]

When the demands of the gospel become part of the gospel presentation, then the gospel will once again be a scandal, and the individual's decision for Christ will be the result of great striving and struggle. Those who are converted will be like Bunyan's man of a stout countenance who fastens his helmet, draws his sword, rushes toward the narrow gate, and fiercely cuts his way through everything of the flesh, the world, and the devil that would oppose him. He will be like a man who wants to build a tower but first sits down and calculates the cost to see if he has enough to complete it.[54] He will be like the king who, before he goes to meet another king in battle, first sits down and considers whether he is strong enough with ten thousand men to encounter the one coming against him with twenty thousand.[55] Furthermore, he will be the opposite of the superficial convert in the parable of the sower. He first hears the word and immediately receives it with joy, yet he has no firm root in himself. His profession is only temporary, and when affliction or persecution arises because of the word, immediately he falls away.[56] The second "hears the

---

52. Hebrews 11:9–10.
53. Hebrews 11:25–26.
54. Luke 14:25–30.
55. Luke 14:31–33.
56. Matthew 13:20–21.

word, and the cares of this world and the deceitfulness of riches choke the word, and he becomes unfruitful" (Matt. 13:22).

Second, so many seem to enter the kingdom with ease because we have replaced Spirit-wrought repentance and faith with empty creedalism and convenient ritual. Therefore the seeker has no need to grapple with the great truths of the gospel or seek to discern whether these truths have become a reality in his life. He is given the ritual of the sinner's prayer to perform and is assured of his salvation because he has performed it. Then, throughout his life, he holds on to that ritual as the basis for his hope of eternal life. For this reason many carnal and worldly people on the street and in the pew are convinced of their right standing before God because of something they did in their past that has little or no impact on their present.

This is where we find the great contrast between the Scriptures and church history on one side and contemporary evangelistic methodology on the other. When evangelism is biblical, the gospel is preached, and people are admonished to repent and believe. Those who manifest an interest in the gospel are taken to the Scriptures for greater clarity regarding the nature of genuine repentance and faith. Furthermore, they are encouraged to examine themselves in light of Scripture to determine whether these twin evangelical graces have become a reality in their hearts. If they find no assurance through the reading of the Scriptures, then the evangelist does not seek to give them assurance by having them perform some evangelistic ritual, "closing the deal," and pronouncing them saved. Rather, he continues to counsel them, pray for them, and—most of all—encourage them to seek God in prayer and in the further reading of Scripture until God Himself has given them the assurance they seek.

This is where the seeker often encounters the greatest battles and finds the greatest need for holy violence. Like the Evangelist of *Pilgrim's Progress*, the modern-day evangelist can only point the pilgrim to the narrow gate; he cannot carry him through it. The pilgrim must fight this battle alone. He must strive against whatever might keep him from surrender. He must wrestle with the Scriptures until he understands them, and grapple with the meaning of repentance and faith until he knows he possesses them. He must even strive with God until God confirms him. The seeker must press on alone until he has found the Lord or been found by Him.

This is when the evangelist will be most tempted to interfere and provide the seeker with some method by which he may gain assurance.

However, any such assurance will be mechanical and natural, and it will thwart the real work of God. The seeker must be left alone to God. He must deal with Christ. He must seriously consider repentance unto salvation and ponder whether such a thing is manifest in his own life. He must consider the promises of God and strive to lay hold on them until a work of the Spirit brings biblical assurance to his soul, the love of God is shed abroad in his heart, and the Spirit of adoption causes him to cry out, "Abba, Father."[57]

After people have made a profession of faith, the biblical evangelist should encourage them with great joy, but not without warning. They must know that if their present assurance is genuine then they will go on with the Lord and, through many trials, grow in sanctification and conformity to Christ. However, if they turn back to the world or continue in carnality without divine discipline, they must question the genuineness of their profession.[58] They must be all the more diligent to make certain about God's calling and choosing of them.[59] They must test or examine themselves in light of Scripture to see if they are in the faith.[60]

The Spirit's work in an individual's soul is a great mystery that demands our complete trust in God's providence. Some people hear the gospel, repent and believe, and gain an immediate assurance wrought by the Spirit of God. Others fight for days, weeks, or even months before they gain a similar assurance. As those entrusted with the gospel, we must be careful that we deal with each case correctly and with the greatest discernment and patience. It is one thing to lead someone through an evangelistic system and pronounce him saved because of his sincere compliance. It is quite another thing to lead him to the promises of salvation and tarry with him until he has truly entered through the narrow gate and God has granted him the wonderful gift of assurance.

---

57. Romans 5:5; 8:15–16; Galatians 4:6.
58. Hebrews 12:5–8.
59. 2 Peter 1:10.
60. 2 Corinthian 13:5.

CHAPTER SEVENTEEN

The Narrow Way

Enter by the narrow gate; for wide is the gate and broad is the way that leads to destruction, and there are many who go in by it. Because narrow is the gate and difficult is the way which leads to life, and there are few who find it.

—Matthew 7:13–14

Matthew 7:13–14 describes not only a gate but also a way, both of which are small and narrow. From this we understand that conversion is not defined merely by a gate through which a person passes but also by the way in which he walks. When we survey contemporary evangelical preaching, it seems that often only half the story is presented.

By God's grace, most of the evangelical world continues to hold to the truth that Jesus is the only Savior and Mediator between God and men.[1] We can also praise God that most remain steadfast in the doctrines of *sola gratia* and *sola fide,* by grace alone through faith alone.[2] However, although there is a great deal of preaching about how to enter the kingdom, little is said about the evidences that prove a person's entrance. We enter into the kingdom by passing through the narrow gate, but the evidence that we have passed through this gate is that we are now walking in the narrow way.[3] We are justified by faith alone in the person and work of Christ. However, the evidence of our justification is our ongoing sanctification.

---

1. John 14:6; Acts 4:12; 1 Timothy 2:5.

2. Ephesians 2:8–9.

3. William Hendriksen writes, "The order 'gate' followed by 'way' is therefore very natural and makes good sense, especially in view of what is probably the intended meaning: right initial choice (conversion) followed by sanctification; or else, wrong initial choice followed by gradual hardening." *Matthew,* 368–69.

The narrow gate and the narrow way are inseparable.[4] The person who enters through the former will find his life defined by the latter.

THE NARROW WAY DEFINED

The word "way" is translated from the Greek word *hodós*, which denotes literally a natural road or traveled way. Metaphorically it refers to a way of life, a course of conduct, or a way of thinking. The word is used six times in the book of Acts as a synonym for Christianity.[5] Thus, we quickly discover that the Christian faith is more than a past decision to accept Christ. It is an enduring faith that alters the course of a person's life.

The word "narrow" comes from the Greek verb *thlíbo*, which means to press or crush as a worker in a vineyard might press grapes or a crowd of people might crush against one another. In the passive, the word means to experience trouble, difficulty, or affliction.[6] Combined with *hodós*, it refers to a compressed, straitened, or contracted way. Various writers and preachers have illustrated the meaning of this metaphor by painting the picture of a narrow gorge where people can walk only single file. On each side are high walls of sheer rock. The confined nature of the path seems to indicate two important truths about the nature of the Christian life: it is a way defined by the will of God, and it is a way marked by opposition, difficulty, and great struggle.

A Way Defined by God's Will

Those who have passed through the narrow gate will walk in the narrow way. They will not walk aimlessly, nor will they be allowed to wander freely in the Vanity Fair and Killing Fields of this world. Their course will be well defined by the will of God, and they will be guarded by His relentless providence. He will teach them, lead them, empower them to follow, and discipline them when they stray. As Jesus taught, His sheep will hear His voice and *follow Him*.[7]

---

4. Hendriksen writes, "It is clear from the description that these—gate and way—should be combined: narrow gate and constricted way, wide gate and broad or roomy way." *Matthew*, 367.

5. Acts 9:2; 19:9, 23; 22:4; 24:14, 22.

6. The noun *thlipsis* is translated as "tribulation" in Romans 2:9 and 8:35.

7. John 10:27.

The notion of a path marked out by God for the conduct of His people is a common theme throughout the Old Testament Scriptures. It is referred to as the way of the Lord, the way of the righteous, and the path of righteousness.[8] This path is marked out by God's commands, and it is the great litmus test of genuine faith. In the book of Psalms, we discover that the way of the Lord and the way of the righteous are synonymous with the way of God's commandments, statutes, precepts, and testimonies.[9] In addition, this path is well worn and hemmed in on both sides. It is cut into the ground by the countless saints that have trod on it from the beginning of God's dealings with mankind. In the Twenty-Third Psalm, David gloried in the truth that God was leading him in paths of righteousness. The word "path" is translated from the Hebrew word *ma'gal*, which denotes a trench or a long, deep, narrow depression in the ground.

Another important truth about the narrow way is that its markers become clearer and clearer as the saint journeys upon it. The book of Proverbs instructs us that the path of the righteous is like the light of dawn that shines brighter and brighter until the full day.[10] When the new believer first sets his foot on the path, the way is often hard to distinguish. However as he continues to walk, the way becomes more easily discerned. Through the renewing of his mind, he begins to understand what God's will is, that which is "good and acceptable and perfect" (Rom. 12:2). The writer of Hebrews tells us that the new believer who partakes only of milk is not accustomed to the word of righteousness, for he is an infant. But as he matures he goes on to more solid food, and through practice his senses are trained to discern good and evil.[11]

The narrow way is marked out by God's will as revealed in His commandments, statutes, precepts, and wisdom. However, we must be careful to understand all of this within the context of the person of Jesus Christ. Jesus told His disciples that He was the way and the truth and the life, and no one comes to the Father but through Him.[12] Therefore, we must constantly be reminded that in this narrow way we follow a person and not merely a code of conduct or procedural manual for life. Propositional truth is absolutely essential to Christianity, and we have been

---

8. Genesis 18:19; Judges 2:22; Psalms 1:6; 23:3; Proverbs 8:20; 12:28; 16:31; Isaiah 26:7.
9. Psalm 119:14, 27, 32–33.
10. Proverbs 4:18.
11. Hebrews 5:13–14.
12. John 14:6.

given great laws, principles, and wisdom to obey.[13] However, they are not the sum of the Christian faith, and if we view them outside the context of Christ, they can lead us down a dangerous path of legalism and self-righteousness. As Christians, we follow and seek to imitate a person.[14] The propositional truths of Scripture have great value in that they explain to us who Christ is and how we are to follow Him, but they are not an end in themselves and can never be detached from Him without doing the greatest violence to Christianity and the Christian. The gist of this warning is summarized powerfully in Christ's words to those of His day who had reduced the faith of Israel to an empty code of conduct. Jesus said, "You search the Scriptures, for in them you think you have eternal life; and these are they which testify of Me. But you are not willing to come to Me that you may have life" (John 5:39–40). Christ cannot be separated from the instruction and commands of Scripture, but neither can these commands be separated from the person of Christ.

A Way Marked by Difficulty

We have learned that the narrow way is defined by God's will. Now we will turn our attention toward a second and equally important truth: it is a way marked by difficulty and struggle. It is not an easy road!

As we have already stated, the word "narrow" comes from a Greek verb that, in the passive tense, means to experience trouble, difficulty, or affliction. Even a cursory reading of the New Testament reveals that the Christian life is marked by these things. If a striving or holy violence is required to enter into Christianity, we can only assume that an equal if not greater striving is required to continue in it. Anyone preaching anything to the contrary is not a true minister of Christ but a charlatan with something to sell.

One of the greatest marks of the early church was the difficulties and afflictions it suffered. Christ and the writers of the New Testament frequently forewarned both seekers and believers that true discipleship would entail great affliction. Jesus warned His disciples that they

---

13. Propositional truth refers to truth that is revealed or communicated by statements or assertions (e.g., "The LORD is one" [Deut. 6:4]; "Jesus is Lord" [1 Cor. 12:3]; "You shall not take the name of the LORD your God in vain" [Ex. 20:7]).

14. Matthew 4:19; 8:22; 9:9; 10:38; 16:24; 19:21;1 Corinthians 11:1; Ephesians 5:1; 1 Thessalonians 1:6.

would be hated by the world and suffer great tribulation because of it;[15] they would be persecuted, insulted, and slandered;[16] and they would be hunted down, condemned, and killed before governors and kings for His sake.[17] The apostle Paul instructed young Timothy that "all who desire to live godly in Christ Jesus will suffer persecution" (2 Tim. 3:12). To the church in Philippi, he wrote that it had been granted unto them not only to believe in Christ but also to suffer for Christ's sake.[18] He encouraged the disciples in Lystra, Iconium, and Antioch: "We must through many tribulations enter the kingdom of God" (Acts 14:22). The apostle Peter instructed the believers scattered throughout Asia that their suffering was according to the will of God, and they should not be surprised at even the most fiery ordeal as though some strange thing were happening to them.[19] In fact, he instructed them that such suffering was the norm for believers and churches throughout the entire world.[20]

From the Scriptures we understand that the Christian's path is narrow and full of affliction, but trials are not without purpose. God designs our sufferings to refine, transform, and make us like His Son. Through the fiery trials of this world our faith is proven genuine and refined to greater and greater degrees of purity until it is as precious as gold.[21] Furthermore, the various trials and tribulations found in the narrow way lead to greater degrees of Christian virtue. The apostle Paul wrote, "We also glory in tribulations, knowing that tribulation produces perseverance; and perseverance, character; and character, hope" (Rom. 5:3–4). James commanded suffering believers to consider it all joy when they encountered various trials, knowing that the testing of their faith was producing endurance, resulting in their greater sanctification and maturity.[22]

In the midst of suffering, the believer is assured that "we know that all things work together for good to those who love God, to those who are the called according to His purpose" (Rom. 8:28). For this reason, the Christian greatly rejoices even though for a little while he must be distressed

---

15. Matthew 10:22; John 15:18–20; 16:33.
16. Matthew 5:10–12.
17. Matthew 10:22–28; Luke 21:12.
18. Philippians 1:29.
19. 1 Peter 3:17; 4:12, 19.
20. 1 Peter 5:9.
21. 1 Peter 1:6–7.
22. James 1:2–4.

by various trials.[23] He knows that the sufferings of this present time are not worthy to be compared with the glory that is to be revealed to him.[24]

The truth that we are God's workmanship and He who began a good work in us will perfect it is both comforting and disturbing. It is a comfort to know that we will not remain as we are, and yet it is sometimes frightening to think of the fires through which we must pass on the narrow way in order to be rid of what God will not tolerate in us. The Messiah came not only to be a delight to His people but also refiner's fire and fuller's soap. He would sit as a smelter and purifier of silver, and He would purify the sons of Levi and refine them like gold and silver so that they might present to the Lord offerings in righteousness.[25] His work of purification among His people would be so intense that the prophet who foretold His coming asked, "But who can endure the day of His coming? And who can stand when He appears?" (Mal. 3:2). One of the great promises of the Old Testament prophecies was that Messiah would cleanse His people from all their filthiness and idolatry.[26] However, this cleansing would not always come through a tender washing, but often through a scrubbing and a scourging. For this reason, the author of Hebrews writes:

> And you have forgotten the exhortation which speaks to you as to sons:
>
> > "My son, do not despise the chastening of the Lord,
> > Nor be discouraged when you are rebuked by Him;
> > For whom the Lord loves He chastens,
> > And scourges every son whom He receives." (Heb. 12:5–6)

To understand the intensity with which the Lord may deal with His children on the narrow way we must focus upon the following three words from Hebrews 12:5–6: "reprove," "discipline," and "scourge." The word "reprove" is translated from the Greek word *elégcho*, which means to convict of wrongdoing or guilt by means of bringing to the light or exposing. It also generally suggests the bringing of shame upon the person convicted. The word also means to reprehend severely, chide, chasten, or punish. The verb "discipline" is translated from the Greek word *paideúo*, which denotes the instruction and training of children. It

---

23. Romans 5:3; 1 Peter 1:6; 4:12–13.
24. Romans 8:17–18.
25. Malachi 3:1–3.
26. Ezekiel 36:25.

often includes, as in this context, the idea of chastisement with reproofs, admonitions, and scourging. The word "scourges" is translated from the Greek verb *mastigóo*, which means to beat, whip, or lash with a scourge. Such language seems too hard or even immoral for the overly sensitive ears of contemporary evangelicalism. Nevertheless, it is biblical language and a reality to anyone who has walked long enough in the narrow way. In fact, one of the great lessons learned by any true pilgrim of the narrow way is that God will go to the greatest lengths and spare no expense to make His children holy. He loves His children and does not hate them; therefore He does not spare His rod but disciplines them diligently in order to deliver their souls from hell.[27]

By faith, the believer submits to this divine work of discipline and even gives his back to the rod. Although for the moment discipline brings great sorrow and even pain, the Christian knows that afterward it yields the peaceful fruit of righteousness, which the writer of the book of Hebrews points out: "Now no chastening seems to be joyful for the present, but painful; nevertheless, afterward it yields the peaceable fruit of righteousness to those who have been trained by it" (12:11). Furthermore, he knows that whether the scourging comes directly from God's hand or a lesser instrument such as the devil or the world, it is all designed by God and directed by His all-wise and omnipotent will. Samuel Chadwick beautifully illustrates this in an observation of a blacksmith at work:

> The smith holds the glowing metal, turning it lest the stroke fall too often upon the same spot, directing the blows that they may descend at the right moment; turning, tempering, regulating till the metal is fashioned to the desired shape. So God holds the soul and regulates the stroke. Sometimes He makes the Devil His hammerman. Satan strikes to smash. God regulates the stroke, and turns his malice to our perfecting, and the Devil sweats at the task of fashioning saints into the likeness of Christ. At the end of the day we shall find that all life's discipline has worked together with grace, and that we stand complete in our identification with the Son of the Father. The glorious purpose will have been accomplished, and we shall be like Him—"I shall be satisfied when I awake with Thy likeness (Psalm 17:15)."[28]

---

27. Proverbs 13:24; 23:14.
28. Samuel Chadwick, *Humanity and God* (London: Hodder and Stoughton, 1904), 90.

Since God's purpose is His people's good, we seek to walk the narrow way and stay within the safety and blessedness of His will revealed in His commandments and wisdom. Furthermore, we also seek to work out our salvation in fear and trembling, knowing that it is God who is at work in us both to will and to work for His good pleasure.[29] Having such promises as these, we discipline ourselves for the purpose of godliness; we cleanse ourselves from all defilement of the flesh and spirit; we pursue sanctification, without which no one will see the Lord; and we perfect holiness in the fear of God.[30] If God would go to any length and spare no expense to transform us into the image of Christ, then we must strive with the same diligence toward the same great prize. In this narrow way, we must forget what lies behind, reach forward to what lies ahead, and press on toward the goal for the prize of the upward call of God in Christ Jesus.[31]

THE BROAD WAY DEFINED

The adjective "broad" comes from the Greek word *eurúchoros* and denotes that which is spacious, broad, wide, or roomy. In the context of Christ's teaching, the "broad way" is the way of fallen and rebellious humans who have denounced or ignored God's claim upon them, thrown off His law, and sought an existence that is independent and autonomous. Several things should be noted about this broad way and the wide gate that leads to it.

First, the broad way is man's path by default. It is a path upon which every member of fallen humanity is born. The psalmist declared that the wicked are estranged from the womb and go astray from birth.[32] The prophet Isaiah cried out that "all we like sheep have gone astray; we have turned, every one, to his own way" (53:6). Nothing is required and nothing must be done to find the wide gate or enter upon the broad way. It is the boulevard beside which Adam built his house, and it has become the inheritance of his children.[33] No sooner are we born than we find the path by our fallen instincts, and, once found, we discover that it suits our

---

29. Philippians 2:12–13.
30. 2 Corinthians 7:1; 1 Timothy 4:7; Hebrews 12:14.
31. Philippians 3:13–14.
32. Psalm 58:3.
33. Romans 5:12.

nature. No striving is required to enter into it or to continue upon it, but everything is required to turn from it. For this reason, Christ admonishes people to strive with the greatest violence to turn from the broad road that leads to destruction and to enter into the narrow gate that leads to life.

Second, the broad way is the path of autonomy. It is the place where the inhabitants of this world take their stand against the Lord and His Christ, saying, "Let us break Their bonds in pieces and cast away Their cords from us" (Ps. 2:3). It is the place where everyone seeks to do what is right in his own eyes.[34] Those who choose the broad way boast that they have freed themselves from the Tyrant of heaven, but in doing so they have subjected themselves to the tyranny of their own depraved hearts. They have traded a heavenly King for six billion unworthy usurpers whose opinions of the truth are as vague as a morning mist and as numerous as the stars in the heavens. They have traded divine law to be governed by their own lusts and have become an unrestrained people rushing headlong into destruction. For where there is no vision or revelation of the law the people are unrestrained, and the way that seems right to them will always end in death.[35] They have taken God from the equation of life and have made absolute truth an impossibility. For this reason the way of the wicked must be broad, because without a moral compass people are condemned to wander aimlessly without rhyme or reason. In the frightening language of Jude, those who reject God's sovereignty in favor of their own become like clouds without water, carried along by winds; they are wild waves of the sea, casting up their own shame like foam; they are wandering stars, for whom the black darkness has been reserved forever.[36]

Although this language is dark and foreboding, it applies to the churchman as well as to the atheist and infidel. Many sit in our churches as confessed adherents of Christianity, yet their lives are lived out on the broad way. They do not seek to know God's will; they do not desire His commands; they do not look for markers of His providence; and they do not walk circumspectly. What is even more disturbing is that they can rest undisturbed in numerous evangelical churches and sit unconcerned under much evangelical preaching. They make every claim under

---

34. Judges 17:6; 21:25.
35. Proverbs 14:12; 16:25; 29:18.
36. Jude vv. 12–13.

the sun to belong to the kingdom, but their continued pilgrimage on the broad way disproves their claim.

Third, the broad way is the path of self-gratification. It is a walkway for all who would put self before God, this world above the next, the immediate over the eternal, and the carnal in place of the spiritual. It is a boulevard that caters to every carnal desire and aspiration of fallen flesh. The Scriptures tell us that people are by nature, lovers of self, lovers of money, lovers of this world, and lovers of pleasure rather than lovers of God.[37] All these things are found on the broad way, and those who walk it are driven by "the lust of the flesh, the lust of the eyes, and the pride of life" (1 John 2:16). For this reason, the broad way may be described as a continual Vanity Fair similar to the one portrayed in Bunyan's *Pilgrim's Progress*:

> Then I saw in my dream that when Christian and Faithful had emerged from the wilderness, they soon saw a town ahead of them, and the name of that town was Vanity; and at the town there was a fair, called Vanity Fair, which went on all the year long. It was named Vanity Fair because all that was sold there was vain or worthless, and all who came there were vain. As the wise saying goes, "All that cometh is vanity."
>
> This fair was no newly established business, but a thing of long-standing. I will show you how it originally began.
>
> Almost five thousand years ago there were pilgrims walking to the Celestial City, as these two honest persons were; and Beelzebub, Apollyon, and Legion, with their companions, seeing that the pilgrims always passed through this town of Vanity, decided to set up a fair here that would last all year long, where they would sell all sorts of vanity: houses, lands, trades, places, honors, promotions, titles, countries, kingdoms, lusts, pleasures, and delights of all sorts, such as prostitutes, wives, husbands, children, masters, servants, lives, blood, bodies, souls, silver, gold, pearls, and precious stones.
>
> At this fair one could always see jugglers, cheats, games, plays, fools, mimics, tricksters, and scoundrels of every kind.[38]

The broad way is filled with every sort of superficial distraction designed to keep people from concerning themselves with what really matters. It offers temptations that create and increase cravings in carnal

---

37. 2 Timothy 3:2, 4; 1 John 2:15–17.
38. Bunyan, *New Pilgrim's Progress*, 108.

people's hearts while at the same time decreasing their capacity for satisfaction. It ensnares people by gross immoralities of the worst sort and even by good things that become deadly idols when they are set above God. The longer people walk on this boulevard, the farther from God they roam, the more vain they become, and the more barren and fruitless their lives.

When people see things correctly they understand that the chief end of man is to glorify God and to enjoy Him forever, as question 1 of the Westminster Shorter Catechism teaches us. When they turn their hearts from this purpose, they lose their divinely appointed dignity. They were created to know God and to explore the infinite wonders of His person and works, but they have chosen to wallow with swine and play with trinkets. They have chosen the downward spiral of the broad road the apostle Paul describes in the first chapter of Romans: "although they knew God, they did not glorify Him as God, nor were thankful, but became futile in their thoughts, and their foolish hearts were darkened. Professing to be wise, they became fools, and changed the glory of the incorruptible God into an image made like corruptible man—and birds and four-footed animals and creeping things" (vv. 21–23).

We live in a culture of men with voracious appetites for all that is carnal and vain. They are described in Scripture as those "whose god is their belly, and whose glory is in their shame—who set their mind on earthly things" (Phil. 3:19). They have traded the eternal for the temporal, heaven for earth, and God for self. They walk the broad road, and they spend their money for what is not bread and their wages for what does not satisfy.[39]

The great mass of humanity, including many who identify themselves with Christ, is on the broad road that leads to destruction. Increasing the problem is that few churches sound the clarion call or warn the wicked of their impending doom. Not only is the broad road of self-gratification not denounced—it is actually defended and promoted. It is even used as a means to attract the carnal multitudes to the Sunday service. Many congregations have become nothing more than a Vanity Fair, and their preachers are nothing more than hawkers of cheap merchandise. Using cleaver sermonettes like pickaxes and spades, they have redirected the broad way so that the carnal multitudes that attend

---

39. Isaiah 55:2.

their churches can pour into heaven as easily as the godly types who take the narrower route. Theirs is a salvation without crosses, afflictions, persecutions, or self-denial. They offer a religion of self-realization and self-promotion, a business venture with God in which a person can keep wealth, luxury, extravagance, and ease-of-life as long as he tithes ten percent. This pilgrimage occurs in a broad and spacious lane where the supposed redeemed walk arm in arm with the world, the grace of God is turned into licentiousness, and the lordship of Jesus Christ is denied.[40] These things must not be! May God once again grant us preachers and shepherds with true instruction in their mouths and no unrighteousness on their lips, who walk with God in peace and turn many back from iniquity.[41] Let us stand by the gates and cry out to all, "And the world is passing away, and the lust of it; but he who does the will of God abides forever" (1 John 2:17).

Fourth, the broad way is the path of least resistance. It is a proverbial "going with the flow." To begin with, there is no opposition from flesh on the broad way. We do not have to strive to enter in. As we have already stated, we find ourselves there by default. We were born in sin, estranged from the womb, and go astray from birth.[42] For this reason, our fallen flesh finds affinity with every fellow rebel it meets on the broad way and heartily approves of every wrong attitude and activity.[43] We must remember that fallen flesh is hostile toward God and cannot please Him.[44] However, it loves the world and willingly harkens to its voice. The flesh needs no prompting to give free rein to its lust and follow the broad road wherever it leads. Therefore, those who would seek to enter upon the road will find no enemy in their flesh, but only a deceptive ally.

Likewise, there is no opposition from the world on the broad way. William Hendriksen writes, "The signs along this wide avenue read, 'Welcome to each of you and to all your friends, the more the merrier. Travel as you wish and as fast as you wish. There are no restrictions.'" [45] Those who walk on the broad way are on the world's boulevard. It is humanity's route, the road of brotherhood, inclusivity, and tolerance. It is

---

40. Jude v. 4.
41. Malachi 2:6.
42. Psalms 51:5; 58:3.
43. Romans 1:32.
44. Romans 8:7–8.
45. Hendricksen, *Matthew*, 369.

an unending festival where mutual flattery is demanded, truth is thrown out the window, and no one is allowed to point out that the emperor has no clothes or that the entire parade is headed toward destruction.

The Scriptures teach that the world loves and listens to it own.[46] When the Son of God came to a world He created and a people He had chosen, they would not receive Him.[47] When the time came for an ultimate choice, the world chose one of its own, asking for the pardon of a notorious thief and murderer and demanding the crucifixion of the holy and righteous One, the Prince of Life.[48] The world is a friend to all who would not be a friend of God. Its hostility is reserved only for those who would dare break truce with it, turn from its path, and join league with God.[49]

Furthermore, there is no opposition from the devil on the broad way. In fact, the road was his design and is directed by his will. According to the apostle Paul, to walk in the broad way is to walk "according to the course of this world, according to the prince of the power of the air, the spirit who now works in the sons of disobedience" (Eph. 2:2). Hendriksen writes, "The [broad] 'way' was built by the devil. His followers travel on it."[50] The saint of God who walks the narrow path will constantly be tempted, tried, and even thwarted in his pilgrimage. The devil will oppose him at every turn and seek to undo his every attempt at progress in the faith. If it were not for Christ's protection, the devil would sift him like wheat and crush him until he cursed God.[51] But to those on the broad way, the devil is a friend, at least for a time, for from his lips drip honey, and smoother than oil is his speech, but in the end he is bitter as wormwood and sharp as a two-edged sword.[52] With his many persuasions he entices men; with his flattering lips he seduces them.[53] But his feet go down to death, and his steps take hold of hell.[54] Those who follow him on the broad way are as an ox that goes to the slaughter, as a fool who goes to his punishment in chains, or as a bird that hastens to the snare. They do not know that their choice will cost them their life, for the devil's house

---

46. John 15:19; 1 John 4:5.
47. John 1:11.
48. Matthew 27:16, 21, 26; Mark 15:7, 11, 15; Luke 23:18; John 18:40; Acts 3:14–15.
49. John 15:19.
50. Hendriksen, *Matthew*, 369.
51. Job 2:9–10; Luke 22:31.
52. Proverbs 5:3–4.
53. Proverbs 7:21.
54. Proverbs 5:5.

sinks down to death and his tracks lead to the dead.[55] None who go to him return again, nor do they reach the paths of life.[56]

Fifth, the broad way is the way of increasing darkness. From the book of Proverbs we learn that "the path of the just is like the shining sun, that shines ever brighter unto the perfect day" (4:18). In contrast, "the way of the wicked is like darkness; they do not know what makes them stumble" (4:19). They are darkened in their understanding and excluded from the life of God.[57] In time, their conscience becomes seared as with a branding iron, their moral compass is taken from them, and they are given over to the lusts of their hearts, to impurity and degrading passions.[58] A terrible judgment falls on men and nations with greater frequency than we may discern or have courage to admit. Although we can never give up on God's grace to save even the worst of sinners, we must warn every person on the broad way that each step brings him one step closer to reprobation, to being turned over and placed beyond all retrieval. It is not a place where he will want to be saved but cannot be, but a place where he will no longer care. At this point, his heart will have been turned into a dry husk and his soul will have become so shallow that the diversions of the broad road are all he needs to fill it.

THE CHRISTIAN AND THE FALSE CONVERT

One of the great truths we must gather from these metaphors of a narrow and broad way is that our walk is the evidence of our conversion. Over and over we must reiterate that a person is saved by grace alone through faith alone. Our right standing before God is not the result of any virtue or merit on our part, but it is a gift of God.[59] Nevertheless, we must also understand that those who have been saved by grace through faith have become the workmanship of God. They have been recreated in Christ Jesus for good works, which God in His sovereignty prepared beforehand so that they would walk in them.[60] Salvation is a supernatural work of God whereby the believer becomes a new creature with new and holy

---

55. Proverbs 7:22–23.
56. Proverbs 2:18–19.
57. Ephesians 4:17–19.
58. Romans 1:24, 26; 1 Timothy 4:2.
59. Ephesians 2:8–9.
60. Ephesians 2:10.

affections.[61] These new affections lead the Christian to walk in the narrow way, not as a forced march but with a willing spirit.[62] Through the regenerating work of the Holy Spirit and His indwelling, the believer has been raised to walk in newness of life.[63] He no longer desires to walk as the Gentiles in the futility of their mind and the hardness of their heart, but strives to walk in a manner worthy of the Lord, pleasing Him in all respects, bearing fruit in every good work, and increasing in the knowledge of God.[64] Though he was formerly darkness, now he is light in the Lord and longs to walk as a child of light—to walk as Christ walked and according to His commandments.[65]

This is the doctrine of regeneration that has been all but forgotten within contemporary evangelicalism, and its rediscovery is essential if the church is to once again preach the gospel. We must decry the empty creedalism of our day and explain that those who believe unto salvation have been born again; they have been regenerated; they have become new creatures who will walk in a newness of life.[66] We must regain the truth that the evidence of justification is the ongoing work of sanctification; that the mark that one has passed through the small gate is that he continues on in the narrow way that is according to Christ's commands and in direct conflict with the flesh, the world, and its devil. Justification is by faith, but the equally important doctrines of regeneration and the relentless providence of God ensure that those who are justified will also be sanctified.

Those who profess faith in Christ and walk on the narrow way should be encouraged and comforted regardless of their many weaknesses and much stumbling. But those who make the same confession yet stroll nonchalantly on the broad way, perusing its sights and buying its wares, should be warned of their reprobation and future condemnation. This is the great task of the pastor and evangelist. It has been granted to the minister of God's people not only to proclaim the good news of the grace of God but also to see to it that no one comes short of it.[67]

---

61. 2 Corinthians 5:17.
62. 1 John 5:3.
63. Romans 6:4.
64. Ephesians 4:1, 17–19; Colossians 1:10; 1 Thessalonians 2:12.
65. Ephesians 5:8; 1 John 1:7; 2:6; 2 John 1:6.
66. 1 John 5:1.
67. Hebrews 12:15.

To illustrate and apply the truths we have considered, we will take a brief look at two men: the Christian and the false convert. In the case of the Christian, we find a person walking along the broad path. Either because he has cast off all belief in God or because he has been anesthetized by some form of religion, he has little concern for his soul. One day he hears a preacher calling out to him with the gospel of Jesus Christ. Though he may have heard the message a thousand times before, he hears something of a voice within a voice. He is awakened to the knowledge of God, his dreadful condition, and the merits of Christ's work. This new revelation of the holiness of God exposes his sin, and he is broken over what he has become and done. His repentance, however, is not unto death, but with the greater revelation of God's holiness and his sin; he also sees for the first time in his life the marvelous grace of God in the face of Christ. He therefore runs to Christ by faith and is saved.

Afterward, the reality of his conversion becomes evident. He sees things differently than before. He also loses many of his old affections, which are replaced by new desires to please God and live in conformity to His commands. At the same time, he becomes painfully aware that there is something within him that is still at war with God and every desire for righteousness. There is still an unredeemed aspect of his person that the Scriptures refer to as simply "the flesh." It sets its desire against the Spirit, and they war against each other so that the new believer soon discovers that the Christian life is a struggle.[68] As he begins his journey down the narrow way, the battles rage around and within him. Sometimes grace makes his feet swift, and he seems to make great progress. Other times it seems that for every three steps forward he takes two steps back. At times, he is even tempted to abandon the narrow way, but God's providence has cut the path deep,[69] and he cannot climb out. Although it is difficult to fight against the flesh, the world, and the devil, the Christian finds it impossible to fight against God. By faith in Christ, he is now God's possession and workmanship. At any given moment in his life it may seem that he is going backward and downward, but God's providence assures that over the full length of the journey he will advance. He will

---

68. Galatians 5:17.

69. In Psalm 23:3, the word "path" is translated from the Hebrew word *ma'gal*, which denotes a trench or a long, deep, narrow depression in the ground. It is well worn and hemmed in on both sides.

struggle with sin, and, at times, he may even fall into grievous sin, but he will not stay there. God jealously desires the Spirit, which He has made to dwell in him.[70] The Great Shepherd will seek him out because He will not lose what the Father has given Him.[71] The Father will deal with him as a son and discipline him with great reproofs and even severe scourging that may leave lifelong scars.[72] In the end, God will perfect the work He has begun, until the Christian, one day, is glorified: "For whom He foreknew, He also predestined to be conformed to the image of His Son, that He might be the firstborn among many brethren. Moreover whom He predestined, these He also called; whom He called, these He also justified; and whom He justified, these He also glorified" (Rom. 8:29–31).

The evidence of conversion in the life of the genuine believer is that he continues on the narrow path of God's commands. With every increasing revelation of God's holiness and his sin, he experiences a greater brokenness. Yet this ever-increasing revelation of his weakness and need does not lead him to despair because with it comes an ever-increasing revelation of the grace of God in Christ. At the end of his days, the believer finds himself on the narrow path, more holy, more broken, and with a greater appreciation of Christ and a lesser trust in self than when he first began.

In the case of the false convert, we find a person walking along the same broad path with little concern for his soul. One day he hears a preacher calling out to him with the gospel of Jesus Christ. For some reason, the message draws his interest. In time, he makes a profession of faith in Christ. At this point, there are two possibilities. At least in some evangelical churches, he would be able to continue on in the broad way and still be assured of his conversion experience and hope of eternal life. His unchanged state and little interest in the things of God would simply be attributed to a lack of discipleship. Like many of the other members who might be equally deceived and to whom he might compare himself, he would continue on the broad path of eternal destruction without warning from the shepherds who are responsible for his soul.

However, if his profession of faith was made in a sound church with a biblical gospel and an understanding of genuine conversion, the matter would take a different turn. The individual would be taught the markers

---

70. James 4:5.
71. John 6:39.
72. Hebrews 12:5–11.

of the narrow way and exhorted to walk in it. At this point, he might quickly reject the demands of discipleship and reveal his unconverted state. However, as is often the case, outward changes may appear in his life. He may exhibit a newfound joy and even show signs of true discipleship. He may strive against the flesh and bear all the marks of a true pilgrim on the narrow way. Nevertheless, the true nature of his case will become evident in time. He will begin to wander from the narrow path and eventually turn from it altogether. He may turn to doctrinal error and deny the fundamentals of the faith. He may cease to strive against sin and return to his vices like a dog that returns to its vomit and as a sow, after washing, returns to wallowing in the mire.[73] Like Demas, his ongoing love for this present age may be rekindled, causing him to desert the faith and return to the world.[74] He may simply fall into apathy, a deep lethargic state from which he cannot be awakened. Or finally, he may wander off to another evangelical congregation where carnal people can prosper comfortably.

Although all these tragedies can occur to some degree in the life of a genuine Christian, the marked difference is that in the case of the false convert, there is an absence of God's relentless providence. There is no biblical manifestation of divine discipline. The person is simply allowed to do what he will. He leaves the path and runs from the fold without any divine intervention to hinder him. By his apostasy he is exposed as a false convert or an illegitimate son. This terrifying truth is clearly set forth by the writer of Hebrews: "For what son is there whom a father does not chasten? But if you are without chastening, of which all have become partakers, then you are illegitimate and not sons" (Heb. 12:7–8).

In the parable of the sower, Jesus describes this unconverted person with the greatest precision. First, his heart is like a stony place upon which the seed of the gospel falls. He hears the word and immediately receives it with joy; yet he has no firm root in himself—which means he is not born again—but his receiving is only temporary, and when affliction or persecution arises because of the word, immediately he falls away.[75] Second, his heart is like a thorny place upon which the seed of the gospel falls. He hears the word, then the worry of the world and the

---

73. 2 Peter 2:22.
74. 2 Timothy 4:10.
75. Matthew 13:20–21.

deceitfulness of wealth choke the word, and it becomes unfruitful.[76] In both cases the false convert differs from the Christian in that he never comes to maturity and brings forth fruit that remains.[77] He is like the plant described by the writer of Hebrews that drinks the rain that often falls on it but yields thorns and thistles and ends up being burned.[78] He is like the tree that does not bear good fruit and is cut down and thrown into the fire.[79] One of the most amazing and disturbing truths about the parable of the sower is that of the four individuals described, only the first rejects the gospel outright. The other three make professions of faith, but only one is truly converted.

THE MANY AND THE FEW

As we come to the end of our look at the narrow gate and broad way, we encounter what may be the most shocking truth of all: that many are on the road to destruction, and only a few find the gate and way that lead to life.[80] This truth becomes even more severe when we realize the proper context of Christ's words.

At first glance, we are prone to think that Christ is drawing a distinction between those who make no public identification with Him and those who do. In such a scenario, the atheists, agnostics, pagans, and cultists are on the broad road that leads to destruction, and those who confess Christ are on the narrow way that leads to life. If this were the case, it would still be true that the great majority of humanity is on the road to destruction. However, the circle that Christ is drawing is even more confined than this. In the context, He is not making a contrast between the irreligious and the religious or even between those who profess themselves outside of Christianity and those who claim to be followers of Christ. Instead, He is concerning Himself only with those who claim to be His followers. He is warning that among those who identify themselves with Him and even publicly confess Him to be Lord, only a few will be saved.

This disturbing truth is proven by the texts that follow in which Jesus gives a stern warning to those who suppose themselves to be His

---

76. Matthew 13:22.
77. Matthew 13:23; John 15:16.
78. Hebrews 6:7–8.
79. Matthew 7:19.
80. Matthew 7:13–14.

followers.[81] First, not every prophet who looks Christian is Christian. The validity of his ministry and confession is proven by his fruit, by the conduct of his life.[82] Second, not everyone who emphatically declares Jesus to be Lord or even ministers in His name will enter into the kingdom of heaven.[83] The mark of genuine faith and true conversion is submission to the will of the Father. Finally, not everyone who listens to the teachings of Christ will be saved from the judgment coming upon the world, but only those who not only hear His words but also act upon them.[84]

From these warnings, it is clear that Christ is not dealing with the great mass of humanity that either ignores Him or publicly denounces Him; rather, He is concerning Himself only with those individuals who claim to know Him and who actually make some public identification with Him. It is among these that only a few will be saved. The rest are like the man who was unprepared in the parable of the marriage feast.[85] He had made a haphazard response to the invitation but did not see fit to obtain the proper clothing so that he could participate in the wedding. Therefore, the king had him bound hand and foot and cast out into darkness. In the same way, Jesus warns that there will be countless individuals who have made some response to the gospel call, yet they were never truly converted, and the true evidences of conversion were never a characteristic of their lives. Although they responded to a degree, although they called Him Lord and even ministered in His name, they will be cast "into outer darkness; there will be weeping and gnashing of teeth." For this reason, Jesus warned that "many are called, but few are chosen" (Matt. 22:13–14).

This is a warning we must heed. We cannot bury our heads in the sand and pretend it is not there. We cannot ignore the reality of the evangelical community in the West. Numerous individuals confess Christ as Lord and participate in every manner of evangelical activity from week to week, and yet their lives are marked by the broad way. They have little or no sense of calling, striving, sacrifice, the renouncing of sin, the shunning of the world, or the pursuit of righteousness. We have devolved into a grotesque and hollow form of what ought to be, and yet now all has

---

81. Matthew 7:15–27.
82. Matthew 7:15–20.
83. Matthew 7:21–23.
84. Matthew 7:24–27.
85. Matthew 22:11–14.

become so common that few even seem to notice. Evangelicalism no longer warns against the Vanity Fair of this world; it has become one of its main attractions. Perhaps the greatest sin of all is that this has happened not in spite of the pulpit but because of it. The contemporary minister is no longer a restraint against these things but often the catalyst for them. Preaching is now carried out by life coaches who teach people principles that they might have their best life now. Church growth experts instruct churches in the matter of how to use carnal means to attract carnal people and to keep them in the congregation by ever-increasing carnality. Evangelism and mission experts have so contextualized the gospel in order to make it accessible and inoffensive to culture that there is no longer much, if any, difference between the two. All the while, multitudes of people who confess Jesus as Lord are drawing ever closer to the day when they will stand before Him and hear, "I never knew you; depart from Me, you who practice lawlessness."

In the midst of all our evangelical noise and confusion and our great boasts regarding the multitudes that stream into our services, we would do well to ponder these truths and this statement from New Testament scholar Craig Blomberg: "The percentage of true believers in places and times in which being 'Christian' is popular is perhaps not that different from the percentage of Christians in times of persecution, when few dare to profess who are not deeply committed."[86]

LIFE AND DEATH

True Christianity is not about trivialities. It is about life and death, heaven and hell, eternal bliss in the presence of God or an eternal existence that horrifies beyond description. Christianity is a religion where the irrevocable destinies of human beings hang in the balance. It is therefore a most serious matter.

In Matthew 7:13–14, Jesus contrasts "life" with "destruction." The word "life" is translated from the Greek word *zoe*. In the context of all of Christ's teaching and that of the New Testament writers, we can conclude that He is not merely speaking of a physical existence or an existence of endless duration. Instead, He is referring to eternal life, that quality of

---

86. Craig Blomberg, *The New American Commentary: Matthew* (Nashville, Tenn.: Broadman, 1992), 132.

life that comes from an intimate and personal relationship with God.[87] It is a relationship that is free, full, and unhindered by the separation and death caused by sin.[88] It is a filial relationship in which the believer is granted the privilege and blessing of sonship.[89] In summary, it is a life of endless duration in the favorable presence of God, and it is granted in and through the person and work of Jesus Christ.[90]

In contrast to "life" is the word "destruction." It is derived from the Greek word *apóleia*, which may also be translated "ruin" or "perdition." Taken in the context of Christ's teaching and that of the New Testament, we can conclude that it does not refer to the termination of personal existence but to eternal or endless punishment in hell. Although a person may have objections to the doctrine of endless punishment and may disregard the New Testament as a flawed document, he cannot reasonably deny that this is its clear teaching. Eternal life and eternal destruction go hand-in-hand. This truth is clearly seen in Christ's description of the final judgment, where He declared, "[The wicked] will go away into everlasting punishment, but the righteous into eternal life" (Matt. 25:46). If the "eternal punishment" of the wicked in hell is not of infinite duration, then neither can we assume that the bliss of the redeemed in heaven is without end.[91]

Hell is the final and full manifestation of God's righteous indignation against the wicked. It is the end result of a great descent that began on the broad way. In hell, all mercy is removed from the sinner, and he is exposed to the perfect justice that was due him. He is also finally and irrevocably given over to the lust of his heart, and his degrading passions rule him without restraint.[92] He is forever excluded from the blessings of God's people; he is without God and without hope.[93] Reflecting this truth of Scripture, the poet Dante writes in his epic *Divine Comedy* that above the gates of hell is inscribed, "Abandon hope, all ye who enter here." The renowned Puritan pastor Richard Baxter declared, "I preached as never sure to preach again, and as a dying man to dying men."[94]

---

87. John 17:3.

88. Romans 5:1; 8:1.

89. John 1:12–13; Romans 8:15; Galatians 4:6.

90. John 14:6; Acts 4:12; 1 Timothy 2:5–6; Revelation 21:3–5, 22–27.

91. Daniel 12:2; Matthew 18:8; 25:41; Revelation 20:10.

92. Romans 1:24, 26.

93. Ephesians 2:12.

94. Richard Baxter, *Poetical Fragments: Heart Imployment with God and It Self* (London: J. Dunton, 1689), 30.

We must understand that there is a gate through which we must pass if we are to be saved. That gate is Christ and Christ alone, and it is faith and faith alone that opens Him to us. Nevertheless, the Scriptures are adamant, even relentless, in their striving to convince us that the evidence of having passed through the gate is that we have become pilgrims on the narrow way.

It is said that from the moment of our birth we begin to die. It is equally true that from the moment we enter into this world we embark on a journey to leave it. For this reason, Christ warns us that there is a narrow path that "leads away" to eternal life and a broad path that "leads away" to eternal destruction.[95] This is a great and terrible truth that must be pressed upon our consciences. The prophet Jeremiah tells us that the Lord sets before us "the way of life and the way of death" (Jer. 21:8). He cries out,

> "Stand in the ways and see,
> And ask for the old paths, where the good way is,
> And walk in it;
> Then you will find rest for your souls."

Let us not be like the stubborn inhabitants of Jerusalem who answered, "We will not walk in it" (Jer. 6:16). As the prophet Isaiah pleads,

> Let the wicked forsake his way,
> And the unrighteous man his thoughts;
> Let him return to the Lord,
> And He will have mercy on him;
> And to our God,
> For He will abundantly pardon. (55:7)

---

95. The phrase "leads to" that occurs in Matthew 7:13–14 is translated from the Greek *apágo*. It means to lead away, as a person being led off to punishment or honor.

CHAPTER EIGHTEEN

The Outward Evidence
of an Inward Reality

Beware of false prophets, who come to you in sheep's clothing, but
inwardly they are ravenous wolves. You will know them by their fruits.
Do men gather grapes from thornbushes or figs from thistles? Even so,
every good tree bears good fruit, but a bad tree bears bad fruit. A good
tree cannot bear bad fruit, nor can a bad tree bear good fruit. Every tree
that does not bear good fruit is cut down and thrown into the fire. There-
fore by their fruits you will know them.

—Matthew 7:15–20

In these verses, the Lord is warning His people about the certain advent
of false prophets and instructing them about how they might discern
them. The apostle Paul gives a similar warning to the church at Ephesus: "For I know this, that after my departure savage wolves will come
in among you, not sparing the flock. Also from among yourselves men
will rise up, speaking perverse things, to draw away the disciples after
themselves" (Acts 20:29–30).

According to Christ, at first glance these spiritual canines will seem
sheep-like and walk within the fold as though they belonged. Nevertheless, they are not what they seem. In fact, they are the opposite. Although
outwardly they have the appearance of a lamb, inwardly they are ravenous wolves. They are cups that are clean on the outside, but full of filth
within.[1] They are carefully painted tombs filled with "dead men's bones
and all uncleanness" (Matt. 23:27). Jude verse 12 describes them as dangerous reefs hidden under inviting waters, spectacular clouds that bear
no life-giving rain, and seemingly robust trees that are rotten at the core
and without fruit. In the words of the apostle Paul, they are evil men

---

1. Matthew 23:25–26; Luke 11:39–40.

and impostors who proceed from bad to worse, "deceiving and being deceived" (2 Tim. 3:13).

The point of all these tragic descriptions is that the inward reality of these men is contrary to their profession: they are not what they seem or profess. They have clothed themselves in a thin veneer of Christianity and have deceived themselves and others with their empty confessions of Christ's lordship.[2] They honor Him with their lips, but their heart is far from Him; they profess to know Him but deny Him by their deeds.[3]

Although Christ is speaking primarily with regard to the hidden character of false prophets and the dangers of being misled by them, His words should not be confined to this matter alone. We would do well to recognize that they also have far-reaching implications for all of us who confess Christ and claim identification with Him. In fact, Christ's words reach to the heart of the Christian religion and address one of its most essential questions: How can I know that I am truly Christian? The answer to this question is as simple as it is profound. Our inward reality is revealed by external evidence; our true identity is exposed by observable deeds; our conversion or lack of it is made known by the fruit of our lives.

AN UNALTERABLE TRUTH

In Matthew 7:16, Christ puts before us a fixed maxim that allows for no exceptions: "You will know them by their fruits." In other words, we will know the genuineness of a person's profession of faith by the conduct of his life.

The word "know" is translated from the Greek word *epiginósko*. In general, the verb denotes a more specific or accurate knowledge of a subject than the common term for knowledge, *ginósko*. It means to know exactly, completely, or through and through.[4] The word "fruit" is translated from the Greek word *karpos*, which literally refers to the fruit of trees or vines. Figuratively, the word is used to denote that which originates or comes from something as a product, effect, or result. W. E. Vines describes fruit as "the visible expression of power working inwardly and

---

2. Luke 6:46.

3. Isaiah 29:13; Matthew 15:8; Mark 7:6; Titus 1:16.

4. William F. Arndt and F. Wilbur Gingrich, *A Greek-English Lexicon of the New Testament and Other Early Christian Literature* (Chicago: University of Chicago Press, 2000), 369.

invisibly, the character of the fruit being evidence of the character of the power producing it."[5]

In the present context, the term *karpos* is used to denote the behavior, conduct, works, or deeds that emanate from a person's character and manifest its true quality. Also, it is important to note that Jesus speaks of "fruits" in the plural rather than the singular, denoting not just one aspect of a person's life, but its entirety. The truth conveyed is that the inward reality of a person will be proven by his actions in all that he is and all that he does in every circumstance. Neither virtue nor vice can be easily hidden, but both will manifest themselves in time.[6]

The certainty of this truth is demonstrated by its repetition in the text. It is significant that Christ begins and ends His discourse on fruits with the same warning: "You will know them by their fruits," and again, "By their fruits you will know them" (Matt. 7:16, 20; cf. 12:33). The righteous will have bouts with sin and even periodic falls. At times, the wicked will perform good deeds and even reflect a semblance of righteousness. However, over time, both the righteous and the wicked will be revealed by their ongoing behavior.

We must realize from the outset that this truth is contrary to the popular teachings of much of contemporary evangelicalism. Not only is it absent from most gospel preaching and counseling, but it is also often openly denied. First, much of the evangelical community has adopted the fallacious opinion of contemporary culture that denies any relationship between inward character and outward behavior, an opinion that gives more credence to a person's confession or feelings than to the facts that either prove or deny them. Furthermore, we have bought into the lie that it is immoral or a violation of human dignity to question any claim an individual might make concerning himself regardless of how contrary it is to the facts. We have accepted as canonical law the saying that you can't judge a book by its cover. However, in doing so, we have also denied Christ's clear teaching that you will know them by their fruits.

It is important to note that when people say that you can't judge a book by its cover, they do not call for a moratorium on discernment, but

---

5. W. E. Vines, *An Expository Dictionary of New Testament Words: With Their Precise Meanings for English Readers* (Nashville, Tenn.: Thomas Nelson, 1985), 133.

6. In his commentary on Matthew 7:16, John Calvin wrote, "Nothing is more difficult than to conterfeit virtue."

rather they warn against making judgment calls based upon mere superficial observation. For example, we should not doubt a person's intellect
or proficiency simply because he did not graduate from an Ivy League
school. But this does not mean that we should not question or even challenge a carnal and wicked person's profession of Christ simply because
we cannot know his heart. According to Christ, the heart can be known
by the outward deeds that flow from it: "For out of the heart proceed evil
thoughts, murders, adulteries, fornications, thefts, false witness, blasphe-
mies. These are the things which defile a man, but to eat with unwashed
hands does not defile a man" (Matt. 15:19–20).

This common departure from the Scriptures should come as no surprise to us. One of the most common traits of those who are disobedient
to any creed they pretend to confess is to argue that religion is a matter
of the heart and cannot be judged by any outward manifestation. Based
on this convenient but false assumption, a person may claim the greatest devotion to God in his heart while committing the greatest atrocities
against His commands. It is for this reason that the Scriptures are full
of warnings against any form of profession without substance. Along
with Jesus' warnings in Matthew 7 and throughout His ministry, the
apostle Paul warns against those who profess to know God but by their
deeds deny Him. He refers to them as detestable and disobedient.[7] James
argues that a faith that does not result in works is dead and of no saving
value. Those who possess such a faith have no hope of salvation.[8] Finally,
we have seen in the first part of this book that the apostle John wrote an
entire epistle so that those who confess Christ might prove the genuineness of their confession by comparing their person and manner of living
to the character traits of a true Christian.[9]

In summary, the genuine believer will bear fruit that remains. For
this he was chosen and appointed, and by this he proves that he is truly
Christ's disciple.[10] Even though he will pass through times of apparent
barrenness due to some besetting sin and the Father's pruning, the work
of divine discipline will serve to make him more fruitful.[11] In the parable
of the sower, Jesus give us some idea of the abundant fruitfulness that will

---

7. Titus 1:16.
8. James 2:14–23.
9. 1 John 5:13.
10. John 15:8.
11. John 15:2; Hebrews 12:11.

mark the life of every Christian when He declares that among His true disciples, some will bear "a hundredfold, some sixty, and some thirty" (Matt. 13:23; cf. John 15:5). It is an amazing thing and a demonstration of the power of God in salvation that even the least in the kingdom will bear fruit thirtyfold![12] As we are told by the prophet Isaiah, the Lord's salvation will bear fruit, and righteousness will spring up with it.[13]

ARGUMENTUM AD ABSURDUM

Argumentum ad absurdum or *reductio ad absurdum* (argument or reduction to absurdity) is a method employed in logic to demonstrate that an opponent's argument leads to an irreconcilable contradiction or absurd conclusion. In Matthew 7:16, Jesus employs a similar tactic in order to refute those who would deny that their inward reality (i.e., what they are) can be known by their outward deeds (i.e., what they do): "You will know them by their fruits. Do men gather grapes from thornbushes or figs from thistles?"

Jesus was an extraordinary teacher, and the Sermon on the Mount is one of the greatest demonstrations of this truth. He was wisdom personified, a master rhetorician, and an unassailable debater. The gospel writer assures us that in any confrontation, "no one was able to answer Him a word" (Matt. 22:46). And when all was said and done, His opponents would walk away amazed, without daring "to question Him anymore" (Luke 20:40).

Jesus employs an illustration that would have been understandable to anyone who was even remotely familiar with the agriculture of the day. He asks the crowd, "Grapes are not gathered from thorn bushes, are they?" We can only imagine the response of the people, who were finally given a question they could actually answer. With possibly an air of condescension they replied, "Of course not! It would be absolutely absurd to even suggest such a thing. It is against nature."

Jesus puts forth a similar question: "Then figs are not gathered from thistles?" Again the crowd responds with a newfound boldness and possibly an air of superiority: "It is ludicrous. There are certain things beyond the realm of the possible. A plant will not yield fruit contrary to

---

12. Matthew 11:11; Luke 7:28. Pastor Charles Leiter, conversation with the author.
13. Isaiah 45:8.

its nature. Anyone who claims to gather grapes from thornbushes or figs from thistles is either out of his mind or lying."

The people feel triumphant. They have correctly answered the Great Inquisitor. They have instructed the Instructor. However, their illusion of victory is brief. Christ's questions were rhetorical in nature. They were not for His benefit, but theirs. He springs His traps and exposes the true intent of His inquiry. He puts forth the inescapable conclusion:

> If it is an absurdity to believe that thornbushes can produce grapes and thistles figs, then it is equally absurd to believe that a person is truly My disciple who does not bear the fruit of a disciple. And if anyone who claims to gather grapes from thorns or figs from thistles is either a lunatic or a liar, then anyone who claims to be My disciple without bearing the fruit of a disciple is equally insane or immoral.

Imagine that a person arrives one hour late for an important appointment, possibly a preacher who was to preach at a large gathering that had been planned for months. When he finally arrives, he is questioned rather harshly about his tardiness. He responds with the following explanation:

> Gentlemen, I left the hotel on time but had a flat tire on the way. While I was changing the tire, a lug nut fell out of my hand and rolled into the middle of the busy highway. Not thinking, I stepped out and picked it up. When I stood up, I realized that there was a thirty-ton logging truck bearing down on me at approximately seventy-five miles an hour. It hit me head on and ran over me. It is for this reason that I am late. I apologize for any inconvenience I may have caused.

Those listening to the explanation note that the speaker's hair is combed and his clothing is neatly pressed. Furthermore, he is without any noticeable harm. For these reasons they can only conclude that the speaker is deranged, deceived, or an extraordinary liar. The basis of their conclusion is the simple fact that it is an absolute impossibility for a unprotected man to be hit head on and run over by a thirty-ton logging truck without some noticeable evidence of such an encounter.

In light of this illustration, the evangelical community is faced with some rather extraordinary questions: Which is greater, a logging truck or God? How is it impossible for a person to have an encounter with even the smallest vehicle without being dramatically changed, and yet it is possible to have an encounter with the living God without even so much as a dent or a paint scrape on a person's character? How is it that so many people claim to have had an encounter with God, yet show so little evidence to back their claim?

There are two primary reasons, one theological and the other practical. The theological reason is that the magnificent doctrine of regeneration has been reduced to nothing more than a human decision. Few understand the concept of the new birth as a supernatural work of God that changes the nature of a person to such a degree that he can be referred to in the Scriptures as a new creature.

The practical reason is that many have received something less than a biblical gospel and have been invited to return to God with nothing more than the repetition of a prayer. They are ignorant of the true nature of repentance and faith and are unaware of the demands of discipleship or the restricted nature of the Christian life. They have yet to pass through the narrow gate, and they continue to blissfully walk upon the broad way. They have been given enough religion to quiet their conscience and enough assurance from their religious authorities[14] to insulate them from any true gospel warnings.

ARGUMENTUM AD HOMINEM

A common tendency among those who profess any form of morality or religion is to deny or ignore the truth that Christ is strongly affirming: the inward reality of a person is known by his fruits regardless of the frequency or adamancy of his confession. The apostle Paul dealt with this problem in his letter to the church in Rome, where he argued at length against the religious Jews who boasted in the law and denounced the immoralities of the Gentiles but were guilty of similar atrocities. They could quote the *Shema* by heart and made great confessions of loyalty to God and His law, but their deeds proved that they were not what they claimed to be. Paul writes in Romans 2:17–23:

> Indeed you are called a Jew, and rest on the law, and make your boast in God, and know His will, and approve the things that are excellent, being instructed out of the law, and are confident that you

---

14. These religious authorities today are evangelical pastors, youth workers, and evangelists whose unbiblical view of the gospel and conversion leads their hearers to a false assurance of salvation and insulates them from any true instruction.

yourself are a guide to the blind, a light to those who are in darkness, an instructor of the foolish, a teacher of babes, having the form of knowledge and truth in the law. You, therefore, who teach another, do you not teach yourself? You who preach that a man should not steal, do you steal? You who say, "Do not commit adultery," do you commit adultery? You who abhor idols, do you rob temples? You who make your boast in the law, do you dishonor God through breaking the law?

This fallacy among the Jews that Paul is addressing among the Jews is rampant in modern evangelicalism. Many evangelicals claim to be born again and to be recipients of eternal life, yet their lives are an extraordinary contradiction to their confession. Not only do they ignore Christ's teachings on this matter, but they often outright deny them and teach the opposite in their place. The false convert will maintain that no one would ever doubt him if they could see into his heart of hearts, where he conceals true faith and love for God. To add insult to injury, he will often appeal to Christ's teachings to chastise anyone who would dare confront him. His favorite rebuttal usually comes from Matthew 7:1: "Judge not, that you be not judged." He is unaware that in his fervor to defend the validity of his conversion he is distorting the Scriptures to his own destruction.[15]

It is noteworthy and disturbing that the false convert's most common response to anyone who would question him is a nearly perfect example of the classical fallacy that philosophers and logicians refer to as an *argumentum ad hominem* (argument to or against the man). This fallacy occurs when a person attacks his opponent's character rather than trying to disprove the truthfulness or soundness of his argument. In this case, the reasoning is that what an opponent says should be discarded because it is the result of some fault in his character or motives. The goal of this strategy is to attack the opponent's character, putting him on trial, so that his argument is ignored.

The false convert often uses this type of reasoning in response to any question regarding the validity of his faith. Imagine the following scenario: An elder notices the growing waywardness of a member of the congregation and decides to confront him. In love, the elder lays out several concrete evidences that have led him to question the congregant's

---

15. 2 Peter 3:16.

conversion. However, instead of considering the validity of the arguments against him or providing an explanation to resolve the misunderstanding, the church member lashes out at the elder. He accuses him of pharisaism and of having a judgmental spirit. He warns him to "judge not, lest he be judged," and admonishes him to take the beam out of his own eye before he tries to deal with the sins of another.[16] Finally, he chastises the elder for even imagining that he can determine what is in another person's heart or suggest that someone is not a Christian. The false convert has managed to shift the focus of the matter away from himself and the arguments against him to place it upon the elder, who, in his opinion, has attacked him arrogantly and without love.

In the end, the false convert has not only denied several of Christ's most important teachings on conversion and the evidence of it but he has also twisted them in order to turn them upon those who have lovingly and selflessly sought to help him. The most tragic thing about this entire scenario is that the seemingly impenetrable insulation against the truth that surrounds the false convert has been created and fortified by much of the preaching that emanates from the contemporary evangelical pulpit.

THE OUTWARD EVIDENCE OF AN INWARD REALITY

What may at first seem to be a quaint saying using metaphors that children can understand is actually one of the most profound teachings regarding the work of conversion and the relationship between the nature and will of man. Jesus declares: "Even so, every good tree bears good fruit, but a bad tree bears bad fruit. A good tree cannot bear bad fruit, nor can a bad tree bear good fruit" (Matt. 7:17–18).

As I have already stated, contemporary man within and without the evangelical community has created an unnatural separation between nature and will. It is an error that lays at the very foundation of contemporary evangelicalism and has created a great weakness through the entire edifice. It has allowed us to divorce what a person is from what he actually does.

When Jesus declared that every good tree bears good fruit and every bad tree bears bad fruit, He was simply affirming the inseparable relationship that exists between the nature of a tree and the fruit that

---

16. Matthew 7:3–5.

emanates from it. Although a good tree may bear fruit that is blemished and a bad tree may bear some fruit that is good, most of their crops will be consistent with their natures. There will be enough good fruit on the good tree to identify it as good and to distinguish it from the bad. As in the days of creation, every tree will bear fruit after its kind.[17]

This inseparable relationship that exists between fruit and nature, characteristics and kind, and what one does and what one is, seems to be understood in every discipline of knowledge except that which pertains to religion and morality. We would wonder about the abilities of a person who could not discern the difference between the basic species of trees by observing their fruits or was unable to distinguish one animal species from the next after a careful examination of their characteristics and habits. When we come upon an animal in a field that does not look like a horse because it has two small legs, webbed feet, and feathers, we conclude that it is not a horse. Our judgment is further verified when we observe that it also does not act like a horse because it waddles with difficulty, swims effortlessly, and flies from north to south and back again. It does not look like a horse or act like a horse; therefore, we conclude that it is not a horse.

However, when it comes to the Christian confession we lose our bearings and trade Christ's teachings for popular clichés. It seems that the evangelical community no longer views conversion primarily as a supernatural work of God wrought through the miracle of the new birth. Therefore, Christians are viewed as those who have merely changed their minds rather than those who have been transformed by the power of God into new creatures with new natures resulting in new and righteous affections. Because of this, sanctification and fruit bearing are viewed as something that may or may not have happened in a Christian's life. We affirm that the God who began a good work in us will finish it, but only if we allow Him to do so.[18] We are His workmanship, created for good works that were prepared beforehand, but the entire divine scheme can be reduced to nothing unless we choose to walk in them.[19] Therefore, some believe a person can choose Christ and be thoroughly justified, yet not choose to go on with Christ in sanctification.

---

17. Genesis 1:12.
18. Philippians 1:6.
19. Ephesians 2:10.

Although it is popular, this opinion is simply not true, but neither is the fatalistic view that would present God as a manipulative and coercive deity who would run roughshod over the wills of His people. Our growth in Christ and our fruit-bearing are dependent upon our volition; however, we must not fail to see that our volition is dependent upon our natures, which have been radically changed through the regenerating work of the Holy Spirit. We decide to bear fruit because we desire to bear fruit, and these desires flow from our new natures. God does not make us willing by manipulation or coercion, but by the act of recreation. It is certain that we will bear good fruit because He has transformed us into the kind of trees that do so.

Christianity is not about us trying to be something that we are not. Although doing righteousness is still contrary to our fallen flesh, it is not contrary to our new natures or adverse to our affections.[20] We are new creations, recreated in the image of God in true righteousness and holiness.[21] We do righteousness because we love righteousness and loathe ourselves when we deviate from it. Although our complete transformation will be consummated at the resurrection, it began on the day of our conversion. Through the new birth, we became new creatures in the fullest sense of the term. These truths must not be treated as poetic or romantic language void of any real meaning but as accurately setting forth the present reality of the Christian. "Therefore, if anyone is in Christ, he is a new creation; old things have passed away; behold, all things have become new" (2 Cor. 5:17).

The reality of the new birth is the doctrinal foundation underlying Jesus' declaration that a good tree cannot bear bad fruit and a bad tree cannot bear good fruit. The truth He conveys is as simple as it is profound: a tree cannot bear fruit contrary to its nature; a radically depraved son of Adam cannot live a life that is pleasing to God; and a regenerate child of God cannot continue in a lifestyle of unbroken rebellion against Him. The pruning work of God in the Christian's life, sanctification, will result in a harvest of righteousness that comes through Jesus Christ to the glory and praise of God.[22] He will learn to walk as a child of light, bearing the fruit of the light that consists in all goodness and righteousness and truth.[23]

---

20. Galatians 5:17. Pastor Charles Leiter, conversation with the author.
21. 2 Corinthians 5:17; Galatians 6:15.
22. Philippians 1:11.
23. Ephesians 5:8–9.

We seem prone to teach only one side of Jesus' remarkable truth about trees and their fruits. We consistently tell the unconverted to put no confidence in the flesh and to cast off all hope of saving themselves through their own works.[24] We rightly inform them that the "carnal mind is enmity against God" (Rom. 8:7). We adamantly assert that it is an impossibility that allows for no exception. A bad tree cannot bear good fruit, and an unregenerate heart cannot fulfill the righteous requirements of the law.

Our defense and proclamation of this remarkable truth is commendable. However, we must ask ourselves why we rarely mention the correlating truth that a good tree cannot produce bad fruit. As it is impossible for the unconverted to live a life that is pleasing unto God, it is equally impossible for a Christian to live a life of unbroken rebellion and fruitlessness before God. God has too much invested in His vineyard to let even one branch fail. He simply will not allow it! His providence will prevail over every weakness of His people and every circumstance that assails them. Although at differing paces and in differing degrees, every child of God will bear fruit.

We are branches and can do nothing in ourselves, but He has engrafted us into Christ.[25] We are subject to fall under our own weight, but He is the faithful vinedresser who prunes us in order to assure our greater fruitfulness.[26] We work out our salvation with fear and trembling, but He is the Sovereign who is at work in us, both to will and to work for His good pleasure.[27] We are children prone to neglect and disobedience, but He is the Lord who disciplines us so that we might share in His holiness.[28] We are always a work in progress, but we are His workmanship, and He who began a good work in us will finish it.[29] However, if we are always barren, then we have not been engrafted. If there is never pruning, then God is not our vinedresser. If there is no progress in sanctification, then we are not His workmanship. And if there is no discipline to match our waywardness, then God is not our Father. "For what son is there whom

---

24. Romans 3:20; Galatians 2:16; Ephesian 2:8–9; Philippians 3:3.
25. John 15:4–5.
26. John 15:2.
27. Philippians 2:12–13.
28. Hebrews 12:9–10.
29. Ephesians 2:10; Philippians 1:6.

his father does not chasten?" And if any be without discipline, they are illegitimate children and not sons (Heb. 12:5–11).

These truths ought to be proclaimed to everyone who confesses the name of Christ and makes a claim to eternal life. While we often choose a more magnanimous motto—you can't judge a book by its cover—we must understand that a good tree cannot bear bad fruit. At any time, a Christian may be running, walking, crawling, sliding, or even falling. Nevertheless, over the full course of his life, he will grow and bear good fruit: "some a hundredfold, some sixty, some thirty" (Matt. 13:23).

CHAPTER NINETEEN

The Dangers of an Empty Confession

Not everyone who says to Me, "Lord, Lord," shall enter the kingdom of heaven, but he who does the will of My Father in heaven. Many will say to Me in that day, "Lord, Lord, have we not prophesied in Your name, cast out demons in Your name, and done many wonders in Your name?" And then I will declare to them, "I never knew you; depart from Me, you who practice lawlessness!"…

Therefore whoever hears these sayings of Mine, and does them, I will liken him to a wise man who built his house on the rock: and the rain descended, the floods came, and the winds blew and beat on that house; and it did not fall, for it was founded on the rock. But everyone who hears these sayings of Mine, and does not do them, will be like a foolish man who built his house on the sand: and the rain descended, the floods came, and the winds blew and beat on that house; and it fell. And great was its fall.

—Matthew 7:21–23, 24–27

Before us is one of the most solemn texts in the Scriptures. It is a fitting conclusion to the Recovering the Gospel series because it communicates to us the seriousness of the true gospel ministry. As we read, we are immediately aware that Christ is not dealing with temporal trivialities, but eternal destinies. In fact, it seems that an eerie, almost frightening wind blows through His words, dispensing the clouds that limit our vision to this world alone. The clearing gives us a brief but startling view of the things that await us on that great and final day when we, along with all mankind, will stand before Christ and hear our fate declared.

From our vantage point we see that there will be a great gleaning and culling of the entire human race. On one side is a great multitude that no one can count, from every nation and tribe and people and tongue. They are standing before the throne and before the Lamb. They are clothed in white robes, and they cry out with a loud voice, saying, "Salvation belongs to our God who sits on the throne, and to the Lamb" (Rev. 7:9–10). These are the people who stand approved of God, and they are invited to enter into the joy of their Master.[1] They are received into the city of the living God by angels and saints made perfect, and they will dwell forever in the presence of God and the Lamb.[2] Every tear is wiped from their eyes, and their long battle with suffering and death and mourning and pain has ended. All of the dreadful things of this fallen age have passed away.[3] In their new dwelling place, they will forever discover that one day in the courts of God is better than a thousand elsewhere, that in His presence is fullness of joy, and at His right hand there are pleasures forever.[4] All the delights and satisfaction of the world they left behind cannot compare to a single moment of the slightest joy they now possess. On earth, they believed Him and loved Him even though He was hidden from their sight, but now they behold Him and rejoice with joy unspeakable and full of glory.[5]

On the opposite side, we see another great multitude that no one can count, from every nation and tribe, people and tongue. Its number is so great that it dwarfs the first and makes it appear as nothing more than a remnant. They have been summoned against their will before the throne of heaven to acknowledge the lordship of the One who sits upon it.[6] Their once bold countenance has been replaced with terror. They are cowed, shattered like earthenware,[7] graceless, and vile. They melt before the throne of God like tiny wax figurines before a blast furnace.[8] They cry out for the mountains and rocks to fall upon them to hide them from the unapproachable light of God and the Lamb.[9] Suddenly, they are silenced, and Christ Himself declares their final sentence: "Depart from Me, you who practice lawlessness!" (Matt. 7:23).

---

1. Matthew 25:21, 23.
2. Hebrews 12:22–24; Revelation 21:23.
3. Revelation 21:4.
4. Psalms 16:11; 84:10.
5. 1 Peter 1:8.
6. Philippians 2:10–11.
7. Psalm 2:9; Revelation 2:27.
8. Pastor Charles Leiter, conversation with the author.
9. 1 Timothy 6:16; Revelation 6:16.

Then, by a divine hand they are cast into hell, and their fearful expectations of judgment are finally fulfilled.[10] In their new dwelling place, they discover that it is a "fearful thing to fall into the hands of the living God" (Heb. 10:31). They will spend an eternity in outer darkness, where there is only weeping and gnashing of teeth.[11] They will drink of the wine of the wrath of God, which is mixed in full strength in the cup of His anger. The smoke of their torment will go up forever, and they will have no rest day and night.[12] They will find themselves housed with demons in a place prepared for devils, where their worm does not die and the fire is not quenched.[13] It would have been better that they had never been born or that they had entered life crippled, lame, and blind than to have been cast with their whole bodies into hell.[14]

We may wish with all our might that these words were mere exaggerations, the figures and hyperboles of a poet. If they came from the pen of Dante, Goethe, or Marlowe,[15] they could be dismissed, but since they are Christ's words, not one jot or tittle is to be ignored.[16] In fact, if His knowledge of the final judgment, heaven, and hell can be believed, then we can be assured that the half has not been told. The end of the world is coming and, with it, a judgment of such magnitude that the ears of everyone who hears of it will tingle.[17]

These truths are why the lighthearted and entertaining preaching of the modern evangelical pulpit is so despicable. How can God's people and their shepherds be so preoccupied with the temporal when so much is at stake in the eternal? "Blow the trumpet in Zion," and sound an alarm in the midst of the church! "Let all the inhabitants of the land tremble; for the day of the LORD is coming!" Surely it is near! (Joel 2:1). Let us pray that God will give us men who have stood on the edge of eternity

---

10. Matthew 5:29–30; 18:9; Mark 9:45, 47; Luke 12:5; Hebrews 10:27; 2 Peter 2:4.

11. Matthew 8:12; 22:13; 25:30; Jude v. 13.

12. Revelation 14:9–11.

13. Matthew 25:41; Mark 9:44–48; 2 Peter 2:4; Jude v. 6.

14. Matthew 26:24; Mark 9:43–47; 14:2.

15. Dante was an Italian poet and the author of *The Divine Comedy*, a poem describing the terrors of hell. Johann Wolfgang von Goethe and Christopher Marlowe wrote separate versions of the popular German legend *Faust*, the story of a scholar who makes a deal with the devil, exchanging his soul for knowledge and pleasure.

16. Matthew 5:18.

17. 1 Samuel 3:11; 2 Kings 21:12; Jeremiah 19:3.

and beheld its severe realities, men who are not afraid to proclaim to the world, "Prepare to meet your God" (Amos 4:12).

THE WORTH OF A CONFESSION

Matthew 7:21 begins with one of the gravest warnings that Christ has ever given: "Not everyone who says to Me, 'Lord, Lord,' shall enter the kingdom of heaven." We must be reminded that Christ's warning is not directed to the self-styled atheist or the infidel. Nor is He addressing those of other religions or those who are openly hostile to His name. Instead, His words are aimed at all who claim to know Him and call Him Lord; those who bear the title "Christian" and who number themselves among His disciples; those whose creeds and confessions would agree with the Scriptures.

Christ's words are for us, and they are intended to pierce our hearts like a lance and to wake us from our dangerous slumber. They demand that we question our assumptions and examine ourselves with the greatest care. Do we know Him? Are we known by Him? Is it well with our souls? Our eternal destinies hang in the balance, and the possibility of self-deception is very great. For many will come before Him on that great day with the greeting, "Lord, Lord," but He will refuse their accolades and declare to them, "Depart from Me; I never knew you." If we ever thought that Christ's previous warnings about the few and the many were exaggerated, we should entertain such thoughts no longer.

Here we are forewarned by the greatest of all authorities. Will we heed His warning? We stand among a great multitude of those who call Jesus Lord, but are we open to the possibility that Christ is speaking directly to us? He has warned us that not all in the camp are true. Will we be like Achan, who thought he could hide among the multitude?[18] Do we think that we can enter into the wedding feast undetected though improperly clothed?[19] Are we open to the possibility that we are deceived and not yet converted, or will we harden our hearts like Judas, who declared, "Surely it is not I."[20]

In this text, Jesus is not addressing secret disciples or those who are ashamed to publicly confess Him. Rather, He is directing His warning

---

18. Joshua 7:18–20.
19. Matthew 22:11–13.
20. Matthew 26:25 (author's translation).

to those who appear to boldly and emphatically declare His lordship. This is evidenced by their declaration, "Lord, Lord." In Hebrew literature, such repetition is used to both clarify and give emphasis. In Isaiah's vision of the throne room of God, the seraphim address Yahweh as "Holy, holy, holy."[21] The intention of the repetition is to give the greatest possible emphasis to God's holiness. Similarly, the repetition in this text is designed to show us that even among those who emphatically declare Jesus to be Lord, many will be rejected and condemned on the day of judgment. This is a terrifying truth that leads us to conclude that a mere confession of faith in Jesus Christ is worth nothing if it is unaccompanied by the essential fruit that proves its genuineness.

THE EVIDENCE OF CONVERSION

If even the most emphatic and frequent confession of the lordship of Jesus Christ is not evidence of true conversion, then what is? We have already looked closely at the answer in two passages of Scripture. In Matthew 7:16 and 20, Jesus tells us that we will know those who are truly converted by their fruits. He declares again in Matthew 7:21 that not everyone who calls Him Lord will enter His kingdom—only "he who does the will of My Father in heaven."

The validity of our confession of Jesus Christ's lordship and of our conversion is evidenced by our obedience to the Father's will. In other words, a person's profession of faith in Jesus Christ and his claim to heaven is doubtful if it is not accompanied by the fruit of a Christlike character and works of righteousness. Even the greatest activity in the Christian ministry along with its accompanying apparent success is not the evidence of conversion.[22]

This truth should come as no surprise to us since it is a common theme throughout Matthew 7. The evidence that a person has passed through the small gate is that he is now walking in the narrow way that is marked out by the commandments of Christ.[23] The evidence that a person has been converted and become a good tree is that he is now bearing good fruit, for each tree is known by its fruit.[24] The evidence that a

---

21. Isaiah 6:3.
22. Matthew 7:22.
23. Matthew 7:13–14.
24. Matthew 7:16–20; Luke 6:44.

person's confession of the lordship of Jesus Christ is genuine is that he is doing the will of the Father and the Son.[25] Finally, the evidence that a person has built his life on the Rock and is safe from the coming judgment is that he not only hears the words of Christ but also does them.[26]

When we go beyond Matthew 7 and look for other Scriptures to affirm the same truth, we find that they are abundant. The apostle Paul exhorts us to examine ourselves thoroughly to determine if we are in the faith.[27] He also warns us of people who will confess that they know God, but by their deeds deny Him.[28] The apostle Peter exhorts us to be diligent to make certain about God's calling and choosing of us.[29] Along with the exhortation, he also provides us with a list of virtues that will be growing realities in our lives if we are truly converted and numbered among God's people: faith, moral excellence, knowledge, self-control, perseverance, godliness, brotherly kindness, and love.[30] To the degree that these virtues are existent and growing in our lives, we can have assurance that we have truly been born again and become partakers of the divine nature.[31] However, to the degree that these qualities are lacking, we should be concerned about our true spiritual condition. As Peter warns, "For he who lacks these things is shortsighted" (2 Peter 1:9). The apostle John wrote his entire first epistle based on the premise that works are the evidence of genuine saving faith and conversion. His epistle contains a number of qualities that will be manifest in varying degrees in the life of every true child of God. To the degree that these qualities are growing and observable realities, we may be assured that we possess eternal life.[32] To the degree that they are lacking, we should be concerned about whether we are truly Christian. Finally, James affirms that works are the product and evidence of genuine saving faith.[33] Although he has often been misunderstood and misinterpreted, he is not denying the doctrine of justification by faith alone set forth by the apostle Paul. Both men are writing about different sides of the same coin. Paul is addressing

---

25. Matthew 7:21; Luke 6:44.
26. Matthew 7:24–27.
27. 2 Corinthians 13:5.
28. Titus 1:16.
29. 2 Peter 1:10.
30. 2 Peter 1:5–7.
31. 2 Peter 1:4, 8.
32. 1 John 5:13.
33. Matthew 13:55; Acts 12:17; 15:13; 21:18; 1 Corinthians 15:7; Galatians 1:19; 2:9.

the cause of justification, and James is addressing the result of it. We are saved by faith alone. However, those who believe have been regenerated by the Holy Spirit and brought under God's providential care. For this reason, we can be confident that every true believer will bear fruit and demonstrate his faith through the works he does. James warns that "faith without works is dead" (2:26), and he challenges those who would say otherwise with the taunt, "Show me your faith without your works, and I will show you my faith by my works" (2:18). For James, those who profess faith and yet bear no fruit are worse off than demons. At least demons have the sense to shudder.[34]

As I have stated, these teachings of Christ and the apostles are not denials of the essential Christian doctrine of justification by faith alone. They are simply affirming the universal truth that the inward reality of a thing is revealed by its accompanying character and deeds. It is also important to understand that neither Christ nor the apostles are teaching that only the most mature believers with nearly perfect fruit can be assured of their salvation. The best Christian among us will be sorely affected by his shortcomings and failings without number. We are all utterly and completely dependent upon grace and the tender mercies of God toward His people. Nevertheless, the true believer's progress in the faith will be the crowning evidence that he has truly been regenerated by the Holy Spirit and is a child of God.

In light of these truths, it is painfully obvious that much of modern-day evangelistic preaching is shallow at best and despicable at its worst. In its superficial treatment of the Scriptures, much modern-day preaching promises salvation to any who will confess with their mouth that Jesus is Lord and believe in their heart that God has raised Him from the dead.[35] However, many preachers do not further clarify this truth with the warning that many—even most—who make this confession will do so in a manner that is void of repentance and faith. To make matters even worse, preachers do not teach those who confess Christ how to determine whether their confession is true. Instead, they encourage them to be assured of their salvation based on their own evaluation of the sincerity with which they called upon Christ and confessed Him as Lord. Many have ignored the clear teaching of Scripture that calls people to make

---

34. James 2:19.
35. Romans 10:9–10.

their calling and election sure by a thorough examination or testing of themselves in the light of Scripture[36] and to determine the validity of their confession by the quality of their fruit.

We must realize that the preaching of gospel promises must be accompanied by gospel warnings. The neglect of either will result in "a different gospel," which is really no gospel at all (Gal. 1:6–7). Throughout the history of Christianity, the most godly ministers were marked by their balanced and consistent warnings to converts and congregants, but in our day such warnings are rare, and in many cases, they are nonexistent. At the moment of our greatest need, when the sword of impending judgment hangs over the heads of so many who confess Christ, few watchmen are willing to sound the horn. They do not alert the wicked, and their pulpits are splattered with the blood of those they refuse to warn.[37]

The need for clear, precise warnings becomes even more evident in light of the superficial, convenient, and man-centered gospel that is rampant in most evangelical churches. We are inundated with a gospel without demands or costs, that not only does not oppose the flesh but often caters to it. Ministers who ought to know better preach a God-dethroning, man-exalting message that can be received with the repetition of a prayer. Then, after only a few minor adjustments, the "convert" is allowed to continue upon the same broad road as before and travel hand-in-hand with a multitude of others who have found the same convenient faith, which is affirmed and defended by the religious authority who leads them and anesthetizes enough of the conscience to make it nearly impervious to the truth.

The greater part of the evangelical culture is held under the sway of its secular counterpart that exalts tolerance, broad-mindedness, inclusivity, and indulgence as the highest and most excellent of all virtues. The evangelical church's members and preachers now pride themselves in their acceptance of one another's doctrinal and ethical departures from the Scriptures without the slightest thought that these variances might be the evidence of their unregenerate state. Is it our love that causes us to be silent in the midst of so many doctrinal and ethical contradictions, or is it our ignorance of the Scriptures? Is it our love that restrains us from warning those who confess Christ but by their deeds deny Him, or is it

---

36. 2 Corinthians 13:5; 2 Peter 1:10; 1 John 5:13.
37. Ezekiel 33:6.

self-preservation and a desire for the approval of men? A person's confession of faith in Christ is not conclusive evidence of salvation. What then is the sign? What are the evidences that a person has truly come to know Him? Jesus is clear:

> "You will know them by their fruits." (Matt. 7:16, 20)

> "Not everyone who says to Me, 'Lord, Lord,' shall enter the kingdom of heaven, but he who does the will of My Father in heaven." (Matt. 7:21)

> "Therefore whoever hears these sayings of Mine, and does them, I will liken him to a wise man who built his house on the rock." (Matt. 7:24)

THE MARKS OF A FALSE CONFESSOR

In Matthew 7:21, Christ is on the throne, and a multitude is standing before Him. However, the scene is not a happy one. In fact, it is one of the most terrifying in Scripture. On earth, this vast multitude called Him Lord, and many of them even ministered in His name, but they are now betrayed by the fruitlessness and disobedience of their lives. Before the throne of Christ, all that was hidden is now made clear.[38] Their confession was hollow, their faith was the faith of demons, and their righteous deeds were like a filthy garment bled through and saturated by the corruption of their own hearts.[39] Their hope of a warm reception and a wide entrance into the kingdom has vanished.[40] Christ looks upon them with a righteous loathing, and cries out: "I never knew you; depart from Me, you who practice lawlessness!" (Matt. 7:23).

From this dreadful declaration, we discover two important characteristics about those who confessed Christ as Lord and yet were rejected and condemned on the day of judgment. The first is that Christ never knew them. The word "know" is translated from the Greek word *ginósko*, which I explained in chapter 14. In this context the verb communicates the idea of intimate union and fellowship. Although these false converts claimed Christ as their Lord, Christ declares that He never *knew* them. This declaration has many possible implications. First, it may refer to Christ's

---

38. Matthew 10:26; Mark 4:22; Luke 12:2.
39. Luke 6:24; Titus 1:16; James 2:19.
40. 2 Peter 1:11.

foreknowledge and election of His people. The Scriptures teach that the name of every child of God was written in the Lamb's Book of Life from the foundation of the world.[41] However, the names of those who now stand before Christ were not found in the book.[42] They were not "elect according to the foreknowledge of God the Father, in sanctification of the Spirit, for obedience and sprinkling of the blood of Jesus Christ" (1 Peter 1:1–2).

Second, it may mean that they were outside of Christ's providential care. The Scriptures teach that "the LORD *knows* the way of the righteous, but the way of the ungodly shall perish" (Ps. 1:6, emphasis added). Christ taught that His sheep would hear His voice, and He would *know* them, and they would follow Him.[43] However, these were not His sheep, and He was not their shepherd. He did not know them, and they did not hear His voice or follow Him in obedience when He called.

Third, and most importantly, it may mean there was no intimate communion between Him and them. It is as though Christ said to them, "You did not seek me during your earthly pilgrimage. In fact, I seldom entered into your thoughts. We did not walk together and delight in each other's fellowship. You did not ask counsel from Me, heed My teaching, or obey My commands. I did not know you then, and I do not know you now!"

It is a common saying among evangelicals that the most important thing in a person's life is to know Jesus. Although there is a great deal of truth in the statement, it may be more appropriate to reverse the order and say that whether we claim to know Jesus is not nearly as important as whether Jesus knows us. Imagine that a man walks up to the gates of the White House and demands entrance. We can be sure that he will be detained immediately and questioned thoroughly. We can be certain that he will not be allowed entrance merely because he confesses to know the president who resides within. However, if the president confesses to know the man who seeks entrance, it will be granted to him immediately and without question. We have already learned that our confession of faith in Christ is worthless apart from the fruit or works that evidence it. In contrast, Christ's confession of us is of infinite value, for it opens a door to us that no one can shut.[44]

---

41. Revelation 13:8.
42. Revelation 20:15.
43. John 10:26–27.
44. Revelation 3:8.

The second characteristic of those who confessed Christ as Lord and yet were condemned is that they were lawless. Jesus tells those who practice lawlessness to depart in Matthew 7:23. The word "lawlessness" is translated from the Greek word *anomía*, which denotes the condition of being without law. It refers to one who lives in violation of God's will out of ignorance, neglect, or willful rebellion. The meaning of the term is extremely important because it sheds light on the nature of a false confession and reveals the reason for Christ's severity. It is as though He looks with disdain upon these false converts and declares, "Depart from Me, you who claimed to be My disciples and confessed me as Lord and yet lived as if I never gave you a command to obey."

No other statement we have considered is so applicable to many of those who claim the title "evangelical." Much of the evangelical community has gradually conformed itself to culture and recreated itself as a convenient religion without demands, laws, or any kind of parameters that might be restrictive to the flesh. Like the ungodly of whom Jude writes, some evangelicals have "[turned] the grace of our God into lewdness and deny the only Lord God and our Lord Jesus Christ" (v. 4). No one can deny that multitudes of evangelicals make a claim to Christ, yet His sovereign will is virtually unknown to them, and its application is absent from their daily lives. There seems to be a great detachment in the evangelical mind regarding the relationship between a person's confession of Christ as Lord and his actual submission to His revealed will. Can a person truly be a loyal subject within the realm of any king, yet not only ignore His commands but also live contrary to them? Many contemporary evangelicals seem to think so.

Although it is true that we are freed from the law to follow Christ and be led by the Spirit,[45] we must understand that neither Christ nor the Spirit are contrary to the law or opposed to it. In fact, the way in which we discern true conformity to Christ and validate the Spirit's leadership in our lives is through what is written in the Scriptures. If we love Christ we will keep His commandments,[46] and if we are following the Spirit we will live a life of highest virtue; "against such there is no law" (Gal. 5:22–23).

God's grace in Christ does not cast us out into the world to live our lives without instruction or to continue walking according to the course

---

45. Romans 7:1–6.
46. John 14:15.

of this world.[47] Instead, we are called to "no longer walk as the rest of the Gentiles walk" (Eph. 4:17–18), but to be conformed to the image of Christ in all things and take every thought captive to His obedience.[48] This is accomplished in part through our diligent study and proper application of the commands, instructions, and wisdom that is found throughout the entirety of the Scriptures.[49] Moses wrote that the commands of God were not an idle word, but the life of the believer and the church.[50] David sang that they were a lamp to his feet, a light to his path, and the means by which a young man might keep his way pure.[51] Jesus confirmed the centrality of the commandments in the life of His people when He declared, "Man shall not live by bread alone, but by every word that proceeds from the mouth of God."[52] The apostle Paul instructed Timothy that the Scriptures not only give us the wisdom that leads to salvation, but they are also profitable for teaching, reproof, correction, and training in righteousness.[53] The apostle John teaches us that one of the greatest evidences of conversion is that we keep God's commandments.[54] He concludes, "For this is the love of God, that we keep His commandments. And His commandments are not burdensome" (1 John 5:3).

In light of the great consensus of the godly regarding the centrality of the Scripture and the importance of its commands, we must ask ourselves why so many evangelicals groan at the mere mention of commandments and fight against them as though they were restrictive and contrary to a life of joy. Why is it that any preaching that even suggests an absolute standard or delineates between right and wrong is considered to be legalistic, rigid, self-righteous, and unloving? The answer is as clear as it is difficult to accept. It is because so many within the evangelical community are unconverted. Although they are dressed in the garb of contemporary Christianity, their unregenerate hearts remain hostile to God and His will.[55] God's Word is burdensome to them because it

---

47. Ephesians 2:2.
48. Romans 8:29; 2 Corinthians 10:5.
49. Psalm 19:10–11.
50. Deuteronomy 32:47.
51. Psalm 119:9, 105.
52. Matthew 4:4.
53. 2 Timothy 3:15–17.
54. 1 John 3:4.
55. Romans 1:30; 8:7.

demands that they do the righteousness they hate, and it is oppressive because it forbids them from doing the wickedness they love.[56]

The apathy, neglect, and even aversion of many evangelicals toward the moral and spiritual absolutes of God's Word is evidence that they have a form of godliness, but nothing more.[57] They have become participants in a twisted caricature of genuine Christianity that is marked by a broad way and leads to destruction. They prayed a prayer and were invited into an appealing community of smiling faces. Each week, they listen attentively to spiritual principles that will ensure for them a better life. They are involved in enough family-friendly activities to have a sense of purpose and keep them entertained. Nevertheless, they are deceived. In their hearts and deeds, they are lawless. They live unaware of God's commands and do what is right in their own eyes. They have found a way to hold onto enough of the world to satisfy their flesh and to embrace enough Christianity to soothe their conscience. However, on that final day they will hear, "Depart from Me, you who practice lawlessness" (Matt. 7:23).

THE GREAT REJECTION

On the great day of judgment, Christ warns us that He will declare to many the most terrifying verdict that will ever fall upon the human ear, commanding those who practice lawlessness to depart from Him. The entire pronouncement is taken almost word for word from a declaration David made in Psalm 6:7–10:

> My eye wastes away because of grief;
> It grows old because of all my enemies.
> Depart from me, all you workers of iniquity;
> For the LORD has heard the voice of my weeping.
> The LORD has heard my supplication;
> The LORD will receive my prayer.
> Let all my enemies be ashamed and greatly troubled;
> Let them turn back and be ashamed suddenly.

Four truths in this text are relevant to our consideration of the final judgment. First, David considers those whom he is sending away to be his

---

56. Pastor Charles Leiter, conversation with the author.
57. 2 Timothy 3:5.

enemies. In a similar manner, those whom Christ will send away on the day of judgment will be His enemies. The Scriptures teach that all people are, by nature, "haters of God," and their minds are hostile to Him.[58] However, we must also understand that this enmity between God and the sinner is not one-sided but mutual. In His holiness and righteousness, God is also opposed to the sinner and has declared war against him: "For if when we were enemies we were reconciled to God through the death of His Son, much more, having been reconciled, we shall be saved by His life."[59] The sinner's only hope is to drop his weapon and lift the white flag of surrender before it is forever too late. Once he has reached the judgment throne of Christ, the olive leaf of peace will have been withdrawn, and the time for reconciliation and peace will have passed. The writer of Hebrews tells us that at that moment, all that will be left will be "a certain fearful expectation of judgment, and fiery indignation which will devour the adversaries" (Heb. 10:27). Although they professed Christ as Lord and held to a form of godliness,[60] He will see through their thin veneer of piety. By their empty confession and neglectful treatment of the gospel, they trampled under foot the Son of God, regarded as unclean the blood of the covenant, and insulted the Spirit of grace.[61] For this reason, they will be gathered like sheaves to the threshing floor and like dry branches to be burned.[62] It is the day of the Lord's vengeance upon His adversaries.[63] They will drink of the wine of the wrath of God, which will be mixed in full strength in the cup of His anger.[64]

Second, those whom David is sending away will depart in great shame and dismay. The word "ashamed" is translated from the Hebrew word *buwsh*, which denotes shame, disappointment, and confusion. The words "greatly troubled" are translated from the Hebrew word *bahal*, which denotes alarm, anxiety, and terror. David's enemies will be cast

---

58. Romans 1:30; 8:7; Colossians 1:21.

59. See also Nahum 1:2; Isaiah 63:10. For a more detailed explanation of this truth see *Romans*, by Thomas R. Schreiner (Grand Rapids: Baker, 1998), 264; and *The Epistle to the Romans* by Douglas Moo (Grand Rapids: Eerdmans, 1996), 311–12. This view is also defended in other respected works on Romans by Robert Haldane, John Murray, Charles Hodge, and C.E.B. Cranfield.

60. 2 Timothy 3:5.

61. Hebrews 10:29.

62. Micah 4:12; John 15:6.

63. Nahum 1:2; Hebrews 10:30.

64. Revelation 14:10.

out bearing their shame, full of anxiety, and utterly terrified. It is an extremely dark picture, and yet this foreshadowing of judgment that we find in David's words cannot even begin to describe the unimaginable shame and terror that awaits those who will be declared reprobate and cast out of the presence of Christ. They will enter the throne room with great confidence and in need of nothing, but they will immediately find themselves to be "wretched, miserable, poor, blind, and naked" (Rev. 3:17). As the land of Canaan vomited out the Canaanites because of their defilement and afterward did the same to disobedient Israel, so Christ will vomit them out of His mouth and drive them away with the greatest disdain and loathing.[65] As those whose faces are smeared with refuse, they will be taken away.[66] They will be covered with reproach and dishonor, ashamed and consumed.[67] As Daniel prophesied about them, they will awake to "shame and everlasting contempt" (Dan. 12:2).

Third, those whom David is sending away are not aware of their impending doom until it is too late. It comes upon them with the swiftness of the sword. At the moment of their greatest confidence, they are turned back. Likewise, those who falsely professed Christ will be unaware and unprepared for the judgment that will fall upon them on that final day. It will come as a dramatic and unexpected turn of events that will turn their entire view of reality upside down. They will enter His throne room thinking that they belong to Him, that they will be well received, and that they will even be honored for their ministries.[68] However, they will take one look into Christ's face and be terrified by what they see. In a moment they will discover their error and fall before Christ as Haman fell before Esther. And like Haman, at the King's word their faces will be covered and they will be dragged from His presence to their impending doom.[69] They will be like the man who entered into the wedding feast improperly clothed and unprepared.[70] He was confident of his acceptance and anticipating the joy of the banquet. However, when he came into the presence of the king, his folly was exposed. He stood speechless as the sentence was passed upon him: "Then the king said to the servants, 'Bind him

---

65. Leviticus 18:25, 28; 20:22; Revelation 3:16.
66. Malachi 2:3.
67. Psalms 71:13; 83:17; 109:28–29.
68. Matthew 7:22; 25:21, 23; Luke 12:37; John 12:26; 2 Peter 1:10–11.
69. Esther 7:8.
70. Matthew 22:10–14.

hand and foot, take him away, and cast him into outer darkness; there will be weeping and gnashing of teeth'" (Matt. 22:13).

Here is a proper place to ask this: How many millions of people will evangelical ministers and ministries send unprepared to stand before the judgment throne of Christ? How many will enter the throne room with confidence founded upon the affirmation of their pastor, only to face Christ's disapproval? How will they then feel about the man who had charge of their souls? He was kind and mannerly to a fault. He was winsome, jovial, and positive. However, he treated their wound lightly and patched over their festering malady with a sinner's prayer and taught them to feel good about themselves in the midst of an affirming spiritual community. He fed them tidbits of morality and filled them with practical principles that they might maneuver their way through life and reap the benefits of it. But he did not prepare them to meet their God! He never told them about the weightier matters of the religion he supposedly represented. They knew nothing about the character of God and the depravity of the human heart. They were unaware of the true nature of Christ's death. They never heard a call to repentance and faith.[71] They were never admonished to make their calling and election sure or to work out their salvation in fear and trembling.[72] He allowed them to be flung out into eternity on a spider's web of religious superficiality.[73] Throughout eternity, he will hear their cries and know he was at least in part responsible for their doom. He healed the people's brokenness superficially, "saying, 'Peace, peace!' when there is no peace" (Jer. 6:14). He was a useless watchman, and their blood is on his hands.[74]

Fourth, those whom David is sending away had caused him untold grief with their attacks against his person and calling. Therefore, their sudden fall would be David's vindication by the hand of God. In a similar fashion, on the day of judgment, Christ will be exonerated from the evil deeds of those who called Him Lord and claimed to be His people but did not do what He said.[75] They turned the grace of God into licentiousness.[76] They committed immoralities of such a kind that did not

---

71. Mark 1:15.
72. Philippians 2:12; 2 Peter 1:10.
73. Job 8:14.
74. Ezekiel 3:17–18.
75. Luke 6:44.
76. Jude v. 4.

exist even among the Gentiles.[77] They lived according to the creed, "Let us do evil that good may come.... Shall we continue in sin that grace may abound?" (Rom. 3:8; 6:1). Because of them, Christ's name was blasphemed among the Gentiles.[78] He was blamed for their evil deeds and mocked as a Savior who could not save; a deliverer who could take His people from Egypt but could not bring them into their own land;[79] a justifier of the wicked who had no power to sanctify them; a builder who began a good work that He could not finish;[80] a God as weak as a woman in her distress who comes to the point of giving birth but has no strength to deliver.[81] All these accusations were railed against Him because of the ungodly, who confessed Him with their mouth but denied Him with their deeds.[82] However, on that final day, all such slanderous accusations will be ended. The truth will be made known that not everyone who said to Him, "Lord, Lord" was known by Him or counted among His brothers. On that day, Christ will be vindicated, and they will be exposed as illegitimate children who acted on their own accord. This is foreshadowed in Moses' vindication of God and his denunciation of disobedient Israel:

> He is the Rock, His work is perfect;
> For all His ways are justice,
> A God of truth and without injustice;
> Righteous and upright is He.
> "They have corrupted themselves;
> They are not His children,
> Because of their blemish:
> A perverse and crooked generation." (Deut. 32:4–5)

The truths that we have just considered are extremely difficult for the modern evangelical mind to receive, but they are nonetheless true. It is a dark subject, but one that cannot be hidden or ignored. As the prophet Amos declared,

---

77. 1 Corinthians 5:1.
78. Romans 2:24.
79. Numbers 14:13–16; Ezekiel 36:20.
80. Luke 14:28–30; Philippians 1:6; Ephesians 2:10.
81. Isaiah 66:9.
82. Titus 1:16.

> A lion has roared!
> Who will not fear?
> The LORD God has spoken!
> Who can but prophesy? (3:8)

Will we hide these things from our hearers? They will curse us in the end! Will we tell them even though they think we are mad? They will bless us on that day! We must throw away all desire for the accolades and approval of men and seek the approval of Christ. We must preach the hard sayings of Christ, even though we are accused of being loveless, angry, morbid, and morose. We must be willing to suffer the temporary wrath of men if it will save them from the eternal wrath of God. We must prepare them to meet their God![83]

THE REALITY OF HELL

We have learned from Matthew 7 that numerous individuals who now confess Christ as Lord will one day be exposed for their false confession and commanded to depart from His presence. This is the culminating warning of all that has been said and the final notice to which we must listen and respond. There are several truths that we should gather from it.

First, we must understand that it is Christ's will that the false convert depart from His presence. There is no evangelical romanticism in this text that would portray Christ as sorrowful and weeping as people throw themselves into hell in spite of all that He would do to impede them. It is Christ Himself who sends them away in wrath and without mercy. During their life, Christ poured out His kindness, tolerance, and patience on them with an abundance that should have led them to repentance, but they hardened their stubborn hearts against Him and stored up for themselves greater and greater measures of wrath to be revealed on the day of judgment.[84] He would have gathered them as a hen gathers her brood under her wings, but they would not have it.[85] He held out His hand to them and condescended to offer Himself to them, but they refused. As He declared through the prophet Isaiah:

---

83. Amos 4:12.
84. Romans 2:4–5.
85. Matthew 23:37; Luke 13:34.

"I was sought by those who did not ask for Me;
I was found by those who did not seek Me.
I said, 'Here I am, here I am,'
To a nation that was not called by My name.
I have stretched out My hands all day long to a rebellious people,
Who walk in a way that is not good,
According to their own thoughts;
A people who provoke Me to anger continually to My face." (65:1–3)

All this Christ had done for them, but they responded with ever-increasing rebellion and continual provocation. He called, but they refused; He stretched out His hand, and they did not pay attention. They neglected all His counsel and did not want His reproof. So now, when they call upon Him, He will not answer, and when they seek Him diligently, they will not find Him. They hated knowledge and did not choose the fear of the Lord; they would not accept His counsel and spurned all His reproof. "Therefore they shall eat the fruit of their own way," and be satiated with their own devices (Prov. 1:24–31). On the day of judgment, Christ's offer of salvation is retracted, and by His command His enemies are throne into hell. This is why He warns:

"And I say to you, My friends, do not be afraid of those who kill the body, and after that have no more that they can do. But I will show you whom you should fear: Fear Him who, after He has killed, has power to cast into hell; yes, I say to you, fear Him!" (Luke 12:4–5)

Kiss the Son, lest He be angry,
And you perish in the way,
When His wrath is kindled but a little.
Blessed are all those who put their trust in Him. (Ps. 2:12)

Second, we should notice that the false converts are commanded to depart *from* Christ. If this does not appear to us to be the most terrifying aspect of hell, then we should question our salvation. To the believer whose heart has been regenerated by the Holy Spirit, the thought of being without Christ is utterly unbearable.[86] Having tasted and seen that the Lord is good and having experienced firsthand that in His presence there is fullness of joy, the believer cannot tolerate even the thought of existence

---

86. Pastor Charles Leiter, conversation with the author.

without Christ.[87] We must understand that the regenerate heart does not think of eternal life primarily as an endless utopia, but as uninterrupted and unmitigated fellowship with Christ. In fact, the believer would rather be in hell with Christ than in heaven without Him. Those who would preach about heaven primarily as a utopia both dishonor Christ and mislead carnal people into thinking that it is the place for them. In spite of all its physical perfections and beauties, heaven would be ruined for them because Christ would be there. His holy and righteous presence would make it intolerable. However, we could fill heaven tomorrow if we could only convince sinful people that Christ was like them or that He was not there.[88] All people want to go to heaven, but most do not want Christ. For this reason, we must warn carnal people that their lack of desire for fellowship with Christ and their apathy toward righteousness is a great evidence that their hearts are yet to be changed and their citizenship is not in heaven. Furthermore, we must warn those who confess Christ yet are more animated by the hope of a future utopia than the hope of the fullness of Christ.

Third, we should notice that the false converts are commanded to depart from the presence of Christ into hell. Some within the evangelical community defend the absence of hell from their preaching by saying that they would rather focus upon Jesus' teachings and the good news of the gospel. However, those who say such things are either purposely deceptive or ignorant of both the gospel and Christ's teachings. In reality, we would know almost nothing about the nature and terrors of hell if it were not for Jesus' teachings. Although the truth of eternal punishment is found in the Old Testament,[89] there are few clear references regarding the matter. The same may be said for the Epistles.[90] In fact, almost all of what we know about the doctrine of hell comes from Christ's teachings in the gospels and from the revelation of Jesus given to John on the Isle of Patmos. It is often said that men who preach on hell are mean-spirited, critical, and unloving, yet this is refuted because the most loving Person who ever walked the face of this earth gave us the most extensive and descriptive teachings on the reality of hell. And if He is to be believed,

---

87. Psalms 16:11; 34:8.
88. Psalm 50:21.
89. Daniel 12:2.
90. 2 Thessalonians 1:8–9; Hebrews 10:26–27; Jude v. 7.

then it is a place of indescribable torment[91] where perfect justice is dis - pensed and the wicked receive the exact measure of the punishment that is due them.[92] It has often been asked why the overwhelming majority of the Scriptures' teaching on hell comes from Christ. The trusted theologian W. G. T. Shedd seems to give the most plausible answer:

> The strongest support of the doctrine of Endless Punishment is the teaching of Christ, the Redeemer of man. Though the doctrine is plainly taught in the Pauline Epistles, and other parts of Scripture, yet without the explicit and reiterated statements of God incarnate, it is doubtful whether so awful a truth would have had such a conspicuous place as it always has had in the creed of Christendom.... The Apostles enter far less into detailed description, and are far less emphatic upon this solemn theme.... And well they might be. For as none but God has the right, and would dare, to sentence a soul to eternal misery for sin; and as none but God has the right, and should presume, so to delineate the nature and consequences of this sentence. This the reason why most of the awful imagery in which the sufferings of the lost are described is found in the discourses of our Lord and Saviour. He took it upon Himself to sound the note of warning.[93]

The Scriptures give many graphic and striking descriptions of hell. Whether they are to be taken as literal has been a long-standing debate, even among conservative scholars. Is hell a place of literal fire and darkness, of brimstone and smoke?[94] If someone denies a literal interpretation of these descriptions in order to diminish the sufferings of the wicked in hell, he is to be dismissed. However, it is acceptable to hold these descriptions to be figurative in the sense that they are an attempt to describe something so terrifying that it goes beyond the capacity of the human mind to conceive and beyond the power of our human language to communicate. To describe the terrors of hell, the biblical writers used the greatest terrors known to man on earth, but we can be assured that hell is worse than anything found on earth. Fire and darkness and brim-

---

91. Matthew 13:42, 50; 22:13; 24:51; 25:30; Luke 13:28; 16:28.
92. Matthew 11:21–24; 16:27; 23:14; Luke 12:47–48; Romans 2:6; 2 Corinthians 5:10; 11:15; 2 Timothy 4:14; Revelation 18:6; 20:12–13.
93. W. G. T. Shedd, *Dogmatic Theology* (Phillipsburg, N.J.: P&R, 2003), 2:675.
94. Matthew 3:10, 12; 7:19; 8:12; 13:42; 18:8; 22:13; 25:30, 41; Jude v. 13; Revelation 20:10, 14; 21:8.

stone and smoke are only a feeble attempt to describe a reality far more terrifying than even these words can convey: the wicked must bear the righteous presence of God and His perfect justice throughout eternity.

We have learned that those who falsely confess Christ are commanded to depart from His presence into hell. However, we must be careful with our language. When we describe hell as an eternal existence without Christ, we do not mean entirely without Christ. There is a common evangelical saying that heaven is heaven because God is there, and hell is hell because He is not. However, this is misleading. It is more appropriate to say that hell is hell because God is there in the fullness of His righteousness and wrath against the sinner. On judgment day, when people are sent forth from the presence of Christ, they will be departing from His favorable presence. However, His frown will follow them throughout all of eternity. The apostle John affirms this truth: "[The unbeliever] himself shall also drink of the wine of the wrath of God, which is poured out full strength into the cup of His indignation. He shall be tormented with fire and brimstone in the presence of the holy angels and in the presence of the Lamb" (Rev. 14:10).

THOSE DESTINED FOR HELL

From the Scriptures we learn that there is an irrevocable and unavoidable judgment coming upon the world. It will be the great and final cull of humanity. The practical application of this truth is that every person on this planet is either destined for eternal glory or for eternal punishment in hell. Although this thought may be obnoxious or repugnant to the great majority of mankind, it cannot be denied that it is the clear teaching of the Scriptures.[95]

In the street and in the pew, people react to the doctrine of hell in a variety of ways. Some deny it outright even though they have a gnawing suspicion that they are wrong. Others are convinced that hell is only for the most abominable people. They believe that even the atheist will escape its grasp if he minds his manners, does the best he can, and is helpful to his neighbor. Still others believe that hell is only for those who adamantly reject Christ, while those who give assent to His claims and

---

95. Matthew 5:22, 29–30; 10:28; 18:9; 23:33; 25:41, 46; Mark 9:43, 45, 47; Luke 12:5; 2 Peter 2:4; Revelation 20:15.

confess Him as Lord are assured of safe passage away from its gates. All these varied opinions lead us to a very important question: Who is destined for hell? The old preachers were fond of saying, "The problem is not that people do not believe in hell. They do! The problem is that no one thinks he is going there."

In Matthew 7, Jesus clearly identifies four groups of individuals who will spend an eternity in hell. We would do well to consider each group carefully and to examine our own lives in light of the characteristics that identify them. There is nothing on earth of greater importance. People may be wrong about many things without doing much harm to themselves. However, being wrong about this matter has eternal and irrevocable consequences.

The first group of those who are destined for hell consists of those who live out their lives on the broad way.[96] Their thinking, conduct, and direction of their lives are not defined by Christ's will. Instead, they are shaped by the opinions and lusts of this fallen age and walk according to them. Although they may wear a thin veneer of Christianity, their manner of thinking and living is contrary to the religion they profess. They love the world, look like the world, and share the same affections with the world. Our evangelical churches are filled with such individuals. They sincerely believe that they have passed through the small gate that is Christ and that their salvation is secure. However, they are unaware that their uninterrupted travel on the broad way demonstrates that they have believed in vain.

The second group of those who are destined for hell consists of everyone whose life is not marked by fruit-bearing and the Father's pruning.[97] They confess faith in Christ, but His character and deeds are not manifest in their lives, nor is there evidence of the Father's sanctifying work through discipline. Those who do not bear fruit simply are not Christians. This truth cannot be minimized or explained away. In the earliest gospel warnings, John the Baptist declared, "The ax is laid to the root of the trees. Therefore every tree which does not bear good fruit is cut down and thrown into the fire" (Matt. 3:10; Luke 3:9). Jesus stood in agreement with John when He repeated the same warning almost word for word: "Every tree that does not bear good fruit is cut down and thrown into

---

96. Matthew 7:13.
97. Matthew 7:16–20; John 15:2.

the fire" (Matt. 7:19). We must realize that our evangelical churches are filled with such people. They bear no fruit and display no evidence of the Father's pruning. They continue on year after year, holding to a form of godliness and denying the power of it by the barrenness of their lives.[98]

The third group of those who are destined for hell consists of everyone whose life is not marked by practical obedience to the Father's will. Again, this is the clear teaching of Jesus, who warned, "Not everyone who says to Me, 'Lord, Lord,' shall enter the kingdom of heaven, but he who does the will of My Father in heaven" (Matt. 7:21). Obedience does not result in salvation; however, it is the evidence of it. In the same way, a life of disobedience is evidence of reprobation. For this reason Jesus will declare to those who are lawless on the final day to depart. He is referring to those who confessed Him as Lord and yet lived as though He never gave them a law to obey. We must understand that there is simply no such thing as a Christian who lives in uninterrupted apathy or disregard for the will of God. To say otherwise is to deny the teachings of Jesus. Nevertheless, our evangelical churches are filled with people who profess Christ and yet live as practical atheists, doing what seems right in their own eyes and being destroyed for their lack of knowledge.[99] If every piece of Scripture in the world were confiscated, it would have no affect on their lives. They are without law. They live under a self-imposed famine of the Word of God.[100]

The fourth group of those who are destined for hell consists of everyone who hears the words of Christ and does not act upon them.[101] Again, conversion is evidenced or proven by practical obedience. Those who have been born again are marked by new and growing affections for the person of Christ. For this reason, they also long to know His will and please Him through obedience. They are awed by the blessing of Christ's Word and humbled by the privilege that is theirs to study it and apply it to their lives. Consequently, they are also ashamed when they find themselves to be apathetic, nonchalant, and disobedient. In a word, the true convert has come to comprehend something of what Jesus meant when He told His disciples: "But blessed are your eyes for they see, and your

---

98. 2 Timothy 3:5.
99. Hosea 4:6.
100. Amos 8:11.
101. Matthew 7:26.

ears for they hear; for assuredly, I say to you that many prophets and righteous men desired to see what you see, and did not see it, and to hear what you hear, and did not hear it" (Matt. 13:16–17).

In contrast, the false convert is unmoved by Christ's teaching because he is unmoved by Christ's person. The Word does not inspire him to wonder, and his heart does not burn within him as it is expounded.[102] He has little real appreciation for the Word of Christ and is untroubled by his apathy and disobedience toward it. Every Sunday morning he hears the teachings of Christ and even assents to their truth, but he casts the Word behind him when he walks out the door.[103] In his case the prophecy of Isaiah is being fulfilled:

> "'Hearing you will hear and shall not understand,
> And seeing you will see and not perceive;
> For the hearts of this people have grown dull.
> Their ears are hard of hearing,
> And their eyes they have closed,
> Lest they should see with their eyes and hear with their ears,
> Lest they should understand with their hearts and turn,
> So that I should heal them.'" (Matt. 13:13–15)

Our evangelical churches are filled with individuals who confess Christ and yet do not hear His Word so as to obey it. Their Christianity can be summed up in a past transaction they made with Christ through the praying of a prayer, but they do not go on with Him into any noticeable depths of devotion and obedience. They have merely done what they were told to do in order to gain entrance to heaven. They sit in our pews with their consciences anesthetized and hear no warning and see no contradiction between what they do and what they claim to be—between who they are and Who they confess.

For the sake of Christ and for the countless multitudes that sit at ease in Zion, not knowing that their judgment draws near, we must repent of what we have done to the gospel and the church. We must throw off the contemporary distortions that have wrecked the greater part of a generation and return to the gospel of Jesus Christ. We must preach with such clarity and earnestness that we who stand in the pulpit might be exonerated on the day of judgment and those who hear us might be without

---

102. Luke 24:32.
103. Psalm 50:16–17.

excuse. Let us heed the words of Charles Spurgeon, who declared: "If sinners will be damned, at least let them leap to Hell over our bodies. And if they will perish, let them perish with our arms about their knees, imploring them to stay. If Hell must be filled, at least let it be filled in the teeth of our exertions, and let not one go there unwarned and unprayed for."[104]

104. C. H. Spurgeon, *The New Park Street and Metropolitan Tabernacle Pulpit* (Pasadena, Tex.: Pilgrim Publications, 1969–), 7:11.